MAKING SERIOUS
MONEY FROM HOME

Sharon Maxwell Magnus is an experienced
journalist. She recently won an Industrial
Journalism Award from the Industrial Society
for her articles on women in the workplace. She
has also won the Catherine Pakenham Award
for young women journalists and the Rosemary
Goodchild award for her articles on women's
health. She was assistant editor of *SHE*
magazine until the birth of her daughter when
she switched to working from home. Since then,
she has become contributing editor of *SHE*
magazine and also works for various
publications including the *Daily Telegraph*,
Sunday Telegraph, the *Independent*, and the
Guardian. She was educated at Olchfa
Comprehensive, Swansea and Christ Church
College, Oxford.

MAKING
SERIOUS
MONEY
from *HOME*

SHARON
MAXWELL MAGNUS

PAN BOOKS

First published 1996 by Pan Books
an imprint of Macmillan Publishers Limited
25 Eccleston Place, London SW1W 9NF
and Basingstoke

Associated companies throughout the world

ISBN 0-330-343718

9 8 7 6 5 4 3 2 1

A CIP catalogue record for this book is available
from the British Library

Typeset by Spottiswoode Ballantyne Printers Limited
Printed and bound in Great Britain

All contact numbers, addresses and specific information
were understood to be correct at time of writing. The business
ideas at the back of the book, are merely general suggestions
and do not imply that they will necessarily lead to business
success, nor any level of future income. This book is not a
substitute for professional advice. Names have occasionally
been changed to protect an interviewee's identity.

To my daughter Samantha, who started me off on this track, Adrian and my mother and father.

Many thanks to Caroline and the many people who freely gave their expertise and time for this book.

CONTENTS

When I tell people what I do the most common reaction is envy. It's not envy of my profession (most people regard journalists as beyond the pale). It is the fact that I work from home.' You lucky thing,' they sigh. 'How did you manage that? I wish I could work from home.' I understand their feelings. My abiding memory of trying to combine a demanding office job with motherhood and a terminally unreliable train service, beset by strikes, is one of constant near panic.

I am not alone. Survey after survey shows that in the hectic nineties, most of those in work feel that they spend far too much time in the office. Not only do we have the longest working hours in Europe, but we compound that with overtime and time spent commuting. (A British Telecom survey found that many commuters spent as much as 1,000 hours each year travelling to and from work. We now spend 1.8 years of our lives waiting at traffic lights – but only ten months talking with our families). No one ever wished on their deathbed that they had spent more of their time in the office, but nowadays most of us are coming to the realization, well before then, that we'd like to spend a lot less time there!

For me, working at home provided an answer to making my life more manageable at a time of immense changes. Indeed, the supreme benefit of working from home is its flexibility – instead of having to commute in the rush hour with millions of other bodies, all frantic to get to work at hours imposed purely for the convenience of the organization, you work when you choose in a way that suits you. If you want to get up early and steal a march on the day in order to spend time with your children after school – you can do so. If you want to spend an hour playing tennis during the day and then catch up in the evening, you can.

But it's not just working mothers and fathers who can enjoy the benefits of working from home. For many small businesses, working from home is the ideal way to 'grow' the business – a way to develop a good idea without incurring huge overheads in the process. 'It was the only way I could start,' says Tim Rustige, who sells second hand computers from his home. 'I started very gradually and couldn't have afforded the outlay for premises.'

'The money I've saved from not having the overheads of an expensive office and storage space has gone straight back into the business,' says Elana Rubenstein, graphic designer and greetings card manufacturer.

During the course of writing this book, I found that most people had one of three similar reasons for working at home: either they needed to work from home because of family commitments (caring for children or for a sick or disabled relative), or they wanted to run a small business cheaply (because they had an excellent idea for one, were unemployed or had been made redundant) or because they simply wanted a better quality of life. A few people had been forced into working from home because of company policy, but they were a small minority. A few, too, had chosen to work from home because they were disabled. Indeed, persuading disabled people to start their own businesses from home, is now being touted as *the* way to reduce the problem of the high level of unemployment among the disabled, although there are potential drawbacks (see chapter 11).

Working from home can be a way of solving many major conflicts: work versus family commitments, innovation versus cost, unemployment versus getting back into the workforce on your own terms. For single parents, who often find it especially hard to combine working and family life, it could provide an excellent solution – provided the parent has a social network. Not surprisingly, people working at home in general report higher levels of satisfaction with their way of life, have 40 per cent more productivity than their office based colleagues and spend less time off ill with minor ailments. They also contribute less to pollution since they do not travel to work by car.

Given these attractions, it is not surprising that an increasing number of people want to work from home. Fortunately, recent improvements in technology such as faxes, modems and conference calling combined with the expense of business properties all make working from home an increasingly feasible option. Almost 30 per cent of firms now have employees who work from home for at least part of the week. Two and a half million people, both employed and self-employed, are already working from home some of the time and that number is forecast to grow to five million by the turn of the century.

And yet. Installing a computer in your front room, switching your phone number and starting work is not all there is to it. Having written this book, I only wish it had been available for me before I started working from home. It would have saved me not only money, time and confusion but a lot of emotional heartache as I struggled to adapt to the different demands of working from home. I imagined, like so many others, that working from home would be a simple matter of moving my working environment. It wasn't. I had failed to realize that working from home requires different disciplines from working in an office. You don't adapt overnight from working in a buzzing organization, surrounded by colleagues and action, to working in the quiet by yourself. Isolation is a common problem for homeworkers, as is overload, motivation and status. 'I sometimes feel I don't quite belong,' says Kim Pickin, a communications consultant. 'I'm not with my children full-time, so can't always take part in the activities arranged around stay-at-home mothers. But at the same time, I don't go out to work with colleagues.'

Kim, like many other homeworkers has developed her own way of dealing with this and is generally very satisfied with her set-up. You can adapt – and adapt brilliantly well – but it helps to have strategies that help you do so. Strategies and tips which I hope this book provides.

Chapters 2 and 8, take an in-depth look at how you can get the most out of working from home emotionally and in your relations with other people. Chapters 3, 4, 5, 6 and 7, look at many of the practical aspects of working from home – from equipping your home office and finding suitable childcare to arranging your finances and deciding whether to set up as a limited company or a sole trader. For the self-employed, market research, taxation, marketing and other essentials are covered in chapters 5 and 6.

This book is crammed with expert advice – expert because it's from the people who've done it – people who work at home, both employed and self-employed, men and women, full-timers, part-timers and from a wide variety of ethnic origins. Over sixty case histories are featured here. The people interviewed come from as far apart as Devon and the Highlands. Some work in inner cities, others in rural areas. Some work at home full-time, others part-time. Some are working very part-time or in cottage businesses, earning perhaps £50 a week. Others are high flyers with five figure turnovers and even profits, employing several staff. They range from craftspeople to consultants, from opticians to sex therapists, from senior management to the shop floor. All have something valuable to say. Some for professional or other reasons have asked for their own names not to be used and where aliases are used, this is indicated.

'My husband told me when I started working from home that I mustn't think like a housewife when it came to selling,' says knitwear designer Jenny Sandler. 'It's advice I'd give anyone – because I had to learn what it meant. Working from home enabled me to fit in my work with the children – but that doesn't mean that it wasn't tough going at times.'

Jenny's business is typical of many at-home enterprises: the hobby that gradually turns into a business and then expands to a much larger entity. In Jenny's case, she started designing sweaters with distinctive patterns, so her young son wouldn't lose them – and ended up designing major collections for Alfred Dunhill. For this sort of enterprise, all too often the tricks of the trade are learnt on the job, by trial and error – and from mistakes.

'I've learnt a lot from my mistakes,' said another homeworker, employed by a small company.' But that doesn't mean I wouldn't have liked to avoid them.' Hopefully, this book will help you avoid some mistakes and give you new ideas to enhance both your working life at home and your personal life too. At the end of each chapter is a list of useful contacts, all of which can help your transition to working at home go more smoothly.

But just how popular is working from home? Although, 'teleworking' (i.e. working from home using technology to link up to a central point) has been much talked about, and although one third of office work is forecast to be done from home by the year 2000, it seems to me that the transfer from office based work to home based work, is likely to be less wholesale than predicted. This is for one simple reason: management resistance to having their employees out of sight. 'Managers are often worried about relinquishing control over their subordinates,' says Professor Cary Cooper of the University of Manchester Institute of Science and Technology, who is an expert in work-related psychology. 'If they can't see them, they feel they may lose some control.'

Working from home does require different management techniques from managing people in an office where you can see exactly what they are doing. Many managers don't want to learn different management techniques – or are simply scared of change. There are firms which have introduced major teleworking schemes (often information technology firms or firms with a direct interest in having more homeworking, such as BT, which has recently started a new teleworking scheme in Southampton), but they are likely to remain a minority. In the main, although more employees will work from home, it will tend to be negotiated in smaller companies at least on a one-to-one, ad hoc basis rather than through formal policies. That means that if you do want to work some of the time from home, much will depend on how you raise the subject with your manager and on his or her particular personality. That is why it is so important to prepare the ground thoroughly – a subject covered in detail in chapter 3.

Although the numbers of people working for an employer from home are set to rise substantially, the majority of those opting to work for home are – and will remain self-employed. Indeed, while researching this book it has struck me that whereas in an office the major difference is between part-time and full-time workers, the major differences in working at home are between the self-employed worker and the worker with a boss, however far away.

Self-employment has many advantages – it is flexible, you set the pace and the agenda, and the rewards are all yours. It also has its disadvantages. You may be a top-notch designer or agent, but you will also be (at least in the beginning) chief book-keeper, tax collector and tea-lady! What's more if the rewards are all yours, so are the risks.

Nevertheless, self-employment is set to rise and rise. According to management guru Charles Handy, author of *The Empty Raincoat*, this is because the company of the future will be pared down to a core group of workers. These core workers will work increasingly long hours for high rewards, but with little life outside the organization. They will perform the organization's essential day-to-day tasks. However one-off or regular projects will increasingly be farmed out to those working on a self-employed basis.

While researching this book, I came across plenty of evidence that this was already happening. Many of the self-employed people I spoke to had either been made redundant or had peeled themselves off from an organization to go it alone. However, it has to be said that I did come across sex differences. At the moment, 70 per cent of homeworkers are women. While many of the women I spoke to had become self-employed homeworkers largely to evade the perceived glass ceiling or to be able to make their working and family life fit better, many of the men had become self-employed after redundancy or had opted to start a business from home because it was the cheapest way.

This is a broad generalization, but it does seem that men and women often have different agendas for wanting to work at home – both of which I hope are addressed here. Many of the people I spoke to had also adopted so-called portfolio careers, doing a variety of jobs, centred around a theme. Michael Levy, for instance, is a potter who also teaches. Elizabeth Newport, a teacher who also helps administer a language agency. Interestingly, although some of the people I interviewed had regarded working from home merely as a stopgap, the vast majority now said that they would not willingly go back to the office, praising the freedom, ease and flexibility of working from home. This tallies with general findings that over 80 per cent of people prefer working at home to working in an office. And no wonder. Handled well, the freedom, flexibility and even time it gives you are far greater than in most office jobs.

For those who feel they would like to work at home – but aren't sure what to do, I hope the section at the back will help. This gives twenty ideas of a range of different businesses that could be started at home. When choosing them, I had two particular criteria in mind:

- That they would involve a sizeable amount of time spent at home. (Gardeners, for instance, might be based at home, but would spend most of their time in other people's gardens so are not included. Ditto financial consultants who, if successful, are largely out and about seeing clients.)

- That they should be the sort of career in which maturity and previous experience in another field present no barriers. That doesn't mean that you won't have to train, or make an investment in your new career, but that when you've completed the course you shouldn't find yourself at a disadvantage just because you are not twenty-one.

There are, of course, hundreds of other options open to those wanting to work from home and perhaps reading through the body of the book and reading about the experiences of those interviewed will give you ideas for other businesses you might set up at home.

Each chapter is divided into sections so that if you want to look at a particular aspect – say insurance (absolutely vital for the homeworker) – you can have a quick glance at the relevant section and take down a useful contact or two.

Above all, working from home should be fun. 'I enjoy what I do,' says copywriter Brian Morris. 'It would be very hard to work as hard as I do at it, if I didn't.' 'Working from home has enabled me to spend time with my children and to use my professional expertise,' says public relations consultant Dana Cukier. 'When it goes well I really do feel I'm getting the best of both worlds.' Katharine Goodison, a former City solicitor, now a milliner agrees. 'Now I'm working for myself, at home, I can't believe I waited so long to do it. I never dread going into work and I still can't quite believe the freedom I have!. What better recommendation could there be?

ONE

Would working from home suit you?

As you've already discovered, there are a great many advantages to working from home. For the majority of people it really can provide the best of both worlds, enabling them to have a fulfilled working life and a happy home life too. By working from home, you can work far more efficiently and cheaply – increasing your hours when the work is there, but taking time off when it's not. Even being able to put on the washing machine during a coffee break can save drudgery at the end of the day.

In fact, working from home sounds so good that you might wonder why millions of people all over the country aren't downing tools and demanding to be given a modem and a home office.

There are two major reasons. Firstly, many employers, being naturally conservative, are suspicious of their employees working in a place where they are not under the boss's beady eye. (This is discussed in more detail in chapter 3.) However, another major reason is that working from home requires very different qualities from working in an office – and that means it doesn't suit everyone. While 80 per cent of homeworkers prefer working from home, 20 per cent are hungering to get back into the office.

So how do the problems of working at home differ from those of working in an office? And how can those pitfalls be overcome? Below we take a look at some of the potential problems a new homeworker is likely to encounter.

MOTIVATION: YOUR GREATEST ASSET – OR YOUR BIGGEST LIABILITY?

Motivation is perhaps the single biggest factor in making the difference between success and failure in any business venture. Surveys have shown that poorly motivated employees, however hard they are worked, consistently produce poorer work than those who may work less hours but have better motivation.

But what gives us our motivation differs with our personalities. For some people, motivation is largely *external*. They work hard because they have external rewards to motivate them – a pay cheque, the approval of colleagues, or a boss breathing down their neck. However, when you work at home, you are largely out of sight – and possibly out of mind – of your boss. (This is the major reason cited by managers for their opposition to teleworking. In a recent Department of Trade and Industry study, many managers said that they did not approve of teleworking, because without a boss to manage employees their work would invariably decline.) Even more challenging, you may actually be your own boss. If you have been the sort of person who regards the boss's holiday as a good reason to down tools yourself, you may well have problems working from home.

You may also have difficulty working from home, if *teamwork* is a major motivating factor for you. If you worked in an office where every success was celebrated by your team and letting the side down was the greatest sin, it may be hard to adjust to the fact that the rest of the team are now fifty miles away – or even that you are now your own 'team'. In order to make a success of working from home, it is vital that you learn to become *self-motivated*. If you lack self-motivation, you may well find yourself getting up too late, working half-heartedly and cleaning the kitchen floor when you should be doing your accounts.

It sounds easy enough, but even the hardest-working employee can feel a sudden drop in enthusiasm when faced with the temptations of domestic life. Lizzie, for instance, was a hard-working veterinary assistant who gave up her job to start a designer knitwear business from home. She'd enjoyed knitting as a hobby and started off with a full order book – but she found working from home sapped her motivation. 'It didn't really work for me,' she recalls. 'Somehow there were always more pressing things that needed doing. I'd go to the shops for my lunch hour – but the hour would turn into an afternoon. I was easily distracted and found it hard to get through the work I had. In the end, I rented premises. It was expensive, but I became so much more efficient and have found it much better for me and the business.'

Many prospective homeworkers share Lizzie's difficulty in getting down to work at home. However, for many it is a teething stage, before they find a *strategy* to give them the same degree of motivation which was previously given by the boss or co-workers.

There are a variety of strategies which you can try in order to increase your self-motivation. They include:

Giving yourself goals to work towards. If you work for a company, these can be agreed with your direct line manager. If you work for yourself, you will need to set them. However, be aware that in order for goal-setting to be successful, the goals need to be:

- Realistic – set them too high and you will only feel frustrated when you fail. Set them too low and you will become demotivated once they are accomplished.

- On-going – once one goal is achieved you need to set yourself another. If you are starting your own business, you may also want to increase the size of your goals as your business expands.

- Have an element of reward or incentive in them. The rewards could be as simple as making yourself a cup of coffee after you've completed a particular task – or they could be much more lavish.

Fiona Bradley, book-keeper and now part-time lecturer at her local Business-Link found that giving herself rewards for work well done was a particularly effective motivator.

Fiona started her business in unpropitious circumstances – she had split up with her husband following the discovery of his affair, her home was in need of massive restoration and she was in the middle of an Open University degree in business studies. Fiona was in dire financial straits, and the turmoil caused by her personal life meant she sometimes found it hard to concentrate. 'I started the book-keeping business from home because I didn't want the children to go to a child-minder and suffer yet more disruption', Fiona recalls. 'That meant I had to do the bulk of my work in school hours and evenings. Given that I had a limited time to do the work I knew I had to get down to it. Most of the time I could because it was a matter of survival. But sometimes stray thoughts would creep in and interrupt.'

Fiona found that the best way to get through such patches was to hold out a 'reward' for her family when she had achieved her goals. 'They started off small – like getting enough money to tile the bathroom – and just grew till the point when I was promising the girls a trip to Hong Kong, if I fulfilled my target. I still managed it.'

Fiona puts her business success down to hard work, 'and a willingness to put on a professional face even when my personal life wasn't right. In the early days, there were times I'd be driving out to a client and would have to stop for a cry. But I'd pick myself up, put my best face on and carry on.'

Fiona's dedication paid off. She was a runner-up in a national business competition and was invited to lecture to other small businesses. 'I never thought of myself as a businesswoman,' she says. 'But I always have been self-disciplined and reliable and I think that helps.'

Making your own routine is another useful self-motivator – just as if you were in an office. You might decide to start work at 9 a.m., take a coffee break at 11.30 and then continue working again ten minutes later, with a lunch break of an hour. Most homeworkers swear that setting yourself a list of tasks to do the evening before is a good way to gee yourself into action. Another is to ensure that you have to make a phone call first thing each morning. 'I make myself a list each night of what I'm going to do the following day,' says Paul Curitz, a computer expert and consultant. 'I never get quite to the end of it, so there's always a list ready for the following day.'

Setting deadlines can also be an excellent way to discipline yourself to work, although they have to be realistic in order to ensure your efficiency. If deadlines are set too tightly, you may find yourself panicking; if they are too loose, you will just amble towards them. If you are working for an employer, or in a service area, your deadlines are likely to be chosen for you. Even if they are not, it is worth pinning your boss or client down and asking them to agree schedules with you.

'I previously worked as a solicitor in the City where deadlines were all important,' says Katharine Goodison, who left her high-flying job to become a self-employed milliner. 'Some of those deadlines were unrealistic, but it was good discipline. Now if I have a client who isn't bothered about exactly when they get their hat, I sit down with them and make them agree deadlines. It helps me and it doesn't upset them.'

Not all of these methods will work for you – but it is likely that at least one of them will. Experiment with them to see which you prefer. Remember, the more motivated you are, the better your results will be.

ISOLATION: LEARNING TO DEAL WITH THE LONELINESS FACTOR

The majority of people who work from home, whether they be working for giant corporations or in one-man bands, work by themselves. On the one hand, that means they are extremely efficient – no interruptions, no joking during meetings, no office politicking around the coffee machine, or gossiping in the lunch break – but it also means that homeworkers can feel terribly alone and isolated.

'I found that working six hours a day at home was worth more than eight in the office,' says Emma Dally, now Publishing Director for The National Magazine Company. 'There are so few interruptions that you are able to work very intensively.'

Although we may not recognize it, the office is a ready-made social network – even if we don't particularly like our colleagues. We tend to talk to them when we arrive in the morning, discuss plans or projects during the morning, gossip at the coffee machine and over lunch. Professor Noel Sheehy, who recently completed a report on homeworking in rural areas, points out that, in offices, 40 per cent of the working day is spent talking, writing, sending memos to each other. 'All the studies in the USA and Europe come up with around the same figure,' he says. 'What we call idle chat and gossip actually keep organizations together.' He also points out that, in offices, the exchange of vital office information often happens on an informal basis – something that is hard to replicate when you are working at home. It is hard to brainstorm if it's just your brain doing the storming.

Most homeworkers, on the other hand, will spend large chunks of their time alone. This is certainly true of occupations like computing and accountancy, as well as creative pursuits such as writing, making jewellery or cakes, graphic design, etc. Even those homeworkers whose work involves a large amount of person-to-person contact, such as counsellors, beauty therapists and recruitment consultants, can end up feeling socially isolated, because although their clients will share problems with them, they in turn have no colleagues to share their own work-related problems with.

Judy Cooper, a psychotherapist has worked at home for twenty years. Her job involves talking to clients and supervision by a colleague. Even so, isolation was a problem in the early days.
'At first, my relations with my clients were too intense. Sometimes I couldn't sleep because I'd be thinking about their problems, over and over again,' she recalls. 'It became very difficult and I sometimes felt quite alone professionally – even though I had supervision.'

Judy found that the way to cope with her isolation was to 'network and also diversify. I joined professional organizations and sat on their committees. I also started writing about my work and doing some research, so that I wasn't always doing the same thing.'

For Judy, getting out and about not only varied the pace of her work, but helped her feel more connected with other people in the field. Joining committees gave her valuable experience and a professional as well as social network – all of which built her confidence. 'It is important to watch that you don't become isolated,' she cautions, 'because it can gradually creep up on you. I had my family around me. My work involves a lot of client contact – but still I felt isolated until I found ways to break that isolation.'

Networking is vital in ensuring that you have human contact and a chance to talk to people who understand what you are going through. Talking to people in similar situations who can offer support, advice, or just a sympathetic ear, is particularly valuable. It may sound daunting, but networking can often be nothing more than getting together with like-minded people for a chat over a cup of coffee, or even going into a client's office for an afternoon just to get to know them. When I first became a freelance writer, I would grumble that I never got to meet my former colleagues any more – until one of them pointed out that she was always available at lunchtime if I would make the time to see her. I took her up on her offer and as a result felt less isolated from my professional contacts. Here are some other easy ways to get your networking act together:

- Join your professional or trade organization. Read their newsletter carefully and make a note of any meetings which might interest you – then go along. In many professions, such as journalism, PR and design, making professional contacts and bouncing ideas off people is of paramount importance. Being active in your professional association will help you do this.

- If you are working for one client or employed by a central office, try and go into that office from time to time, even if it is not strictly necessary. Talking to your boss, colleagues and clients can give you a better insight into what is happening while you are not there – and give you the feeling of being part of a team.

If you are self-employed and working alone, you will need to strive harder to keep in touch. Here are some suggestions:

- Take at least one professional or trade magazine. It will keep you abreast of developments in the field and help you feel more in touch with what's going on.

- Your local chamber of commerce represents local businesses and can be a good forum for networking. Each chamber has its own agenda. In a small town, they may organize such things as the local Christmas lights as well as providing business advice. In a bigger town they may provide detailed advice on how to export successfully and have a huge reference library. The chamber of commerce is often consulted on matters of public interest in addition to hosting talks and business seminars. Other locally based organizations such as the Rotary Club and Round Table raise money for charity, and generally consist of local business people. There is also a growing number of organizations specifically catering for small/home businesses. The Federation of Small Businesses is well-established and has a range of benefits for members. The Breakthrough Centre in London, runs a variety of personal development courses with a new age flavour for small businesses. They also offer a telephone helpline to members. For women, there are many professional organizations with specific sub-groups aimed at helping women to network. For example, Women In Management has a small business section which you may find useful. The Women's National Commission has a fairly comprehensive list of women's organizations.

- Another good way of keeping in touch is to take journals which are designed specifically for home or teleworkers. One designed for all homeworkers is *Home Run*. Published monthly, it is full of useful advice, inspirational case histories and money-saving ideas. Journals specifically for teleworkers are dealt with in the next chapter.

- Try to find out, through the local chamber of commerce, Training and Enterprise Council (TEC) or Business Link, about other homeworkers in your area. 'If I meet someone else who's working at home and like them, I invite them for lunch and ask them to bring along a friend who's also working at home' says Mary Montague, a theatre designer. 'We tend to go out rather than stay in and just have a laugh. The lunches have got bigger over the years and there's now a troupe of regulars.'

- Using your work skills in a voluntary capacity is another good way to build social networks – and could also be a useful source of future clients. Linda Greenbury, a careers counsellor, found that serving on the Women Returners Network committee gave her not only a lively social interest, but a real degree of credibility and experience. 'I also ran some free introductory workshops through local groups I belonged to, and some of those people became my clients or recommended others to me.'

- Keep up your outside interests. It is easy, when you are busy, to devote more time than you planned to work, and to let friends and hobbies drop. This however, will only intensify feelings of isolation when you have quieter periods. Take time out for hobbies or for groups that encourage social contact. A local charity, or a sports club with lots of social events, can all be vital in helping you establish a new network of friends and prospective clients. You might want to join a special interest group such as Parents At Work (for working parents) or even a local branch of your favoured political party.

● Listening to the radio can make you feel less isolated – if it doesn't distract you.

However, even if you do all these things, there may well still be days when you feel trapped and lonely. 'I listen to the radio, network with other homeworkers, but there are still days when I feel down,' says Katharine Goodison, milliner. ' If I feel really low, I take off to an art exhibition, or go out looking at window displays. Something pleasurable, but in some way related to my work. I always find that getting out cheers me up and gives me new inspiration.'

So make a gap in the day – even if it's just to wander down to the local shops or stroll round the park. Most workers have coffee breaks and lunch hours, so give yourself the same perks. Working at home shouldn't mean incessant slavery.

SEPARATING WORK AND HOME

A recent survey by the psychology department at Swansea University found that the major difficulty experienced by people who had just started working from home was the inability to separate their work and home life. That was not just because they themselves found it hard, but because family and friends found it equally hard to accept that the person who was previously 'mum' or 'dad' at home was now also a worker. 'They found it very difficult to accept the change in roles,' says Professor Osborne. 'It was hard for partners and kids to comprehend that the person who had previously been available when at home, no longer was, and that they had a new role inside the home.'

Indeed, family members and friends often expect homeworkers to perform duties they would never ask of them if they were in an office. 'I live in an isolated rural area and on the days I work at home, I am often subjected to a variety of demands,' says Val Tyler, a management trainer for the Industrial Society. 'I've even had farmers knocking on the door to ask me to help them round up lost sheep or help herd cows. On the days I'm in the office, they wouldn't dream of phoning me and asking me to come back to help them!'.

Being asked to round up stray sheep during office time might seem way out, but being expected to do household tasks because you are 'on site' is far more common. 'My husband is very supportive,' says Judy Magnus, a piano teacher. 'But the assumption is that if there is any domestic task that requires doing, I'll be the one who can make the time to do it.'

Elissa, a computer programmer found that pressure from her family was so severe that she was unable to work properly and had to look for an office job. 'When I was at work, everyone understood that. But the minute I was working at home, it was as if I was spending all day twiddling my thumbs. I didn't mind doing the school run more frequently, but then my mother also expected me to drop her off to her day clubs, instead of getting the bus. My daughter started expecting an after-school chauffeur service and my husband went on domestic strike. Suddenly, if there was any task to be done – whether it was collecting the dry cleaning or even buying a pint of extra milk – it was down to me to do it. It got to the point where I had to get a job away from home to get them all off my back.'

An unsupportive family can wreck even the most well-laid plans for working at home. The problem is that part of the attraction of working at home is that it does enable you to spend more time with your family – but that doesn't mean they have a right to squeeze out your working time.

Checking out your family's attitude to homeworking is vital before
you start. If you are a woman who has taken a few years out to raise your
children, you may encounter opposition from children and partner to
the very idea of your returning to work. After all, if they have all
enjoyed the situation up to now, they may well be unsympathetic to
having less of your time and having to do more round the house –
especially if it means the end of the hot cooked meal on the table. If this
is your family's attitude, it is worth finding out whether working at
home will soften the blow (you will be more easily available in a crisis
and spend less time commuting), or whether it will actually mean that
the family will ignore your work commitments. Comments like 'well, at
least you'll be able to iron my shirts then,' or 'so you'll still be able to
take me to my after-school clubs' are dead giveaways.

If your family thinks working at home means working when it is
convenient to every member of the household bar you (normally
between the hours of midnight and 3 a.m.) you may find it easier to
make a complete break and take an office job.

Not all situations are so extreme. If you have already had an office
job and are now planning to work at home, your family is likely to be
grateful for the extra flexibility this will give you. Even so, it is vital
to talk through the change in your work with them. It may even
be advisable to have a trial period, before you make the final decision,
just to ensure that everyone knows how the changes will affect
them.

Once you have started working from home, beware of taking on
too many commitments. You may well find that one of the joys of not
commuting is being able to take your daughter to Brownies or going to
the gym with your brother, but it is unwise to take on a whole raft of
family commitments before you know just how time-consuming your
work will be.

In order to make sure family and friends understand that what you
are doing is *real* work, not something you do in between everything else,
it is best to establish some ground rules:

- If you are working for an employer, stress to your family that you are an employee and that your boss expects exactly the same degree of commitment as in an office job.

- Be firm, but fair. Telling your mother you cannot take her to the day centre every day, because those times will cut across vital appointments, is far more effective – and less hurtful – than merely saying no. Make sure your family understands that you cannot do certain things because you have work commitments, rather than because you don't want to. Alternatively, if refusal will cause family ructions, you could try compromising – say, offering to take mother to the day centre once a week. Be aware, however, that giving in too easily can lead to more emotional blackmail.

- Explain to your family what is in it for them. If you are the major breadwinner, your family will soon grasp that in a choice between paying the mortgage and taking Johnny to piano lessons, there is really no alternative. However, even if your wages are secondary to the family income, point out how useful the money will be in terms of 'goodies' such as family holidays, computer games etc. – provided you are left alone to earn it. 'My husband was very reluctant to have me work at home, because it is an intrusion into our family life,' says May, secretary to a medical consultant. 'But when he began to see that I was earning as much as I had in a job, that I was seeing more of the kids and was enjoying myself, he gradually came round.'

- Keep some sort of office hours. You may start at eleven and finish at three, or work from three till eleven. It doesn't matter – provided you have some form of routine and stick to it. Make it clear that during these hours, you do not welcome disturbance from anyone who is not a client.

- Keep personal phone calls to a minimum. If a friend phones for a chat, explain politely that you are working and arrange a time that is clearly out of office hours to return the call. He or she will soon get the message. If your friends really can't leave you alone, you'll have to let the answer-phone take your messages and return them when it is convenient to you.

- Try to ensure that your family do not answer calls during work time. If it is unavoidable, try to instil in them the importance of a good telephone manner. An important client who puts in an initial call only to be greeted by 'yeah, so who are you then?' will not be impressed.

- Learn to separate your work self from your home self. 'Sometimes pupils' parents phone in the middle of the washing up,' says Judy Magnus, piano teacher. 'But I always make sure I take my apron off before I answer them, because it makes me feel professional. Similarly, I always change out of my "domestic" clothes and into my work suits before my pupils arrive. They are only children and so probably wouldn't notice the difference, but it helps me separate the different parts of my life.'

There are a variety of 'tricks' you can learn to separate home and work selves. Some women put on their make-up before going into their home office, just as they would do for an office job. Some men always put on a suit, even if they know they won't be seeing any clients that day. Yet others plan a strict diary with hours allotted to different tasks and a lunch hour.

Alternatively, you can remind yourself that in an office-based job you would have a finishing time and that you have to apply the same rules to working at home. This problem will be dealt with in detail in chapter 8.

'Phil' runs a specialist agency from home, but has found it tough going.
'When I used to go into an office, the kids were used to me coming

back and playing with them,' says Phil who feels his family's attitude has been the major block to successful working at home. 'They haven't really adapted to the fact that daddy is working while he's at home – even though I lock the door.'

Phil also feels his wife is resentful of the hours he spends on his business. 'I suppose she could understand it if I had a boss who was pushing me into working the hours I do, but it's the fact that it comes from me that upsets her,' he says. ' She sometimes says she'd rather I earned less and spent more time with the children, but it's not how it works.'

Phil, however, does feel that he misses out on being with the kids. 'They only have one childhood and I know I should spend more time with them.' However, when he is busy he feels fully occupied with work and when he is quiet, he feels obliged to spend all his time drumming up more. 'I don't really feel in control because I'm always waiting for someone to ring me,' he says. 'I suppose I haven't adjusted to that.'

Phil thinks he might look for premises soon – although he knows that financially he'll be worse off. 'But I think taking things out of my home might make things easier with the family and I think it will also mean I'll be taken more seriously.'

A SPACE OF YOUR OWN

Before you even start working from home, it is vital to consider exactly where you will be working and to ensure that you have one space that is always used for your work. The setting up of a home office is considered in detail in chapter 7, but some basic points are worth bearing in mind:

● Having a space of your own makes it much easier to separate your work life from your home life.' I tried working in the front room, but it meant that when I sat down to watch the TV, I couldn't help seeing all my papers and all the things I was meant to be doing the next day,' says May a medical secretary. 'It became very hard not to take them up and just have a quick browse through. Once I transformed the back room into an office, I could at least shut the door on my work and walk away.'

- If you have a space of your own, you are far less likely to be drawn into family life when you are meant to be working. 'Working with the children in the same room was impossible,' says Sally Wilkins, who started her baby-sling business on her kitchen table. 'I just couldn't concentrate and they all wanted my attention anyway. As we didn't have a spare room at the time, I found the only solution was to work when they had all gone to bed – often into the early hours. But at least I had my own space then.'

- Having a space of your own will also mean that your work life doesn't literally spill into your family life. It is difficult to live with boxes of papers on tables, or half-knitted garments that have to be moved whenever a visitor arrives. 'At first my friends thought it was fun to have dinner surrounded by hats,' says Katharine Goodison. 'But I found it uncomfortable.'

- If work and personal matters are kept too close together, you are also likely to find them getting muddled up, resulting in lost papers, documents etc. I first realized the importance of keeping work and family life absolutely separate when I left a tape of an interview lying around the dining room. My one-year-old promptly unravelled the tape, resulting in the complete loss of the interview.

- In some professions it is vital to have a space of your own in order to reassure people that you are a professional. This is particularly true in any area which has a great deal of client contact, such as being an optician, chiropodist, counsellor, beauty therapist, or consultant who expects to entertain clients at home. Most clients will want a degree of privacy that cannot be achieved with family members trying to live or eat in the same room.

● Many occupations require a great deal of equipment that needs a permanent home (e.g. a piano teacher needs space for a piano, a computer consultant needs a permanent station for a computer.) If you cannot find a permanent space for the equipment you need to carry out your professional duties, you will not be able to make a success of working from home.

● You will need to contact your building society (or other mortgage lender) if you plan to establish a home office. They are unlikely to raise any objections if you do not wish to alter the property, and if you do they will probably be the first in line to offer you home loans. A few properties also have restrictions preventing them being used for *any* form of business use – even if the use doesn't create noise or extra traffic and uses only a small part of the house. However, one civil servant whose work has brought him into contact with many home businesses says that 'People anticipate problems like planning and restrictive covenants, but in terms of owner-occupier houses most of the time there is no problem, provided the work isn't disturbing the neighbours.'

However, if you intend to convert a large part of your home into working space, you may also need planning permission. See chapter 3 for more details.

For council tenants and those living in privately rented properties, there are often restrictions on working at home. It's worth finding out before you start, though bear in mind that occupations which don't attract any commotion (mail order, word-processing, consultancy) are more likely to find favour than those which do (running a minicab service, tea shop etc.). 'Officially, our tenancy agreement says that the property must be used only for residential purposes,' says one housing officer, who doesn't want to be named. 'But, to be honest, if someone wants to knit, do office work – quiet things which involve very little traffic – we're not bothered. It's when the neighbours complain or the work starts to take over the whole property that we have to act. The most common complaint is of someone starting a car repair outfit out the front.'

If your work involves little traffic, few visitors and is largely invisible, the chances are that you won't bother anyone. However, you may need to do a lot more research into the official attitude if your work is highly visible and possibly disruptive.

Michael Levy works as a potter supplying Habitat and other major stores. He also teaches.

'Space is the big problem for me,' he says. 'Yesterday, I had two part-timers in and there was no room for me in the workshop at all, so I had to do the paperwork.' Michael has a workshop at the end of his garden, which he feels is a much pleasanter environment than the alternative of an industrial unit. 'And much cheaper too!'

He feels that it's important to 'start small and gradually add space as you get bigger. Doing it the other way round makes you much more vulnerable to the bills.'

Michael rarely feels isolated because he has employees coming into his home to work for him and also teaches. 'It could be depressing stuck here by myself all day,' he says. 'But that rarely happens. Having a variety of things to do also means that I'm always pretty enthusiastic about what I'm doing.'

DEALING WITH LACK OF SECURITY

If you are fully employed by a company or on a contract, this will not be an issue for you apart from the initial negotiation of your terms and conditions (see chapter 2 on persuading your manager to allow you to work from home). However, if you are self-employed, there is no doubt that lack of security is a major issue and it may be one that will never be completely resolved. This is because however successful you become, there will always be good times and mediocre – if not bad – times, and as the owner of the business, you will take the brunt of this. However, there are ways you can minimize the lack of security experienced by self-employed homeworkers:

- Set yourself realistic targets over a reasonable time-frame. If you previously earned £100 a week in your previous job, but set yourself the task of earning £200 a week each and every week from the day you start work, you will give yourself unnecessary stress trying to achieve it and may end up feeling depressed if you don't.

- Learn to average out your earnings. Being self-employed is not like earning a salary where you get a set amount paid every week or month. A self-employed person may earn a great deal one week, nothing the next, so it is important to average your earnings out over a period of time. Setting yourself monthly or even three-monthly targets will be better than weekly ones. Remember it takes time to build a business. Not even Anita Roddick or Richard Branson made a fortune in their first few months.

- Talk to other self-employed people about how they cope with peaks and troughs. If you can chat with a self-employed friend or family member about your difficulties, you will soon find that you are not alone and they may be able to offer constructive advice.

- Keep an eye on the market. If other people in your field are going through a boom time and you are in a slump, you may have reason to worry. However, if things are bad everywhere, it may be unrealistic to expect your business to be expanding by the week.

- Keep yourself busy. If you have a quiet week, rather than spend it fretting, work on new strategies for increasing your market share, call prospective clients or network to find some new ones.

If you still haven't decided whether you are right for homeworking try this just-for-fun quiz to assess whether you are likely to thrive – or skive – if you work at home.

Am I an office lover or a home bird?

1   How do you feel about office gossip?

a   Office gossip? I am the office gossip.

b   Well, I do like to know what is going on.

c   Couldn't care less, it's all trivial anyhow.

2   How do you feel about your colleagues?

a   Indifferent.

b   Good for an occasional laugh.

c   The best thing about working here.

3   How do you think your family would react to your working from home?

a   They'd be open-minded.

b   They'd love it – I'd be able to play with the kids more.

c   It's not something they've ever thought about.

4   A new employee is brought in at your level, but with a much more interesting-sounding job title. How do you feel about it?

a   I'm off to see the boss in the morning about this.

b   Mildly narked, but I'll consider whether to make a fuss about it.

c   Not that bothered. The job itself isn't as interesting and the pay is the same.

5   How good have you been at adapting to change in the past?

a   I don't like change.

b   It takes a bit of getting used to.

c   I like constant change and variety.

6   How easy did you find it to do your homework as a child?

a   Provided it was interesting I got down to it.

b   I got down to it eventually.

c   Never did it unless forced.

7 If your boss goes away on holiday what happens to the quality of your work?

a Slides a little, because s/he never leaves clear instructions.

b It's a semi-holiday for me – until the day before the return.

c My work improves because I have freedom to do things the way I want to do them.

8 How would you describe yourself socially?

a The life and soul of the party.

b Reasonably outgoing.

c A bit of a loner.

9 How organized are you?

a Very.

b Moderate.

c Not at all.

10 Do you have many interests outside work?

a Yes – lots.

b One or two.

c No.

11 A client you've previously got on with suddenly withdraws her work with no clear explanation. How do you feel about it?

a Lousy – I must have done something dreadfully wrong.

b Puzzled – so I'll question her about why she made the decision.

c Furious – she needs her brains examining!

12 How easy do you find it to say no when friends and family request a favour?

a I am quite firm if I can't do a favour, but I help out if I can.

b I always give in.

c They wouldn't dare ask.

SCORES

1 a 0, b 2, c 1	5 a 0, b 1, c 2	9 a 2, b 1, c 0
2 a 2, b 1, c 0	6 a 2, b 1, c 0	10 a 2, b 1, c 0
3 a 2, b 1, c 0	7 a 1, b 0, c 2	11 a 0, b 2, c 1
4 a 0, b 1, c 2	8 a 0, b 2, c 1	12 a 2, b 0, c1

Score 16–24 You'd probably love working from home. You are self-disciplined, confident in your own abilities and while you are able to work on your own you are sociable enough to be able to market yourself to strangers and keep your family happy. Go for It!

Score 9–15 You've got a lot of potential as a homeworker, but perhaps there is one area that might cause you problems. Is it that you love the cut-and-thrust of the office and its politics? Or is it that you find it hard to make contact with people (something you have to psych yourself up for as a homeworker). Or do you need a bit of a push to get you going in the morning? Think about the qualities needed for homeworking before you start.

Score 0–8 You might have difficulty with working from home – either because of communication problems (either with family or colleagues) or because you need to have the approval and presence of others to work best. If you have to work at home (perhaps because of company policy or to save costs) you might need to do some emotional – as well as practical – preparation.

Useful addresses

Association of British Chambers of Commerce (London), 9 Tufton St, London SW1P 3QB. Tel: 0171 222 1555

The Breakthrough Centre, 7 Poplar Mews, Uxbridge Road, Shepherds Bush, London W12 7JS. Tel: 0181 749 8525

Carers National Association (for anyone caring for a relative at home) 20–25 Glasshouse Yard, London EC1A 4JS. Tel: 0171 490 8818

Federation of Small Businesses, 32 Orchard Road, Lytham St Annes, Lancs FY8 1NY. Tel: 01253 720911

Gingerbread, 16–17 Clerkenwell Close, London EC1R 0AA. Tel: 0171 336 8183 (self-help groups for single parents)

Home Run (the magazine comes out about ten times a year and owners Andrew James and Sophie Chalmers are very helpful), Cribau Mill Llanvair Discoed, Chepstow, Gwent NP6 6RD. Tel: 01291 641222

National Council for One-Parent Families, 255 Kentish Town Road, London NW5 2LX. Tel: 0171 267 1361 (advice and support for single parents)

Ownbase, 68 First Avenue, Bush Hill Park, Enfield, EN1 1BN

Parents At Work, Fifth floor, 45 Beech St, Barbican, London EC2P 2LX. Tel: 0171 628 3565 (for working parents; also provides some support for working parents with special needs children)

Rotary International of Great Britain and Ireland (RIBI), Kinwarton Road, Alcester, Warwickshire, B49 6BP. Tel: 01789 765411

Round Tables (National Association of) Marchesi House, Embassy Drive, Birmingham, B15 1TP. Tel: 0121 456 4402 (men only but does have associated Ladies Circle)

Women In Management, 64 Marryat Road, London SW19 5BN. Tel: 0181 944 6332

Women's National Commission, 4th Floor, Dept of Education and Employment, Caxton St, Tothill St, London. Tel: 0171 273 5486

company is likely to increase. However, Professor David Birchall of Henley Management College, who has been studying teleworking, has found that firms where employees work remotely all the time are few and far between. He believes that in the future there will be more homeworking – but that it will be for part of the week, with employees going into a central office or local centre at least a couple of times a week. These local centres – 'telecottages' are already popular in many rural areas and seem likely to grow in the future.

WHY WORK FROM HOME?

For employees, there are a whole host of reasons why they may want to wish to work from home at least part of the time. These fall into several categories:

- The work can be done more efficiently at home. Interruptions in the office, or workplaces fraught with politics, can make it hard to concentrate.

- Quality of life issues – wanting to spend more time with the family; the need to care for a sick or disabled relative.

- Relocation – either of the company or of a spouse, or a wish to relocate to ensure a better quality of life.

- A wish to avoid a long, stressful commute – this is likely to become ever more pressing with traffic on the roads set to double in the next twenty years. Even now, most commuters spend two hours a day getting to and from work.

- Equal opportunities issues – e.g. to ensure that disabled people have the chance to take up employment.

A better quality of life?

Stephen Jupp works for Digital Equipment Corporation, a pioneering information technology company, and has been working from home in Hertfordshire on and off for over seventeen years. He started on an informal basis 'because my boss was very open-minded and appreciated that I felt it would be easier to concentrate on some of my work outside the office.'

Gradually, it became clear that much of Stephen's work could be done at home – enabling him to avoid a strenuous commute. 'The biggest relief was when they took away my desk at the office', he says. Although Stephen's reasons for wanting to work at home were largely practical, he has also found that 'working from home has enabled me to play a greater part in my local community. I take stuff to the post office and have a chat with local people. If I have a tricky problem and need time to think, I might walk the dog and stop for a chat with the people I meet. I firmly believe that teleworking can do a lot to revitalize local communities.'

In fact, Stephen even believes that teleworking could save your marriage. 'What happens at the moment is that one partner goes off to the office and becomes involved in the politics and the social life there, while the other partner is more home based with a totally different sort of life. As a result, the office worker may come to feel that his office life is more interesting and becomes more enmeshed with that. That means the partners end up becoming more and more distant from each other with the result that the marriage is weakened or even breaks down because they have nothing in common any more. When you are both at home, you are both involved in life at home.'

Stephen only commutes into head office once every couple of months – although this is where his secretary is based. She is one of around 3,000 staff who work from the office – the other quarter all working from home.

An office with a view. David Silk a management tutor, was motivated to work from home, largely because he'd long cherished a dream of working from a peaceful rural area – in this case, the Lake District.

However, Henley Management College, which employed him as a tutor, was situated several hundred miles from where he wanted to live. He solved the dilemma by becoming self-employed working on a variety of projects, but he still does some work for his old employers, tutoring their distance learning courses. This was made possible by computer software which enables him to comment on chunks of work or questions by accessing a central computer. However, he also visits Henley several times a year to keep in touch. 'If I hadn't worked there for so long, I would go in more frequently,' he says. 'But as I know the people I'm dealing with and have a good relationship with them, it's quite easy to communicate by e-mail and phone. I do think however, that you need to have a good relationship with the people you are working with in order to work from home successfully. Do I enjoy it? Of course!'

THE EMPLOYER'S VIEWPOINT

From the employee's perspective, the advantages of working from home are apparent. However, employers are much more ambivalent. A large number – probably the majority – will accept employees working from home some of the time on an informal basis. This is particularly true in the case of those firms which already encourage flexible working (e.g. job-sharing, part-time working) who are likely to see homeworking as just another option in their raft of employment options. A survey for the former Department of Employment found that very large firms (over 200 employees) and very small firms (under 20 employees) were most likely to encourage teleworkers. However, firms of all sizes had staff who worked for some of the time at home.

A few companies will adamantly forbid any homeworking at all, either because they have a culture which is inimical to it, or because the occupations within the company are inappropriate for homeworking (see list below).

There are also a small number of companies who have formal policies about homeworking and encourage teleworking. Burger King, for instance, first became interested in homeworking when their head office in Miami was hit by a hurricane. Homeworking became a necessity, but worked so well that it was quickly adopted for certain jobs elsewhere (not the behind the counter jobs of course!). Digital Equipment Corporation, for instance, have many employees working as teleworkers based at home or in local telecottages (small business units with a large amount of equipment). Cable & Wireless are also in the process of moving some employees into their homes and out of the central office. Both British Telecom and Mercury Communications have introduced various teleworking and flexible working experiments. Indeed, it does seem that certain types of industry are more open to homeworking than others. The types of company which seem to be pioneering the way include:

1 Financial (banks, building societies and financial services companies such as Allied Dunbar and National Westminster Bank).

2 Telecommunications and information technology (BT, Mercury, IBM, ICL, Digital).

3 Media (TV producers, editors, journalists, authors – a recent survey reckons a third of media employees are based at least part-time at home).

4 Government (national and local such as the Borough of Enfield, Sutton and Oxfordshire County Council for example).

5 Small consultancies.

Before you decide definitely that you want to work from home, check through personnel as to whether your firm has a policy on homeworking. If not, try to find out whether anyone else in the firm is working from home on an informal basis. 'One of the conditions of allowing me to work from home was that no one else should know about it,' says 'Janet' who works for a large publishing house. 'I thought that was unfair but agreed. Fortunately, my colleagues leaked the news for me and there are now several other people doing the same thing. To be honest, I think the fear that I would open floodgates hasn't happened because not everyone wants to work from home. But also I think that once management saw that I was actually managing, their fears subsided.'

If you cannot find anyone working from home already, you may need to prepare yourself for an uphill struggle. You will have to accept that the number of firms who will allow you to work from home full-time and supply your equipment, without a very pressing reason, can be counted on the fingers of two hands. So before you take the plunge and ask your boss, consider whether you are suitable for homeworking either part- or full-time.

IS HOMEWORKING RIGHT FOR YOUR OCCUPATION?

1   Is where you work an important part of the job?

>   **A: NO**
>   **B: YES**

If clients always expect to see you at your place of work, it may be difficult to transfer to homeworking. A doctor working in a casualty department, for instance, is unlikely to be able to work outside the hospital for any length of time, since patients expect to be treated at the hospital and that is also where support staff are based. On the other hand, if much of your work is *location independent*, i.e. can be done anywhere, you are much more likely to be able to work from home for some of the time.

2   **How much necessary face-to-face contact do you have on a daily basis?**

>   **A: NOT A LOT**
>   **B: A LOT**

A manager of a large branch library spends most of his day interacting with members of the public, who expect to see him on site. Similarly, if your work requires delicate face-to-face negotiations, it may be necessary to hire a meeting room, rather than speak with someone on the telephone from home. However, it has to be said that the Norwegian diplomat who brokered the Israeli–Palestinian peace deal invited both parties into his home for much of the undercover negotiations. Both said how much they enjoyed the homely and relaxed atmosphere.

3   **How much specialist, expensive equipment do you need to do your job?**

>   **A: NOT A LOT**
>   **B: A LOT**

And would your company be prepared to pay for it if you work at home? Who would insure it? Who would be liable if a client injured themselves falling off the chair in your dining room? (see chapter 7 for more details).

4   **How important is it to be able to bounce ideas off people in an informal, unplanned way throughout the course of the day?**

>   **A: NOT IMPORTANT**
>   **B: IMPORTANT**

The more you enjoy exchanging ideas at the coffee machine, and walking around the office to see what's going on, the less suitable you will be for homeworking.

5   How much of your work can be done alone?

> A: A GREAT DEAL
> B: NOT MUCH

The more work that can be done alone, the more likely you will be able to do it from home.

6   How much benefit do you get from observing your boss in action during the course of a working day?

> A: NOT A LOT
> B: SOME

In many industries training is almost entirely on the job, with juniors being expected to learn by watching seniors – something that's difficult if you are not on site. On the other hand, if you are already experienced in your work, you may not have much to learn from watching your colleagues or direct boss. It is worth noting that computer firm ICL only allows people to telework if they already have five years experience in their area, i.e. they are confident and are not on a steep learning curve.

7   How much day-to-day supervision do you require?

> A: NOT A LOT
> B: A LOT

The less you need, the more suitable your job is for working at home.

8   How much day-to-day supervision do you need to do?

> **A: NOT A LOT**
> **B: QUITE A BIT**

If your juniors are extremely well motivated, or also have the option of flexible working, you may not need to be on site all the time. However, if they are poorly motivated, untrained or resentful of your privileges, out of sight can become out of mind.

9   Does your company have a policy about homeworking? Are other people already working from home on an informal basis?

> **A: YES**
> **B: NO**

If the answer is yes, your company is already willing to take the idea of homeworking on board and are more likely to listen to you.

10   How much processing of information does your job require?

> **A: A LOT**
> **B: NOT MUCH**

Information based occupations such as economists, researchers, journalists and computer boffins are all likely to be able to do some work from home.

The more A's you have, the better your chances of working from home successfully. If you score more than five B's, think again – it sounds like your occupation is firmly tied to the office or factory.

Another way to assess whether you are suitable for homeworking is to analyse the nature of your occupation. The management consultants, Fresh Solutions, who specialize in setting up teleworking schemes for employers, have found this method useful in working out whether employees could work from home at least some of the time. They distinguish four categories of workers:

- **Specialists** by dint of their specialization often work alone. Technical writers, designers, academics etc. can all do a large proportion of work from home.

- **'Nomads'** travel from client to client or site to site in order to do their job. They could make their central base their home, rather than doing unnecessary travelling into an office. Sales teams, architects, marketing managers, would all fall into this category.

- **Managers** could spend part of the week at home, doing those tasks which require quiet – writing speeches or preparing presentations, compiling reports or doing budgetary tasks.

- **Clerical staff** could do tasks such as routine administration, data-processing and compiling lists from home.

Even if you know that your job is 100 per cent suited to working from home, you still need to ask yourself some hard questions about whether your personality is suitable for homeworking. See the quiz in chapter 1 or ask yourself briefly:

How suitable am I for homeworking? If you get a buzz from being with people, love to be in the thick of things and can remember just who's dating who in which department, homeworking may not be right for you. The same applies if much of your social life is based around the office or your place in the hierarchy is very important to you. On the other hand, if you are a self-starter, enjoy your own company in limited doses and find it easy to concentrate, you may be well placed to work from home. Confidence in your ability, self-discipline, a good network of local social contacts and enough space to work are all vital for a homeworker. 'I thought that I would spend more time working at home than I actually did,' says Ken Davey, who initiated Mercury Communications flexible work project. 'I used it for writing reports and initiating strategy, but I came to realize how much of my job depended on interacting with colleagues.'

How supportive are my family? Working from home, even part-time, does alter the family dynamics. Children will have to be taught to understand that mummy or daddy are not available for play and that they must be quiet if clients come. Some may even need to be taught how to take messages, although one disillusioned teleworker quoted in *The Telecommuters* by Francis Kinsman, said that 'you might as well open the window and shout out your message to the hills as expect my kids to answer it.'

It is vital to discuss the possibility of homeworking with your family *before* you discuss it with your boss. A recent British Telecom report cited the case of one spouse who became so fed up with her husband holding client meetings at home that she interrupted one meeting by pouring a bowl of cold water over her husband before silently walking out again!

'It's a difficult area,' says Joanna Foster, Head of the BT Communication Forum. 'There need to be distinct boundaries between work and home life that are accepted by everyone in the family.'

How hard am I prepared to fight in order to work at least part of the time from home? It's a good idea to know when you are prepared to give up the fight – will it be at the first refusal, when promotion prospects are jeopardized, or when you hand in your resignation? Clare, an editor on a trade magazine, had asked her boss several times about working part-time from home – and had always been turned down. However, after the birth of her second child, her maternity leave replacement left, and Clare was asked to return to work early to help out. She agreed – on condition that she be allowed to work from home at least two days a week. 'Once they saw it was working, they made it a permanent arrangement. The down side is that they cut my pay on the basis that it was less convenient for them. I was upset about it, but it was better than traipsing into the office.'

Cutting your wages because you work at home might be drastically unfair, but it is quite possible that an employer will offer this as a trade off. If you are a member of a union, they may be able to intercede on your behalf. Otherwise it is up to you to decide how much you are prepared to sacrifice.

Why do I want to work from home at all? If you want to work from home in order to escape a boss who makes Mussolini seem liberal, or to avoid cut-throat office politics, then maybe what you need is a change of employer, rather than a change of scene. On the other hand, if you enjoy your job and respect your employer, but the daily commute is getting you down, or you miss seeing your children, homeworking could be a solution. 'For me, working some of the time at home was a way of easing myself back into work after a career break,' says Judy Greavey, Human Resources Manager (Retail Services) of National Westminster Bank. 'When I'm at home, I might stop work when the kids come home from school and then work again in the evening, once they've gone to bed.'

> **'Estelle' was one of the first managers in her firm to take part in a pilot programme of homeworking.**
> She opted to work three days at home and two days in the office. 'I was the first person at my level to take part in the project,' she recalls. 'My boss was very supportive, firstly because it was his project, but

also because I was just coming back after maternity leave and he wanted to keep me.'

But Estelle feels the experience was not a success. 'Don't get me wrong. I feel teleworking could work, but it needs a lot of support – and I didn't get that. They'd rushed headlong into the project without thinking about it. For instance, whenever there was a fault with my computer, I had to take it back into the office to have it fixed. They hadn't arranged with anyone to come out and fix it. No one even showed me how to run the equipment that was meant to connect me with the office, so I was always going wrong with that. I had to set it up myself.'

Estelle also found it hard to adapt to her new relationships with her colleagues. 'I felt like a spare part and they were always joking that I probably spent my time playing with the baby.'

Matters came to a head when Estelle 's department was reorganized and she gained a new boss. 'He thought working at home was just a waste of time and made it clear he didn't approve.'

Despite her bad experiences, Estelle feels that homeworking can work. 'It did work, in fact, for the people who were more senior. They were senior enough to demand the support they needed – people coming out to them – and no one dared suggest they weren't working. I think it can work very well, but in a way you need to be prepared for it. It would have helped enormously if someone had gone through the possible problems and how to handle the new relationships with my colleagues.'

HOW TO PERSUADE YOUR BOSS TO GIVE WORKING FROM HOME A TRY

- First, do your homework. Find out if anyone else in the organization is working – or has worked – from home. Your union as well as the personnel department may know. If so, arrange to have a drink or meeting with them, to find out how they tackled the subject, how the arrangement works or, if it has stopped, why it ended.

'When I decided to move to the Isle of Bute, in Scotland, I thought I'd have to leave the bank,' says Kevin Attwood, Strategic Planning Development Officer for Nat West who now works two days from home, and three in London. 'In fact, I kept the move so quiet that when I told my boss I'd moved to Scotland over the weekend, he was flabbergasted. When we had lunch I said flippantly, that if I'd got my act together I would have come up with a strategic plan for teleworking. He told me to come up with a proposal. I rung up people in the bank who were already working from home some of the time and talked to them extensively before coming up with my plans. Listening to their experiences helped me make a convincing proposal.'

- Marshall your arguments. Do as much as research as you can about homeworking and the arguments for it. *The Teleworker* magazine also has lots of information about teleworking and how to manage it.

- Be clear as to why you need to work from home on a regular basis. Some situations – like moving several hundred miles away – are easy to explain. Most employers will also understand your reasoning (although that doesn't necessarily mean they will be sympathetic) if you need to care for a sick relative or child, or if you are disabled.

- Pick your moment carefully. Choose a time when you will not be interrupted, when the boss is not in a hurry and when you feel comfortable.

- Beware of committing yourself to a non-fallback position. Do not threaten resignation unless you really mean it. Suggest that you try homeworking for a trial period – say a couple of months. You may also find it easier to phase in the homeworking. 'My boss and I agreed that at first I'd work one day from home, then two and then three,' says Kevin Attwood. 'We both agreed that working two days from home was enough for both of us, but at least we had that flexibility.'

- Be prepared to be flexible in your demands – you cannot expect flexibility of your employer if you are not prepared to be flexible yourself. However, if not being allowed to work from home will mean you having to leave – in the case of relocation, pressing family commitments or a severely reduced train service, for instance – make that clear. Many firms are prepared to try tele- and homeworking rather than lose a valued employee. This is particularly true if you have been employed by the company for a considerable period of time. Newcomers and casual workers may find it much harder.

- Explain clearly just what jobs you plan to do from home, e.g. writing reports, assessing market research, processing data, thinking about issues, reading, answering letters etc. You may also need to reassure your boss as to the suitability of your home and related issues, e.g. how you intend to ensure client confidentiality. (The London Borough of Enfield insists that those homeworkers working on community charge files have lockable filing cupboards, for instance.)

- Suggest ways in which your output can be monitored. The most common gripe of those managers who use homeworkers is that they are hard to manage and cause communication difficulties. For that reason, it's very important that you develop a strategy which makes your manager feel that s/he will know what you are doing – and can talk to you about it. You might for instance suggest completing a certain number of tasks in a day, or ask for the quality of your work to be measured. It's a good idea to fix a meeting to go over what work has been done at home. But remember, one of the prime rules of working from home is that *output* (i.e. what you accomplish) is more important than *hours worked* (how long you can sit at a desk).

- Explain how you intend to keep in touch with the office. A survey for the Department of Employment and Education found that the most common ways for teleworkers to keep in touch were:

1 mailings

2 meetings

3 informal approaches

4 the telephone

5 memos.

Even if no one contacts you, make it your business to keep in contact with them.

- Tell your boss what is in it for the company. S/he may be interested to learn that repeated surveys have shown that people working from home are up to 40 per cent more productive, the quality of their output is improved and they work harder than office-bound employees. They also take fewer days off sick, largely because they are less exposed to other people's germs while commuting. It may also interest your employer to know that employers who already encourage homeworking report the major benefits are cost savings. Indeed, the Economic and Social Research council estimate that the average saving per employee is estimated at £1,500–£3,000 a year – largely because they save office space. 'I don't care quite frankly if people working from home do drink coffee some of the time or play an occasional round of golf,' says Ken Davey of Mercury Communications, who piloted their independent location working scheme. 'What I care about is the quality of work produced and if they can do that work best at midnight, that's OK by me. There are areas – like those which require client contact – where you do need to work a more regular day, but that's not always the case.'

This is an enlightened attitude, likely to lead to productive and happy employees. However, it has to be said that not all companies are so open-minded. Some of the most common excuses (rather than valid reasons) for turning down any form of homeworking include:

- **It's not been done before – so it's not being done now.** An illogical argument, since followed through this would lead to total stagnation in the company.

- **If you do it, everyone else will want to do it too.** Not necessarily. Many workers prefer to work in the office. If everyone, irrespective of their circumstances, wants to get out of the office as quickly as possible, there must be something badly amiss in the office itself.

- **I like you where I can see you.** This is shorthand for 'we don't trust you to do your work properly without supervision'. Only you can know if this is fair comment.

But don't despair. Carefully handled and researched, you have a good chance of sympathetic response if you have checked out the issues dealt with above. According to one Department of Employment survey, the qualities most likely to persuade an employer to allow someone to work from home at least part of the time were:

1 Self sufficiency (listed by 45 per cent of employers)

2 Maturity (listed by 25 per cent of employers)

3 Already experienced (15 per cent)

4 Suitable home (9.4 per cent)

5 Communication and time management skills (9.4 per cent).

Self-sufficiency and maturity have already been discussed. Clearly, it is also important for those working at home to be trained/experienced, in that there is much less help on hand for a homeworker than for someone working in an office. In fact, one of the enduring problems of teleworking is how to cope when your equipment breaks down! For this reason, most firms with a formal policy on teleworking have support staff and back-up systems in place.

However, it has to be said that at the moment, the majority of firms have no cohesive policy on working from home. But that doesn't mean it's not happening. What appears to be happening is that certain departments or even individual employees are being allowed to work from home in response either to their demands or the particular set-up of the department. This form of working from home is neither officially encouraged or discouraged, but seems to depend largely on the whim of the managers concerned – and the determination of employees. If you feel your working life could be substantially improved by working from home, take a close look at your firm and ask yourself whether it has taken on other forms of flexible working – part-timers, job-sharing etc. If the answer is yes, then the chances are good that you will be able to persuade them to let you work from home – at least some of the time.

SO YOU'VE PERSUADED THEM!

Congratulations! Now you will have to consider the nitty-gritty of arrangements necessary for your new working style to develop smoothly. The union for skilled and professional workers MSF have introduced some guidelines for homeworkers to ensure their health and safety at work. They may be a counsel of perfection – particularly if you are only working at home on a very part-time or informal basis – but they are worth bearing in mind. They include:

- Homeworkers should be employees of an enterprise and not deemed self-employed. (It is vital that this is understood when you start homeworking, as you will lose out on a host of employment rights if you become self-employed.)

- To avoid isolation, contracts of employment should require homeworkers to attend the office periodically.

- There should be a separate room available at home for working, a separate telephone and payment for additional costs.

- There should be regular meetings between homeworkers. Electronic mail and telephone links with other homeworkers should be provided at the employer's expense.

- There should be regular weekly liaison discussions between a homeworker and his or her supervisor/manager .

- Homeworkers should enjoy the same rates of pay and employment benefits as office based workers, including childcare provision and family leave. They should be included in career development and appraisal schemes, including training programmes.

- All computer equipment should be provided, paid for and serviced by the employer, who will be responsible for installation and compliance with health and safety requirements. The employer should also accept legal responsibility for any accident or injury.

- Health and safety advisors and trade union advisers should be able to visit homeworkers.

- There should be a defined number of working hours.

- Homeworking should be voluntary with the right to return to the office.

These guidelines will, of course, be more honoured in the breach for the foreseeable future. But even if your boss has only agreed to let you work from home a couple of days (or more) a week on a trial basis, you will still need to establish some basic details: who provides what equipment and who pays for what. Who will pay for business phone calls (an itemized bill is essential). You will also have to make sure that you indicate your whereabouts on each working day, so the boss knows where to contact you. Having agreed these fundamentals, you will then need to be aware of the more general demands on you that working at home can make.

Communication skills are important for anyone who is self-employed, but those working as employees of a company at home also need a whole range of communication skills that are more sharply honed than their office colleagues. For one thing, they need to be able to *communicate effectively over the phone* with colleagues. Gesticulation, nods and shakes of head are only useful if your colleague can see you. It's a good idea to phone your boss several times in the day – particularly at the end of it with a synopsis of what you have been doing. That's so they know that you have been working. Once you are back at the office, talk about – and show – what you've been working on at home. Ask for feedback if no-one offers it.

Homeworkers also need to work especially hard at ensuring they know what is going on within the office and *avoiding isolation..* When BT conducted a teleworking experiment, allowing some of its Inverness operators to work from home, they found that one of the main grumbles was that the operators felt they were not kept up to date with company news the way they had been in an office. For those who work only a couple of days at home, this can still be a problem. It pays to phone in on your days out and to take part in any social events in the office. When you are in the office, make sure everyone knows that you are there – and keep your wits about you. 'I make sure that when I'm in the office, I listen very carefully to what's going on,' says Helene Hook of the computer firm ICL. Kevin Attwood of Nat West Bank has formalized the process by having an updating meeting with his boss every week.

Stephen Jupp of Digital Equipment finds that one of the most effective ways to communicate with colleagues in the office is to arrange meetings, 'but to be sure that I know exactly what I want to achieve before I go into the meeting. If you are meeting infrequently, there are no second chances.' He also phones up colleagues frequently for a chat about what's going on.

Finding out what's going on in the office is vital if you are to feel you are playing an important role in company life. Far from being unimportant, office gossip is often the chief way in which company news is transmitted. Job vacancies, resignations, changes in company policy, are often widely known through office gossip long before they are officially announced.

According to Cary Cooper, Professor of Occupational Psychology at the University of Manchester Institute of Science and Technology, being *less visible* in the office can mean your chances of getting promotion are severely affected. He suggests that the only way for homeworkers to be sure they are remembered is to keep in touch – whether it's by phone, fax or email.

Organizing yourself for the home-to-office run

There is nothing more annoying than getting to the office and discovering you've left the vital papers at home, or vice versa. However, good organization and knowing what tasks are allocated to what environment can solve that. Pam Block, who works as an accountant for Oxfordshire County Council, rigorously divided her day up into office tasks and home tasks. 'I came into the office every morning and used that time for meetings, time with my staff – people oriented work. Then I left work to be home for when my children came back from school. In the evening, when they'd gone to bed, I used that time to do tasks that required concentration – spreadsheets, writing reports etc.'

Pam found that it was vital to keep a note of just what materials were at home and what in the office, so she could be sure of having everything where it was needed.

Now that her children are older she has eased herself back into an office job. 'Working part-time in the office enabled me to get back into the swing very quickly. I have to say though, that working at home is very efficient. It is a lot harder to find time for concentrated work when you are in the office and being interrupted all the time!'

Homeworkers can also find out that they *miss out on opportunities for training* – simply by not being informed on time. The solution is to ensure that your boss knows just how keen you are for any training – backed up with periodic reminders if necessary. If you are expected to operate computer equipment that you are not used to, make sure you get training on it before you start working at home – and that you are entitled to help from the office support systems.

It is important to realize that colleagues may *feel jealous* of your flexible working arrangements. You may make life very difficult for yourself if you insist on rhapsodizing about your life in the country and how you spent the preceding afternoon out walking, if you know your in-house colleagues are trapped in a grimy inner-city office. This is one occasion where discretion may be the better part of valour. Indeed, when Ken Davey of Mercury introduced his Location Independent Working Scheme, he was well aware that other employees might view his team as 'leading the life of Reilly, coming and going as they pleased and working when they wanted to.'

He challenged this by explaining to colleagues in the office that working at home and on the move did present its own drawbacks and risks. Even so, he admitted in a paper on the subject that 'our real problems have been in managing our peers who still see us as having special privileges, despite explanation. It may be that this is the price you have to pay – if so it may signal that those who are not working flexibly are keen to adopt flexible working practices too.'

The moral of the story is that if you are one of the very few allowed to work from home, it is a good idea to play up the difficulties, rather than tell everyone about how you were on the golf course when they were slaving over a hot desk!

One of the major difficulties of homeworking is that it is very easy to *overwork*. Without exception, everyone I spoke to for this chapter felt that they had worked harder at home than in the office. 'I find that I sit down at 9 a.m. and, because I'm concentrating really hard and don't get any interruptions, I look up and suddenly it's 2 p.m.,' says Stephen Jupp. 'I haven't had any lunch, my back and neck are stiff and I suddenly become aware that I've worked flat out.'

It is vital to build breaks for yourself in the day – just as you would in an office. Set an alarm clock to go off at lunchtime if necessary. Try to get up from your word processor at least every hour and walk round and stretch your legs. It is also important to leave your work behind when your day is officially finished. If you find this difficult, make up your own ritual. One man I know takes his tie off when he feels his day is officially ended. Another woman goes out of the house, walks round the block and then re-enters. These may seem extreme rituals, but without commuting time or distance from the office, you do need a way to learn to switch off. It is also important that your colleagues understand that although you are working at home, that does not mean you can be interrupted all the time. Tell them when you are working – and be firm about when you are not. This is vital, as according to Professor Noel Sheehy of the University of Belfast, who has made a study of homeworkers, people working at home can end up routinely overloaded. This is because employers find it much harder to gauge how much work a homeworker is doing. 'When you're in an office, you can look round and see that Jane is buried under a sheath of papers, or that Fred is walking round looking as if he has the weight of the world on his shoulders. You know just by looking who is busy and who is not. It's much harder to tell that down a telephone line.'

He also points out that homeworkers can be a victim of office politics – if someone is strenuously resisting taking on a project, it is much easier to post it off to an out-of-sight homeworker than have a face-to-face confrontation about it.

Another important issue is *security*. If you work in an area where you are frequently dealing with confidential documents, it is vital to have facilities for locking them away. Leaving them on the coffee table could be a serious breach of confidentiality. You also need to be aware of your own security. Social workers, council tax collectors and others who work in sensitive areas may need to take extra precautions to protect themselves. This means, at the least, being careful about whom you give your home address to, refusing to see clients alone unless specifically pre-arranged and getting yourself a good alarm and security system. A separate business line might also be a good idea. (See chapter 6 for other thoughts on security.)

This may sound daunting, but remember – over 80 per cent of employees who are working at home believe that their quality of life has been improved by homeworking. Making sure you know the pitfalls before you start can maximize your chances of avoiding them and increase your chances of success. Homeworking will only be a success if you – and your employer – are equally pleased with the arrangement. As Pam Block, accountant for Oxfordshire County Council, remarks: 'working part of the time from home and part of the time from the office not only helped ease me back into work, it also meant I didn't miss out on my kids and was very efficient into the bargain. I think that's a good deal all round!'

Useful addresses

British Telecom (has a range of user-friendly booklets on homeworking)
Tel: 0800 800854
Fresh Solutions, Haultwick Farm, Haultwick, Herts, SG11 1JQ. Tel: 01920
438001

MSF, 33–37 Moreland St, London EC1V 8BB. Tel: 0171 505 3000

Mercury Communcations (has an interest in promoting teleworking and has information for homeworkers) Tel: 0500 500 194

National Association of Teleworkers, Tel: 01404 42327

New Ways to Work, 309 Upper St, Islington, London N1 2TY. Tel: 0171 226 4026 (information on working at home from the employers' perspective)

The Teleworker Magazine (excellent for keeping in touch with the latest in technology and training)

The Other Cottage, Shortwood, Nailworth, Gloucestershire, GL6 OSH. Tel: 01453 834874 (the Telecottage Assocation can also be contacted at **The Telecottage Association, WREN Telecottage, Stoneleigh Park, Warwickshire, CV8 2RR.** Tel: 01203 696986

THREE

On your marks – the count-down to setting up your own business from home

There are all sorts of reasons to start up a business. It may be that you have worked for someone else, but now want the rewards that working for yourself can bring. This is often why professionals such as solicitors, accountants, architects and even GPs decide to set up their own practice. It may be that you have spotted a gap in the market and just have to follow it through, or it may be that you have been made redundant and self-employment seems the best – if not the only – option.

All the predictions are that self-employment will grow as companies continue to shed staff and replace them with outside contractors who are employed on one-off jobs or specific projects. In Charles Handy's fascinating book, *The Empty Raincoat*, he predicts the growth of small organizations with a very small permanent staff – but with a whole host of outside sub-contractors being brought in for one-off projects, all of whom are already self-employed.

Whatever the reason that you are considering self-employment, there is one overriding consideration: *cost effectiveness*. Premises are a major overhead and when you are starting a business you want to keep overheads down as much as possible. It's fine to take premises when you are making tens of thousands in profit and employing a team of staff. It is quite another matter to shackle yourself to renting an office, when your business is in the embryonic stages and your outlay is more than your income. What's more, there are tax benefits in working from home as you may be able to get tax deductible expenses for some of your heating, lighting and telephone bills.

BRICKS AND MORTAR

One reason why people mistakenly rent expensive premises, is that they feel the clients will be unlikely to give their business to someone working from home – the supposition being that grandiose offices give an air of success which attract a client. Andy Unger, Chair of the Young Solicitors Group, (an increasing number of whom are already working from home), is sceptical about that argument. 'I think that nine times out of ten, the client does not care where you are working, provided the job is done as they want it, on time and at an acceptable price.' He also points out that since clients rarely arrive unannounced, it is easy enough to arrange appointments either at their offices (often something for which a client is extremely grateful) or at a suitable meeting room.

Andrew James, publisher of *Home Run*, also feels that working from home, but hiring a meeting room for important appointments, can be an ideal solution. 'The meeting room can be at a venue convenient to you both. There is normally tea and coffee laid on and you might have a lot more space than if you were in a cramped little office somewhere.'

While most businesses can be adapted to working from home, there are certain constraints. If you have the sort of business which carries a lot of stock (although you would be unwise to carry much stock until the business has proved itself) you need somewhere to store it. It is also vital that you have a room, or at the very least a set space, set aside for your work and yours alone. If you are dealing with clients on a regular basis, say as a counsellor, optician, GP or therapist, then a separate consulting room is vital. If you haven't the space for one, you may either have to consider abandoning working from home altogether, or look for a new solution, such as converting a shed to an office – but it needs to be well built, as clients are unlikely to have faith in anyone who entertains them in a shack with a leaking roof. One GP has a deluxe surgery cum shed in her garden. There are also legal requirements and planning considerations to take into account. It is wise to be aware of these before you set up the business.

WILL YOU BE ALLOWED TO WORK FROM HOME?

If you own your home there may be *restrictive covenants* which make it difficult for you to work from home. However, as someone has to enforce those covenants against you, this is only likely to be a problem if you are planning to change the character or nature of your home substantially. Beavering away in your study is unlikely to cause a problem; turning the whole of the downstairs into a restaurant might. Much the same rules apply if you are renting your property or are a council house tenant (see chapter 2 for more details).

One way to forestall any possible trouble is to keep the neighbours informed if there is likely to be occasional disruption. If you are a mum at home with children and intend to become a childminder, then it is likely that you already have a constant procession of young children trooping in and out of the house, so becoming a childminder will not make much difference. (One of my previous neighbours ran a playgroup, but it took a long time for me to realize it was a playgroup rather than children visiting.) On the other hand, if you have lived alone with your cats for ten years, but decide to open a large nursery, your neighbours might well notice the difference and become difficult if not consulted. They could also seek to force you to get planning permission – and then oppose the application – so it is well worth trying to head off trouble by finding out what the planning requirements are in advance.

Most neighbours will not notice the difference if you are

teaching/researching/doing consultancy work. If you want to run a shop-front type business, or a tea shop from home, they may be more wary.

If, alas, you are one of the unfortunates who have neighbours who complain if they hear a goldfish blinking, you have a major problem. Brace yourself for a battle royal should you decide to work from home in any way that is vaguely visible.

PLANNING PERMISSION – WHO NEEDS IT?

In general, you will not need to apply for planning permission if working at home, *provided* the character and use of your home remain substantially residential. This means that you can have an office, run a catering business etc. from home, *as long as most of your home is used as a home.*

However, if you intend to use a large part of the house for work or a couple of rooms exclusively for work (and that includes the garage and shed) then you may in certain circumstances need planning permission. A lot hangs on the world *exclusively*. You can help yourself avoid this trap by having a few domestic activities that are done in working areas. According to the Department of the Environment's booklet on planning permission, the key questions are:

1 Will your home no longer be used mainly as a private residence? If the answer is **YES** planning permission will be needed.

2 Will your business result in a marked rise in traffic or people calling? If the answer is **YES** planning permission will be needed.

3 Will your business disturb your neighbours at unreasonable hours, or create other forms of nuisance, such as noise or smells? If the answer is **YES**, then planning permission will be needed.

These questions are, of course, highly subjective. You might say that someone who has never had any visitors at home and then starts a business with one client now has a 100 per cent rise in traffic outside their home, but it is highly doubtful that they would need planning permission.

If in any doubt, contact your planning officer at your local council and discuss it with him or her informally. If you need to apply for a formal decision, you will need to pay a fee. If permission is granted, you will receive a *lawful development certificate*. If the certificate is refused, then you may need full planning permission.

Fighting for the right to work at home

Planning permission disputes can, unfortunately, be both tiring and depressing. Michael Parker, who runs his caravan accessories business from home, endured months of worry when his neighbours reported him to the council for causing added traffic and disruption. 'They logged twenty-two cars and said that this was an enormous rise in traffic outside the house,' recalls Michael. 'Fortunately, I was able to prove that twelve of those cars belonged to family and friends, while five of them belonged to officers from the council who were investigating me!'

Michael had bought his house precisely because it was situated close to a light industrial estate, so the prospect of having to move out was not enticing. He decided to fight the planning permission order. 'The best move I made was joining the Federation of Small Businesses, who gave me legal advice and also suggested getting in an independent planning officer,' he recalls. 'He was a breath of fresh air. The minute he got involved, the council started to back off. I won but it was a struggle.'

When should you apply for a formal decision? You should do so if you are unsure whether the character of your house might change (or that your business may cause disruption, increased traffic etc.), but suspect you will have a fight on your hands. If you intend to make jam from your kitchen, it is only the worst of neighbours who would suggest that you are causing noxious smells (unless you are a very bad jam-maker). However, if you do have the neighbours from hell on site, a legal development certificate might well stop them in their tracks!

If in doubt, the Royal Town Planning Institute suggests that you contact your local planning officer for advice. Planning permission can be a lengthy process, although nine out of ten small business applications are successful.

A useful booklet, which gives more details about planning permission, is the catchily titled *Planning Permission: A Guide for Business* available free from the Department of the Environment. The Royal Town Planning Institute can give you the name of a planning consultant, who may be able to help you should you need to fight for planning permission.

Even if you do not need planning permission, you may need to pay *business rates*. See chapter 7, and the section on B & B in chapter 9 for more about this.

THE VALUE OF MARKET RESEARCH

Once you have decided to run your own business from home, you need to decide on the type of business you are going to run. You may, for instance, already be self-employed and merely looking to save costs by working from home. Or you may be a professional – such as solicitor, barrister, architect, accountant, optician or management consultant – looking to start up on your own.

Alternatively, you may have a brilliant idea for a new product or service – or intend to buy an on-going business. Whatever your thoughts, it is vital to do some thorough market research before you even think of handing in your notice – or doing a business plan. If you have already been made redundant and are desperate to start your own business, doing market research will prevent you from making costly mistakes.

What is market research? At its most basic, it means establishing that someone wants to buy what you want to sell. At a more refined level, it can also be used to find out just who your target customers are, how much they are prepared to pay for your services and how often they need them. For instance, if you are selling antique grandfather clocks, you might be quite content if every potential customer purchases one item in a lifetime. However, if you are selling children's clothes and find that potential customers only intend to buy one item in a lifetime, it is back to the drawing board for you!

MARKET RESEARCH – THE TECHNIQUES

1   **The questionnaire**   One simple way to establish whether there is a demand for your services is to give a questionnaire to those people who you think will be most interested. Kiren Darashah, a clothing designer, had a hunch that there was a gap in the market for specialist children's clothes. 'I'd hear people complaining about gaps in the market, or talking about it on the street,' she recalls. 'But I hadn't done any market research to back up my instinct.'

Kiren made up a very small range of clothing and then took it round to local mother and toddler groups, homes and workplaces, where there were a lot of parents. She gave everyone who looked at her clothes a questionnaire asking their personal details (including their children's birthdays), their opinion of her clothes, where they normally bought their clothes and how much they expected to pay. From this information, she was able not only to decide how to develop her line, but also how it would be priced and where it would be sold (she started off by using party-plan and mail order).

Kiren feels that the questionnaire was invaluable both in allowing her to get her business off the ground and in helping her present a plausible *business plan* (see below). 'I use market research all the time,' she says 'because you have to be aware if the market changes. If my customers can afford less than they used to, I need to know about that and I need to know what they like and what they don't. Market research gave me the courage of my convictions, but also helped me tailor my ideas to the market – there is no point making something no one wants.' Kiren feels it is largely as a result of market research that she went from a customer base of 0 to 350 within her first year.

A questionnaire can be useful not only if you are trying to sell a product, but also if you want to sell a service. If, for instance, you plan to start a book-keeping service, it might well be worth leafleting local businesses with a questionnaire about how they get their books done now and what they look for in a book-keeper.

TIP: It is notoriously difficult to get back questionnaires from clients. You may get a higher response rate if you offer a prize or incentive, however small.

2 **Keeping your ear to the ground – trade journals, networking, foot-slogging** Another method of market research is to read widely around your subject. This can be useful in finding out if a gap in the market exists, if an existing business is a good bet, or if your service is likely to attract clients. Read your trade journals to see if anyone has a similar idea, who is selling what and what businesses are doing well. If you want to find out a particular company's turnover, you can do so at Companies House for the payment of a small fee – provided they are a Limited Company.

Go along, too, to professional or trade events. Linda Greenbury, a careers counsellor, found that by joining various professional associations, she was able to get a better idea of what sort of problems were likely to occur on the career front, while

Andy Binfield, a wood turner, regularly used craft fairs to talk to colleagues. 'I'd ask them about which fairs were worth doing and see if I could get a consensus. But I also did market research on the areas the craft fairs were in. For instance, I keep a track of local unemployment patterns. A fair may do very well one year, but if the major employer shuts down the next year, you can bet that fair won't do well at all. It's worth doing that sort of market research, because going to a craft fair which doesn't pay is an expensive mistake.'

TIP: Where to start your market research if you are exploring a relatively unknown area? The best place to start is in a large reference library, probably your county or city one. These libraries contain lists of all sorts of information – from back copies of newspapers (and their business pages) to reference books on virtually every topic under the sun and a whole host of directories. There is even a Directory of Directories!

Make friends with the librarian, as they will have a fount of local knowledge at their finger tips – or know where to find it. It is also a fair bet that if a librarian doesn't know, she'll know a man (or woman) who does. Universities, careers services, certain major companies and hospitals also have libraries which may be open to the public.

Foot-slogging is also a good method of doing market research. If you want to find out if there is enough demand in your area to start a sandwich service, walk round the local industrial estates, find out how many staff are in each building and ask them when they come out what they normally do for lunch. You may discover that they all have staff canteens – in which case you need to go back to your drawing board and think again. Be aware, too, that each locality has its own character – which may affect both the pricing of your product and the product itself. There is no point trying to charge thousands of pounds for items which you hope to sell in areas of high unemployment. Heather Grant, part of the duo who run the catering business Lewis and Grant, has found that even tastes differ in parts of the country. 'You can do some interesting market research just by talking with other caterers. We've discovered that people outside London tend to like bigger portions and that certain dishes which are popular in metropolitan areas aren't popular outside. Times change too. In the eighties, sweets weren't really fashionable; now a lot of caterers are finding that everyone wants gooey deserts – comfort food for recessionary times, I suspect!'

3 **Suss out the competition**   One way to find out more about your chosen area is to look at the competition. If, for example, you are thinking of buying a business, you would be unwise to accept the vendor's word that she just wants a rest, but has a brilliant business, without doing some market research. As well as talking to her current clients, you need to find out about other competitors to get an idea of how viable the business is.

If you are planning to launch yourself as a beauty therapist, look in the Yellow Pages to see how many local salons there are. Then go round and find out what they are offering. Perhaps you can offer something extra/cheaper/different. You need a *USP* (unique selling point) to ensure that your service – or product – will be a success.

It is also worth talking to competitors if you bear two points in mind – they will generally overstate how successful they are; and they will not give you any information likely to prejudice their own business.

4 **Putting a toe in the water**   One way of finding out how business is likely to develop is to dabble a toe in the water and see what customer response is. This approach is particularly useful for things like crafts, where buying is often on impulse. One very small scale way to test the waters is to become part of the WI markets. This is a co-operative run by the Women's Institute, with goods being sold on stalls for a couple of hours each week. Or you might exhibit your wares at the school or hospital fete, or even take a stand at a trade fair as Louise Morrey did for her collection of

painted wooden animals. 'I talked to giftware sellers about the various trade fairs and visited a few, then took a stall,' says Louise, who sells her hand-painted gifts through the National Trust as well as other outlets. 'I got interest, but I also used prospective customers' comments as a way of researching what they wanted. You have to make what the customer wants. There is no point otherwise. I discovered the customers wanted useful items – decorated watering cans, brushwear, footstools – so that is what we make.'

If you plan to offer a service, talk to potential customers, although be aware that initial enthusiasm might not translate into offers of work. 'I asked all my old clients if they'd give me work,' says one consultant. 'They all said yes, but when I actually set up, very few delivered. Now I learn to take a conservative estimate of responses.'

Mike Conroy, Manager of Small Business Services for the Midland Bank says that many people don't like to actually say that they don't need a particular service 'so they say "that sounds interesting" and the prospective small business person interprets that as a yes. When the business person comes to start up, however, the number of people who actually buy the service or product is far less than expected. That's why I always ask people how they have arrived at their prospective sales figures. The vaguer their answer, the more suspicious I am.'

The moral is that when it comes to starting up, doing your market research is vital. But it pays to be pessimistic and take the worst-case scenario, as revealed by your research, at least as seriously as the glorious future that might result if all your best-case forecasts turn out to be true.

The benefits of research
Christine Buckingham, set up her ironing service when she felt the one she was using was ripping her off. 'They'd charge £6 if my

husband answered the door and £10 when it was me!' she says.' I was furious.'

However, Christine, a nurse, didn't want to go into the business without thorough research. So she talked to colleagues at the hospital and also examined the area she wanted to work in thoroughly. 'There are lots of big families around there who want the ironing done – lots of women who work and a prosperous area – so I thought I'd be in with a chance.' She also rang up other agencies to get an idea of pricing before she started off.

'We were careful about where we advertised,' says Christine. 'We chose schools, newsagents windows and surgeries because we knew that's where our audience would be.' The business grew steadily, although ironically Christine doesn't do any of the ironing herself. 'It's my sister-in-law who's keen on ironing. Can't stand it myself.'

Christine feels that her market research has paid off. 'This is a business like any other and you need to know just who you are going to appeal to and what you are going to do to make them come back to you.'

THE PRICE OF SUCCESS

Market research is also invaluable in *pricing* your product or service. Ron Flounders, of Hertfordshire Business Link, which offers free advice to start-up businesses, says that all too often people work out their pricing 'back-to-front'. They ask themselves how much they need to earn, what their costs are, and then price the product accordingly – regardless of what the market will pay. In fact, what you need to do is market research to establish what price the market will pay, then work out your costs and from that see whether it is worth going into business at all.'

Pricing will depend on a number of factors, including *the local rate for the job* – which you can establish by looking at competitors, trade journals etc. You can also find out using a questionnaire exactly what people are prepared to pay – a method of operation which Kiren Darashah of the Ben Go Tig children's clothing company, found exceedingly useful. 'I discovered from my questionnaire that my proposed price point was too high, but by adapting the designs, materials and finishings, I was able to make clothes at an acceptable price point, which ensured they sold a lot better than they would otherwise have done.'

CAN YOU MAKE A PROFIT?

Of course, you also need to ensure you make a profit. That means working out what your costs are. Costs come in two categories – fixed costs and variable costs.

Fixed costs are those costs you have to pay however many sales you make – or even if you don't sell anything. For instance, a beauty therapist would have to pay for a couch, even if she failed to attract a single customer. A consultant would have to pay telephone bills, even if none of the calls result in any work. Fixed costs often include: stationery, heating, lighting (over and above your domestic use), interest on loans, insurance premiums, leasing or hire payments, depreciation of equipment you have purchased, and advertising expenditure.

Variable costs are the costs that vary according to what you produce. For instance, if you are a potter, clay is a variable cost, because the more pots you make, the more clay you need. The price of clay in itself may vary from day to day and depending on the quantity you buy at once. Variable costs include materials, petrol and postage.

Add all your costs up – then add what you feel is a reasonable margin/labour cost. Does it tally with what the market is prepared to pay? If not, you will either have to find a way to reduce costs, or rethink your idea totally. 'Pricing is very difficult,' says Carola Brassey, a cake decorator, 'because people are only prepared to pay so much for a cake, however many hours you may have worked on it. That's why I always work out how long a job will take before I quote.'

'Working from home means that I can often undercut the competition, because my overheads are less', says accountant Nick Weedon. 'People who have expensive premises have to charge for that.'

One problem which people often have when starting off – particularly those who are transforming a hobby into a business – is that they are unwilling to charge friends a realistic rate for their product. This often means the business flounders through their goodwill. If you are setting up a business, you must charge a rate which is both acceptable to the market *and* covers your costs and still gives you an income. A true friend who wants the goods will be prepared to pay the market rate, rather than using you as bargain basement.

It is also important to be aware of the break-even point. Even if you do not do your books yourself, you should be aware not only whether they are showing you profits or losses, but where those profits and losses are occurring. It is perfectly possible to have one highly profitable item – and one which is holding your entire range down.

'I always worry about people who tell me the reason they will succeed is that they are going to charge less than the competition,' says Mike Conroy, the Midland's Small Business Services Manager, 'because there may be a reason the competition charge as they do – like that's what it takes to make a profit. And when people tell me they are going to be cheaper than a major supermarket, somehow I doubt it. Oddly enough, putting up your prices can actually make the business a success because you actually need fewer customers to break even – even if you do lose some. And there are some services where people are suspicious of cut-price rates, because they think cut-price rates equal poor quality. And quality is often the key to success.'

He suggests that if you are having problems with your pricing, rather than reducing prices, try to add value – an extra bottle of wine with your gourmet take-away if the customers buy two in a row or an extra hour of gardening for anyone who buys ten hours worth of your time.

He feels it is also important never to underestimate your costs or the time taken. 'If a mail order firm promises you that the good will arrive in 72 hours and they arrive in 48, you think they've done a marvellous job. But if they promised you the goods in 24 hours and they arrive in 48, you think they are hopeless.' The same applies to price. Conservative estimates are the best ones.

HOW TO GET GOOD ADVICE

Once you've done your market research and worked out if you can make a profit from the business, the next step is to take advice. This will not only confirm whether your calculations are realistic, but can take a lot of the pain out of setting up. The good news is that there's lots of advice available – and much of it is free. What's more, experts on small businesses reckon that over 60 per cent of small business failures could be avoided if only people took advice in three areas – money, management and marketing.

1   **TECs/LECs**   A good place to start is your local *Training and Enterprise Council (TEC), or Local Enterprise Council (LEC) in Scotland*. These can also put you in touch with other helpful agencies, such as your local *Enterprise Agency* and *Business Link*. You can find them through your telephone book, Yellow Pages or local library. The Department of Trade and Industry also has a hotline.

    The service provided by the TECS and LECS varies from region to region, but in general they should offer at least a few of the following:

- Enterprise awareness seminars, or courses, to alert prospective businesses of the requirements and pitfalls of starting a small business – and some training in these areas.

- An introduction to business skills such as book-keeping, marketing, training.

- Information about loans and grants that may be available to you. For instance, SOLOTEC, the TEC for South London, provides a comprehensive list of sources of finance for businesses in their area.

- A personal business advisor, to talk through your plans for your business, (although you may have to pay for this.)

- Some TECs or Business Links can put you in touch with any start-up *grants* for small businesses. The discretionary Business Start-Up Scheme offers financial assistance and training to long-term unemployed people who are thinking of starting up a business in certain areas. You need to provide an acceptable business plan and the amount you are 'paid' varies between TECs – with a maximum of £90 a week for 66 weeks, although it can be as little as £20 a week for 26 weeks. Other TECs provide grants towards the cost of consultancy for your business. There are also grants for areas which are reckoned to be in special need of assistance.

- The Enterprise Initiative Consultancy Scheme enables small firms who meet certain criteria to employ consultants they might otherwise not be able to afford, in areas such as design, marketing etc. However, this is of most use to those businesses that have already set up. For more details contact your local Business Link or TEC.

Paul Mitterhuber, an osteopath who recently started his own practice, went on a two-day course at his local TEC. 'It was really worthwhile, because they talked a lot about marketing, which gave me some good ideas for doing some marketing and PR of my own – perhaps getting the local paper involved, or local celebs.'

Elizabeth Newport, a former teacher now helping to run an accommodation agency for foreign students, feels that a course by her local TEC aimed specifically at women was 'the best thing I could have gone on. It was brilliant not only in giving practical advice, but in making my confidence grow.'

2   **Banks**   Another useful source of advice is banks, most of whom have a free start-up pack that they can make available to small businesses as well as a small business advisor. It is well worth chatting to local banks, before you decide to go ahead with your project, even if you do not plan to get finance from them at the time of setting up. The chances are that sooner or later you will need the advice/lending facility of a bank and the more informed you keep your bank, the more helpful they are likely to be. If you plan to ask for a loan, you could try rehearsing your business plan on a bank other than your own. If they snap you up, you are then in an excellent negotiating position with your own bank. If they do not, they may be able to tell you why not.

3   **Trade or Professional Associations**   Your trade or professional association can be an excellent source of advice. Verna Wilkins, who runs the highly successful Tamarind Books specializing in children's books featuring positive images of black children, says that much of her advice came from other publishers. 'They let me in on how to get good agreements with distributors, passed on tips about bookshops and generally told me just what publishing was. I had a lot of lunches with people, went to plenty of meetings and generally got out and about. I not only learnt a lot about the business but I made some very good friends!'

Such advice is generally free, although you will normally have to pay a fee to subscribe to the professional organization.

The *Association of British Chambers of Commerce* can also be a good source of advice, as can organizations like the Federation of Small Businesses, who provide a free legal advice line to their members. Again, you will need to pay a joining fee. If you live in a rural area, The *Rural Development Commission* has a major role in helping rural businesses to start up. Other government help can be found through the *Department of Trade and Industry* and *Local Government Offices*. The DTI, in particular, has a useful series of booklets for small firms including *A Guide to Help for Small Firms* which not only gives details of grants and loans, but covers services to help *Innovation* and *Technology* based firms.

4   **Legal Advice**   If you decide to go into partnership, or become a limited company, you will definitely need legal advice. However, in the meantime, it is well worth considering the *Lawyers for Business* scheme, which offers a free legal consultation to businesses who are setting up or established. Contact the *Law Society* and get their *Lawyers for Business* leaflet to find out who is taking part in the scheme locally.

5   **Citizens Advice Bureaux**   Your local Citizens Advice Bureau may also be able to help with basic financial problems. Many branches can also provide, or have access to, a debt counselling service.

MONEY, MONEY, MONEY – WHAT YOU NEED AND HOW TO RAISE IT

It is a sad fact of life that most small businesses require capital to start up. There are a few businesses which require only the minimum of equipment and stationery (journalism, PR and teaching, for instance), but most will require some form of outlay either for equipment, for stock or both. Then there are other considerations. You may need a budget for advertising, for accountancy and legal fees, or even for adapting your living room.

Before you even try to raise money, it is well worth thinking about the minimum amount needed. If the business is in the fledgling stage, try to keep only to the bare essentials – there will be time for a mahogany desk and state-of-the-art printer at a later, more successful stage.

Once you've worked out what you need, the next item on the agenda is how you are going to raise it. Here are some ideas:

Your own savings

Using your own savings is an excellent way to start a business, as it doesn't mean incurring debt or risking other people's money. However, it is normally only an option if you have planned the business for some time. Jennie Woodcock, who owns Bumper Jeans, a children's jeans company, always knew that she would one day be self-employed, ' so I had something put aside for when I needed it.' She started her company largely on her savings.

Sell, Sell, Sell

Selling certain of your possessions is another good way to raise money. You might decide to trade in your expensive car and buy a cheaper one, sell an heirloom or even furniture. It is also possible to trade in certain life assurance policies, provided they are of sufficient value. Louise Morrey, whose hand-painted goods are sold by the National Trust, raised initial funds this way.

Family and Friends

Family and friends can be an excellent source of capital – or an unending source of grief. The key is to establish what they expect for the money they are giving you. Do they regard it as similar to a charitable donation and expect no return, other than your success? Or are they throwing their long-cherished savings into the venture in the expectation that you have a product which will make them rich? Before you accept their money, make sure you both understand:

- whether it is a gift or a loan

- whether it is to be repaid without interest or not

- whether your family (or friends) expect to have a stake in the business – or even shares – in return for their money – or whether they are trusting you to go it alone.

If the arrangement is a business one, i.e. they expect some form of return for their investment, or you are selling them shares in the business, then it is vital that you see a solicitor and put the arrangement on a business footing, so there is no misunderstanding. Hell hath no fury like a family at war with itself over money, as Peter (not his real name) knows. 'My cousin lent me £5,000 to set up a mail order business. I thought of it as a long-term loan. He didn't. He called the money in just when I needed it to really get the business off the ground and we had a real row about it. We haven't spoken since.'

That doesn't mean that borrowing from friends and family is doomed to failure. Sally Wilkins started her baby-sling business on the back of a £100 family loan for materials – and now has a turnover of £250,000. It is just that you should all know the score before you begin.

> **David Fox started up his own business organizing residential tuition for foreign students with £1,000 of his own money. He is also a business studies teacher.**
> 'A lot of people think that starting a business means borrowing from the bank. But the way I look at it is once you take a loan, you are no longer working for yourself, because you are working to pay the

interest off. I felt that if I jeopardized my savings, well, at least it stopped with me,' says David. However, he acknowledges that if you need to buy a large amount of stock to start with, a bank loan may be your best option. David thoroughly enjoys his business, but some aspects have surprised him.

'I discovered that as your business grows rather than the level of investment dropping off you need to up it. It's a bit like going backwards up an escalator. Now, however, the money is not the overriding priority. I enjoy the business. I suppose it's my baby.'

Raising money by selling shares – or a stake – in the venture

Venture capital generally means that an outside party invests in your business, in return for a stake in it, although you are more likely to find a buyer for an established business than for a highly speculative one. Nevertheless, there are exceptions. 'Angels' often invest in theatre productions where there is no cast-iron guarantee of success. Based on this idea, there are now business angels who will invest in start-up businesses. Contact them through the British Venture Capital Association. Your TEC may also be able to give you a list of local firms which act as introduction agencies for small businesses and potential investors. Two schemes to look out for are LINC (Local Investment Networking Company) and EIS (Enterprise Investment Scheme). Another way of raising money is share buy-back schemes where you sell shares, but agree to buy them back at a later date. You can get more details through an accountant.

If you are interested in selling shares in your business, it is vital to consult an accountant and a lawyer. It is also worth reading the Department of Trade and Industry's free brochure *Finance without Debt, A Guide to Sources of Venture Capital under £250,000.*

Getting a grant or low-interest loan

There are thousands of grants and low interest loans available for small businesses. The problem is finding out what they are and whether your business qualifies. Some fields are more liberally provided with grants than others. For instance, the Crafts Council has a setting-up scheme which allows selected craftspeople to receive a grant of £2,500 for maintenance and up to £5,000 for equipment (they pay half of equipment costs), provided they apply within two years of setting up. While this would not cover your start-up costs entirely, it could certainly be a very useful addition. Other areas where grants may be forthcoming include:

- **Business ventures related to the Arts (and certain crafts)**
  Many regional Arts Councils provide grants/loans to people just starting work in the arts, or to specific projects. The criteria vary from area to area. In one part of the country, for instance, grants may only be available to those working in the visual arts. In another part of the country, there may be grants for those working in a wide variety of arts-related fields. In some areas, the main thrust of the grants may be to encourage artists – or craftspeople – to market their work more aggressively. Other areas may be more interested in providing training. Grants on offer can range from several hundred to several thousand pounds. You can find out more about what's available in your area by contacting your regional *Arts Board or Council*. The *Arts Council of Great Britain* will be able to tell you which is your nearest. Keep an eye out too for any grants being advertised in arts, crafts, or media sections of newspapers and magazines. The *Arts Funding Guide*, available from good libraries, has a comprehensive list of available grants for those working in the Arts.

- **Business ventures related to tourism** In certain areas – particularly Wales and Scotland – there may be grants/loans available for people who wish to set up projects that will attract tourists. Bed and breakfast accommodation could well qualify, as could specialist tours – although the exact criteria vary from year to year. If you live in Scotland or Wales, contact the relevant Tourist Board. In England, the DTI has regional enterprise schemes for projects creating employment.

- **Grants for farmers** are sometimes offered by the Ministry of Agriculture, Fisheries and Food for those who are planning to use their farms for uses other than farming – and are in environmentally sensitive or otherwise specially designated areas. Check with the Rural Development Commission (see below).

- **Business ventures for young people** *Livewire*, sponsored by Shell UK, is a competition for entrepreneurs aged 16–25, with prizes for those who win at regional and national level. Business advice is offered as part of the award, but you may also win a cash prize of several thousand pounds.

- The **Prince's Youth Business Trust** offers a mixture of loans and grants to people under 30. There are discretionary grants of up to £1,500 for equipment, as well as start-up loans. The Prince's Trust also provides 'go-and-see grants' of up to £500 for those under 26.

- **Business ventures in rural areas** The Rural Development Commission gives grants for turning unused rural buildings into productive work areas, e.g. turning a disused barn into a workshop. However, they will not fund more than a quarter of the cost.

- **Business ventures in areas of high economic deprivation** Certain areas have earmarked funds to establish new businesses – although they tend to favour those businesses that will create jobs. Your TEC, Enterprise Agency, or Business Link will have details of whether there are local grants and what you need to do to qualify. It may also be worth talking to the Economic Development Officer at your local district or county council, as there are many regional grants. For example, both *British Coal* and *British Steel*

offer low interest loans in areas that have been affected by pit and
steel closures.

- **The Royal British Legion** also has a loan scheme for former
  servicemen and women who are currently unemployed, but want
  to start their own business. The application has to go through the
  local branch, but more information is available from the Royal
  British Legion Village.

- If you need vocational training (or want to train someone else)
  before you start your business, you may be interested in a **Career
  Development Loan** or **Small Firms Training Loans,** which
  are government schemes run through Barclays, The Co-operative
  and Clydesdale Banks. This is a low interest loan for training
  lasting up to a year. Your TEC or LEC will have more details.

- The Government also runs a **Loan Guarantees for Small
  Business** scheme for people working in various fields who are
  unable to get a conventional loan, due to a lack of security or track
  record. This guarantees a loan at a considerably lower rate of
  interest than would be provided by a bank. However, it is only
  available to businesses which have been going for more than two
  years and which fulfil certain criteria. For more details contact the
  Department of Trade and Industry.

These are just a few of the grants and loans currently available –
although the number and type change all the time. Your local TEC,
your bank's small business advisor, the local chamber of commerce and
your professional association may know of others that could be made
available to someone in your line of work. Many charities also give
grants and it is worth taking a look at the *Directory of Grant Making
Trusts,* available in major libraries, if you think your project might
attract charitable funding. Also worth looking at is the *European
Community Funding for Business Development,* published by Kogan Page.

The National Westminster Bank also has a very useful small business information directory, available to those who complete their free business start-up forms.

Dealing with the banks – what you need to know

If you discover that you cannot raise all the costs of starting a business by yourself, you may well decide to go to a bank for a loan. These generally take one of three forms:

1   **The Overdraft** This means that the bank allows you to draw money which isn't in your account, up to an agreed amount. It sounds an ideal solution for an embryonic business, but there is a catch. The bank charges interest. That means you not only repay the bank the amount you were overdrawn, but you also have to pay them added interest – and the rate can go up. An overdraft is useful for cash-flow problems, and many businesses rely on it for that reason. But you must be aware that the bank does expect to be paid back with interest – and that they get to choose when!

2   **The short-term loan** This is a loan normally given to you for a period of up to five years. The interest rate is often fixed (so it's worth timing the loan for a time when the interest rate is forecast to go up rather than down). Short-term loans are often a good way to purchase expensive equipment, stock etc.

    The bank will want to be assured that they are going to get their money back so will generally ask for security, i.e. something they can take if you stop repaying them. You might offer them a life assurance policy, if it is worth enough, but many borrowers do end up offering their homes as security. Be aware, though, that this means that if the business goes bust, you will lose your home as well.

3   **A medium-term loan** works in much the same way as a short-term loan, but it is paid back over a longer period of time.

It has to be stressed that banks are not charitable institutions. They can – and will – call in their debt if they believe that the business isn't going to be able to pay back. If you have given your house as security on a loan, the bank will have no qualms about repossessing if they decide to call the loan in. For that reason, it is a good idea to be very cautious as to the amount of money you borrow, and to avoid using your home as security if you possibly can.

Having said that, the banks want your business to succeed rather than fail, simply because that way they get to recoup their money, plus interest. For that reason, they are also pretty careful as to who they lend their money to. They will want to see a convincing *business plan* (see below), to reassure them that you are a reasonable bet. If no bank wants to lend you money, it might be that they can't recognize genius when they see it – but it is also possible that they sniff a dud. If you are turned down for a loan, find out why before you charge off – and then decide if you can learn anything from their answer.

Banks are very keen to attract prospective small businesses which they believe will succeed. Most offer a package of goodies such as reduced or even free banking for a certain period, so it is worth sounding out the best deal.

Cash flow – what it is and what it means

Even if you managed to obtain adequate finances for your business, one of the biggest traps is cash flow. Cash flow basically means the movement of money *into* your business (from the sale of your goods or services) and the movement of money *out* of it (to suppliers, the bank, other creditors and employees). The relationship of these two flows is very important. Many businesses go under because although they are owed a lot of money they do not have enough in hand to pay the bank/their own debts. There is nothing more frustrating than knowing you are owed £5,000 but not having enough cash in hand to pay for the weekly shop.

I know, because I've been there. When I started up as a freelance writer, I needed enough money to tide me over six lean weeks before my invoices started to be paid: two weeks while I was setting up and writing my first pieces, four weeks minimum before the invoices started to be paid. The first time I was freelance, I failed to bargain for the time it took the publishers to pay me – and had to live on baked beans as a result. The next time, I'd put enough money away to tide me over.

It is vital to ensure that your cash flow is healthy enough to keep the bank happy and make yourself a living – even if that means dipping into savings to begin with. There are few businesses which make money on day one; even fewer which can expect their bills to be paid by day two.

You can calculate cash flow by estimating all the money you expect to receive in a month – and everything you have to pay out, including expenses such as childcare, telephone bills etc. If you get in less than you pay out (even if you are owed more) then you will have a deficit (or negative cash flow) for that month. Remember, too, to make a note of when big bills – like the tax and NI bills – are due.

Let's take an example of a tricky cash flow. Say you plan to make wooden apples. Your supplier requests payment thirty days after the wood has been delivered. Your bank loan interest has to be paid on the same day. It takes you fifteen days from the date of delivery to make up the apples and get them installed in Apples Are Magic, the shop which has agreed to sell them. They have also agreed with you that they will pay for their apples thirty days after receiving them. This means that you somehow have to pay the wood supplier and bank well before you receive any money from the shop. Now this may be fine if – in the intervening fifteen days before payment was due – you not only made up apples but went to a craft fair and sold a previous batch off. But it's bad news if you don't have any money in the kitty.

Calculate your cash flow carefully, not only for the business plan, but to ensure that your business is viable. Incidentally, once you are trading, it is vital that you chase debtors and chase them hard. A paid bill in the hand is definitely worth two unpaid-for orders of work.

Ron Flounders, of Hertfordshire Business Link which gives advice to business start-ups, points out that small business people are often reluctant to call debts in, on the basis that they may not get work from the client again. However, if you do not get paid for your work – you are giving it as a gift. A customer who doesn't pay up is worse than no customer at all, because you've had to incur costs to service them. If, for instance, you are a piano teacher who has a pupil who doesn't pay for his lessons, you will have lost out twice. Not only will you not be paid for the lessons you gave, but you have lost out in that you could have had another pupil during that time. The golden rules for small businesses should be:

- Discuss payment terms when the work is taken on. Confirm them in writing in order to ensure that you have a binding contract, i.e. you can sue if it isn't fulfilled. Your terms of payment should be included on any quotation, order, invoice and statement.

- Remind your client that money is owed if they don't pay on time.

- Remember to bill promptly – paperwork may be tedious but it's the only way to ensure you get paid.

- Try to make firm sales rather than selling on a sale-or-return basis.

YOUR BUSINESS PLAN

Every bank and lending institution will require a business plan before they commit themselves to lending you money. A business plan basically shows that you have established that there is a market for your product/service and that having established sufficient demand, you have a good estimate of what your costs will be, as well as your sales volume, cash-flow and likely profit (although the last is often optimistic).

Business Link advisors say that the same mistakes crop up time and time again. 'The major mistake we see on business plans is that people have failed to do their market research – and the banks say the same. People believe that if they don't sell as many as they hoped they just have to work harder. Wrong. If the market for your product is only a hundred people, then all the hard work in the world won't increase that.'

It is, of course, hard to project exact profits and loss. But with thorough market research and realistic pricing you can work out a rough estimate. 'My business plan was almost a piece of fiction ' says Verna Wilkins of Tamarind Books. 'But the bank could see that I'd done my homework and that there was a demand for the books I wanted to produce. I also was prepared to ask what was needed to make my proposition work and that showed them I meant business.'

Remember, a business plan is not just to impress the bank. Its essential purpose is to prove that the business is viable and to act as a reference point while you are establishing the business. Although business plans vary, they should include:

1 A clear description of the type of business. If you are running a cleaning agency, say so. The bank won't be edified by a description of yourself as a domestic operative sub-contracted supply agent. If your business has a unique selling point, explain what it is. If you have training and well-established contacts in the field make a note of that too.

2 A description of the premises (i.e. your home) and any key staff (i.e. you and any employees).

3 Details of the product or service. Again, try to keep it simple.

4 Details of market research conducted. How it was done and what it established. How you intend to use that market research in order to market your services/product and estimate sales demand.

5 Details of the competition – and how or why you intend to offer a better service/product. If, for instance, you are setting up a mobile hairdresser when there are three mobile hairdressers in the same street, you need to prove to the bank that there is a demand for your service.

6 Financial information, i.e. fixed and variable costs you expect to incur, including details of any equipment you have bought/intend to buy, the cash-flow forecast, pricing and profit margin and volume of sales. Remember to include such things as childcare, extra electricity and telephone bills in your costs – it all mounts up. Of course, it is hard to know exactly what you will sell – but try to make a stab using the market research you did. If in doubt, err on the side of caution.

7 Each bank has its own form, which may also require other information, such as the estimated break-even point, turnover etc.

If your business plan is turned down, find out why. Even if you decide to go ahead with alternative financing, it is a good idea to find out why the bank feels your idea isn't viable – is it merely that your business plan isn't well presented, or do they believe you don't have enough collateral?

Once you have done your market research, got all the advice you can and found some finance, you are well on the way to the next stage – getting the business up and running.

Useful addresses _____

Arts Council of Great Britain, 14 Great Peter St, London SW1P 3NQ. Tel: 0171 333 0100

Association of British Chambers of Commerce, 9 Tufton St, London SW1P 3QB. Tel: 0171 222 1555

British Coal Enterprise Ltd, Edwinstowe House, Edwinstowe, Notts NG21 9PR. Tel: 01623 826833

British Steel, London Office, Canterbury House, 2–6 Sydenham Road, Croydon CR29 2LJ. Tel: 0181 686 2311

British Venture Capital Association, Essex House, 12–13 Essex St, London WC2R 3AA. Tel: 0171 240 3846

Companies House, Crown Way, Cardiff, S. Glamorgan, CF4 3UZ. Tel: 01222 388588 (for England and Wales)

Companies House, 37 Castle Terrace, Edinburgh, EH1 2EB. Tel: 0131 535 5800 (for Scotland)

Companies House, IDB House, 64 Chichester St, Belfast BT1 4JX. Tel: 01232 234488 (for Northern Ireland)

Crafts Council, 44a Pentonville Road, Islington, London N1 9BY. Tel: 0171 278 7700

Department of Environment, 2 Marsham St, London SW1P 3EB. Tel: 0171 276 0900

Department of Trade and Industry (has a list of publications designed to help small businesses) Ashdown House, 123 Victoria St, London SW1E 6RB. Tel: 0171 510 0169 or (general queries line) 0171 215 5000

Details of TECs, LECs, Enterprise Agencies and Business Links can be obtained from your local Job Centre, or Library.

English Tourist Board, Thames Tower, Black's Road, London W6 9EL. Tel: 0181 846 9000

Enterprise Publications (provide useful booklets, including one on making a business plan) Tel: 01954 261040

Federation of Small Businesses, 32 Orchard Road, Lytham St Annes, Lancs, FY8 1NY. Tel: 01253 720911

Highlands and Islands Enterprise, Bridge House, 20 Bridge St, Inverness, IV1 1QR. Tel: 01463 234171

Law Society of Northern Ireland, 98 Victoria St, Belfast BT1 3J2. Tel: 01232 231614

Law Society of Scotland, 26 Drumsheugh Gardens, Edinburgh EH3 7YR. Tel: 0131 226 7411

Law Society, 113 Chancery Lane, London WC2A 1PL. Tel: 0171 242 1222

Livewire Awards, Tel : 0191 261 5584

Northern Ireland LEDU, LEDU House, Upper Gallwally, Belfast, BT8 4TB. Tel: 01232 491031

Princes Youth Business Trust, 18 Park Square East, London NW1 4LM.
Tel: 0171 543 1234

Royal British Legion, Small Business Advisory Service and Loan Scheme,
The Cottage, Ordnance Road, Tidworth, Wiltshire SP9 7QD. Tel:
01980 847753

Royal Institute for Town Planning, 26 Portland Place, London W1N
4BE. Tel: 0171 636 9107 (*Planning Permission: A Guide for Business*,
published by the Department of the Environment, is available from your
local council)

Rural Development Commission (look up your nearest branch in your
local telephone book) or telephone the Head Office on: 01722 336255

Scottish Enterprise, 120 Bothwell St, Glasgow G27JP. Tel: 0141 248 2700

Scottish Tourist Board, 23 Ravelston Terrace, Edinburgh, EH4 3EU. Tel:
0131 332 2433

Wales Tourist Board, 2 Fitzalan Road, Cardiff, South Glamorgan, CF2
1UY. Tel: 01222 499909

Welsh Development Agency, Pearl House, Greyfriars Road, Cardiff, CF1
3XX. Tel: 01222 222666

Women's Institute Markets Dept, 104 New Kings Road, London SW6
4LY. Tel: 0171 371 7960

FOUR

Childcare for
the homeworker

There is one ingredient in a working parent's life which is more important than any other. It makes all the difference between feeling happy and competent in your work and being miserable and frustrated. It is quite simply childcare.

Many people (particularly women) imagine that by working at home they can dismiss the need for childcare. They imagine the baby gurgling by their feet while they get out a report or log some statistics. In fact, while you are busy on the report, any unattended child able to crawl will generally have managed to find something unsuitable to do – like playing with the knives in the dishwasher or crawling up work surfaces. Elizabeth, a secretary, tried working from home without childcare for a short time, 'but it was too stressful. I'd be making arrangements for a client and would turn round to find Joel had spilt all my make-up or was trying to eat the cat's tail! It was too much.'

'I can't tell you how many people tell us they want to work at home, so they can work and be with their children,' says Andrew James of *Home Run*, the magazine for homeworkers. 'And every time they say that I get a sinking feeling. Business and looking after children can't be done at the same time.'

There are a few exceptions. You may, for instance, be doing work which requires no concentration and can be easily put aside, or you may be working extremely part-time and able to do your work after your children have gone to bed. Be warned, however, doing one job straight after another, is not a long-term recipe for happiness, although it can be a way to start up your business if money is very tight, as Sally Wilkins found out.

Sally manufactures the very successful Wilkinet Baby-Sling. She now employs eleven people and has a turnover of £250,000. But when she started twenty years ago, she worked from her kitchen table. 'I found the only way to stop one of my children – and I have eight – disturbing my work or removing my materials was to work when they were asleep. I used to get up at 3 a.m. and work till 7 to get some peace. It was helpful in getting the business started, but it made me totally exhausted and grumpy.'

'John', who runs a mail order service also tried looking after his daughter while his wife was at work. 'But she'd start to drop the ice-cream I'd given her to keep her quiet, just as someone was giving me the biggest order of the day. There were times I just had to walk out and leave her in the room screaming. I used to think to myself thank goodness we don't have a videophone!'

Looking after your children by day and working by night is one solution, albeit not a permanent one since it is likely to leave you too tired to concentrate on either your business or your children. It also means that expansion is impossible. But if you intend to work for more than a few hours you will need childcare of one sort or another. However, homeworkers do have an advantage here in that they can normally control their hours better than parents who have to face long journeys beset by traffic jams or delayed trains.

The disadvantage of being a homeworker, particularly if you are self-employed, is that you may need to work on a particular project which requires different hours from those you normally work – or you may have busy times when you need more childcare than you normally require or slack times when there is very little to do – but the childminder has to be paid. In these cases, a network of friends, relatives and evening working may help you over the busy times, but you may have to take the slack times on the chin unless your childcarer is remarkably flexible. If you have also previously worked for a large company where there was a staff crèche, you may find it hard to adapt to having to find your own childcare at first.

If you have decided to work from home in order to be on hand while continuing to work, you may find that it is easy to feel jealous of your carer. After all, you planned to work from home specifically to spend more time with the children and instead, here you are typing up reports, while your kids are at the childminder's having fun in the paddling pool! There is no easy answer to this. Suffice it to say that you probably see more of your children than you would if you were working in an office. Secondly, if you need – or want – to work, then you may have to accept that working from home is the best compromise rather than perfect solution.

HOW TO CHOOSE CHILDCARE

The four main questions to bear in mind when you're looking for childcare are:

- What qualities do I require in a childcarer?

- How much can I afford to pay?

- How many hours do I need childcare for?

- What method of childcare will best fit in with my business?

You might for instance, be meeting a lot of clients on the premises – in which case having your child darting around the house when they come in may not be ideal – unless you are running a childrenswear outlet. If you are a counsellor, therapist or pursuing another occupation where clients require peace and quiet, you will generally find that you want childcare that is out-of-house, a childminder or nursery rather than a nanny.

On the other hand, if you enjoy hearing the sound of children in the background, if you want to be free to join in or you like to know exactly what your carer is doing you may want an in-house nanny/mother's help or au pair. Libby Purves, the writer feels that one of the joys of working from home is being able to listen in to the kids' activities and switch off from work for a while.

If you do intend having in-house care then you must train both child and carer not to interrupt you while you are working. A closed door, which must be knocked on, is an easy way to establish boundaries. If that isn't possible, perhaps you can arrange for carer and child to be out when you need to concentrate most intensely. If you have a very young child, it is worth making sure your business line is out of their reach or you may get unexpected interruptions!

What sort of childcare is available? A great deal, except that most of it is very ad hoc. Britain has the worst state provision of child and nursery care in Europe, so most people have to rely on a variety of sources which they find – and finance – themselves. Below I give some options.

Relatives
In this country relatives are the greatest childcare providers, with partners heading up the list followed by grandmothers. A relative is often the first choice for childcare if much of your work involves weekend or unsociable hours, e.g. if you want to exhibit at craft fairs, or if you are a therapist many of whose clients come to you in the evening. If you are using your partner as childcare in this situation, this may be an ideal arrangement – provided you make sure you see each other as a couple occasionally. If you are using other relatives, such as grandmas or sisters, matters become more complicated.

Costs: Generally free.

Pros:

> You know the carer well and have an idea of how they will look after the child.

> A relationship of trust with your childcarer.

> The building of an ongoing loving relationship between carer and child which will benefit both of them.

Cons:

> Potential for disagreement about childrearing methods – particularly if an older relative is looking after the child. It is worth bearing in mind that attitudes towards various aspects of childcare including breastfeeding, diet, discipline have changed in the last twenty years and you cannot expect your carer to have kept up with all these changes.

> Feeling indebted – if you are uncomfortable with the fact that all the benefits seem to be flowing one way, this can stifle your own relationship with the carer.

> If grandma/dad has to get a full-time job, or becomes too old to care for your child, you will need to look for another carer and may never feel that anyone else matches up.

> Lack of a formal contract means that you have to be careful not to impose and must allow the carer to have a life of their own. For this reason, using a relative may be best suited to those working part-time. If your spouse is your childcarer then you should also beware of getting to the situation where you have no time together because you are both continually working to different schedules.

If you fall out, you not only lose your childcarer but a good relationship with a family member.

Childminder

Childminders are the most popular form of paid childcare in the UK. By law, they must be registered with social services. A childminder is often a mum herself, who looks after children in her own home. She can take no more than three under fives (including her own child), or five under eights, which means that childminders are often an ideal form of childcare for older children who can go to the childminder after school and during holidays (although you may need to find a holiday scheme for some part of the time).

Registration is your guarantee that your childminder has at least passed some sort of very basic test, (although you *must* check her out thoroughly for yourself). Childminders are registered with the local authority who carry out police and social services checks on every adult member in the house, and then carry out an inspection of the home in order to ensure that it is clean, safe and child-friendly.

In the past childminders have had an undeservedly bad name. Although there have been cases where childminders have injured or abused the children in their care, this is rare. The majority of childminders give the children in their care warm and loving attention and the National Childminding Association, their national body, aims to improve standards even more.

Costs: Childminders charge per child, either on an hourly or weekly rate. Costs vary widely across the country ranging from as little as £1.50 an hour to as much as £4, although generally childminders are the cheapest form of paid childcare. Childminders are generally self-employed which means their tax and national insurance contributions are down to them.

Pros:

> Your child will have a home-from-home. A warm relationship with another adult in your own locality.

> Your child will learn to socialize with other children from an early age and will have a ready-made group of friends. This is particularly valuable for elder or only children.

> Your child will be safely cared for outside your home – leaving you to work without distractions or interruptions.

Cons:

> The convenience factor – you have to take the child to the minder. If, for you, one of the major attractions of working at home, is the lack of commuting time, then you will hardly want to spend an hour getting your child to the minder. Finding someone good close at hand is a pressing requirement. You will also need to get your child to your minder at an agreed time – whatever your personal schedule, although the minder may be flexible – which is something to check at interview.

> Your child will get less individual attention than care on a one-to-one basis. You might be happy with this if the other children are loving and receptive to your child, but how will you feel if they bully your child or you regard them as a band of ruffians?

When flexibility is at a premium

Angela Davies, a colour consultant works two days a week, but is often called on to do extra presentations to companies or has an unexpected booking. This can make childcare very difficult. Her partner helps out at weekends and evenings, 'but I've also been very lucky in finding a childminder who's great with my child and very flexible too. If I let her know as soon as I do, the chances are that she'll be able to take my daughter for some extra hours.' Angela thinks this is because she looked carefully for a childminder who could be flexible. 'I was clear about what I needed from the outset and it has all worked out very well.'

Nanny – live-out and live-in

Nannies are characterized by the fact that they come to your house and look after your children alone. Other than that, they are a disparate group. They may have a qualification, such as an NNEB, (which means following a two-year training course), or a PPA or NVQ (shorter, more vocationally based qualifications) – or they may simply have oodles of experience. They may be as proper as Mary Poppins or very down to earth. Whatever their personality, it is vital you take references to ensure you get a good standard of care, although it has to be said that working from home will give you a good idea of how your nanny treats your child.

This is both an advantage and a disadvantage. Some nannies get very sniffy about the idea of a parent 'snooping' on them. Most, however, are quite happy with the arrangement – provided you are not constantly interfering or changing their routine. Sarah, a nanny recalls one homeworker who didn't keep her side of the bargain. 'We agreed that we'd all have lunch together – the two kids, myself and the mum. That would have been OK, but instead she kept popping down at irregular intervals. Of course, the child wanted to be with mummy and would then get upset when she'd disappeared again. I'd just have got her settled, when she was back again. It didn't really work out.'

Helping your childcarer make the switch from office to home

Rosemarie Ghazaros is a marketing consultant who employs a nanny for her children. She says that when she switched to working at home it required some readjustment on both her and her nanny's part.

'She is an excellent nanny, but she was used to having the house to herself. For my part I had to learn not to be looking over her shoulder, checking she was doing things the way I would.'

Rosemarie, adept at negotiation in her professional life, found the best way to ensure harmony, was for them both to agree the times when the nanny would have sole charge, the times when Rosemarie would take over, or when everyone would spend an afternoon together. 'I think that being clear about what's going on makes everyone feel happier,' says Rosemarie.

She has found the arrangement works very well. 'My nanny is very flexible, but I also try to be generous with her about holiday time, days off and so on.' Rosemarie feels that she has an advantage in that she has a large element of control over her workload and so can keep her nanny informed about her working hours. 'I think that trust between nanny and mother is essential and letting her know what's going on is part of that.'

If you work very variable or unsociable hours then a live-in nanny is one of the most flexible forms of childcare you can have, as she will normally be able to accommodate her working pattern to yours – provided you give her sufficient notice. Most people use nannies where at least one child is under school age, as they can be expensive for school age children. However, it is possible to arrange a nanny-share (sharing a nanny with another family) in order to cater for school age children or if the cost is too expensive.

Nannies will not do 'heavy housework', but will do all the essentials for the children in their care e.g. laundry, ironing, and making up food. Some will also do minor tasks for the household such as shopping.

Cost: Expensive for one child but may work out surprisingly similar to a childminder for more than one as nannies expect to be paid by the job rather than per child. Prices vary enormously, but expect to pay anywhere between £100–

£300 a week net for a live-out nanny depending on locality, qualifications, experience etc. For a live-in nanny expect to pay anywhere between £85–£250 net. You also have to pay tax and national insurance, which can add a sizeable whack. If you pay your nanny £200 a week, the total cost to you will be nearly £300. If you share a nanny you each pay a proportion of her salary, making this a less expensive option.

Pros:

Lots of loving one-to-one attention for your child. She may also take your child to activities such as baby music or toddlers groups.

Professional expertise for you to benefit from.

Convenience and flexibility. Home childcarers can often tailor hours, days-off etc. to suit yours.

Your nanny will still look after your child when the child is ill.

Cons:

Nanny and child can become isolated.

If she is very experienced (or opinionated) you can end up feeling inadequate or have blazing rows about childcare methods.

The I-can't-bear-to-lose her factor: if your nanny is excellent you may find yourself offering her bigger and bigger salary rises and bribes to stay on. A few nannies do take advantage of a mother's dependence and many, particularly live-ins, expect to move in on a regular basis.

Loss of privacy if you have a live-in nanny. You will have to share your lives with a third adult. If she has a major emotional crisis, you can be sure that you'll get to know every twist of the tale. You may also find yourself feeling rather cramped if you are already working from home and do not have a lot of space. When she is in the house with the children, you may find it difficult to concentrate on your work.

A nanny-share can save on cost – but you need to be sure that you have the same ideas about discipline, childcare and holidays as the other family or there may be major disagreements.

Mother's help

A mother's help is an unqualified person, who will look after children in their own home. They are best used for short periods of time or to help out when you are around and *can be disturbed*. For that reason, a mother's help is often a good choice for women working at home part-time.

Pros:

Reasonably priced care in your own home – could be very useful for school age children.

Cons:

Not necessarily the best care for long periods of time.

Nursery or playgroup

It used to be that nurseries were just for children of three plus, giving them a pre-school education. However, an increasing number of nurseries now take babies from upwards of six months (although the educational content is, of course, limited for the youngest children). There is no agreed standard for nurseries, but the best are excellent. Nurseries are required, by law to have one carer to three under fives.

Some use the key-worker system where one nursery nurse takes special responsibility for certain children. There is a school of thought which believes that nurseries are not suitable for children under two, but many mothers feel their children are well-settled, loved and happy within them.

Another option for two to four year olds is a playgroup. These normally run for a half-day session, so would suit part-timers best.

Costs: Depends on the type of nursery. Local authority nurseries are often free, but places tend to be reserved for children on the at risk register or, at a pinch, for the children of single mothers. For private nurseries, costs can range from £45–£165 a week although many charge by the session.

Pros:

Stimulation of other children and adults.

The number of people working in a nursery means that it is unlikely to close because of staff sickness.

Cons:

An institution, rather than a home.

You will have to get baby and yourself to the nursery in the morning and collect her again.

A lively nursery could be intimidating for a shyer child.

Lack of continuity if there is a high turnover of staff – a relationship with one caring adult is very important for the under twos.

Your child will have to stay home if they have an illness.

CHILDCARE FOR SCHOOL AGE CHILDREN

For older children, there is a variety of childcare. Childminders (see above) will often take children after school and in the holidays, and a nanny may be an option if you have younger children who will need her during school-time as well. Worth considering too, are after-hours and holiday schemes. These are run either by local schools, councils or private organizations and are designed to cater for the school age children of working mothers and fathers for at least part of the day. You can find out about local schemes through the library, school or word of mouth. They are often reasonably priced. However, if your child is shy he or she may find it a bit daunting to be with a group of comparative strangers for several hours a day. An au pair, see below is another option.

When is a child old enough not to need care? This is a very individual decision, but one which working at home can help smudge. Hilary Simpson, for instance, Principal Personnel Officer for Oxfordshire County Council often works at home during the holidays. Her elder daughter Eleanor, a teenager is also at home. 'She knows she can call on me if there are problems, but at the same time I'll leave her alone to have space of her own. I'm both there and not there, which is good for us both.'

Au pair

An au pair is a young woman (although the Foreign Office also now accepts male au pairs) who comes to the UK from abroad, to combine learning the language with live-in childcare and light household duties. By law, an au pair must be 17 plus, can only work for five hours a day and must be given time off for language tuition. Au pairs need not necessarily have any childcare experience at all and they are not qualified. This makes them unsuitable to undertake the care of young babies unattended. This may not bother you if you are doing the sort of work where you can be interrupted at regular intervals, but may well be a problem if you regularly need to be closeted with your clients (e.g. if you are a counsellor, accountant etc.) or need to go out to see clients. Au pairs are best suited to the homeworker with older children or who works part-time.

Costs: Au pairs are paid around £35 per week pocket money.

Pros:

Flexible – they will undertake household tasks as well as caring for children. Hours can also be varied.

They have youth on their side – which may mean they have the energy to spend hours playing rough and tumble with lively school kids. The best may also build a real rapport with the children in their care.

Could be useful for after-school and holiday care.

Cons:

Inexperienced.

Their lack of maturity can lead to them having personal problems which may interfere with their ability to care for the children. You may also find yourself in loco parentis – having to worry about their boyfriends, the times they come in etc.

Lack of continuity – au pairs can only stay for a short period.

How much responsibility should an au pair bear? 'Caroline Smith', an optician, has been using au pairs for seven years.
'When my children were little, I had a childminder and an au pair because I think they need back-up when you have little ones,' says Caroline. She feels that working at home is a distinct advantage if you

have an au pair. 'You are there if they have problems, you have more time to explain things to them and you can also make them feel more welcome.'

However, Caroline does not regard her au pairs as cheap labour. 'There are limits on the hours they are allowed to work – and I keep to them. I think that if you treat au pairs badly you won't get the best out of them. I have heard of people who made their au pairs clean the loos twice a day!'

Caroline regards her au pairs as helpful family members and says she has only rarely had problems, 'but then the fact that I'm around and it is made clear that I will be around, may pre-empt problems that would otherwise occur.'

Caroline has had such good relations with several au pairs that they still come and see her when they visit Britain. 'I believe that if it's handled well, the year should work well for both employer, children and the au pair herself.'

FINDING YOUR CARER

When to start looking

It is worth starting the search for your carer between four to eight weeks before you need them. If there is a public holiday such as Christmas or Easter intervening, eight weeks is best. Any less and you may find yourself running up against your starting date and unable to find the sort of carer you want. However, if you start looking too far in advance, you may find the childcarers in your area will not know if there are any vacancies, or, in the case of nannies, if they wish to move on.

Where to look

This will depend on the type of childcare you are looking for. However, there is one method which should never be overlooked as it is often the most reliable. This is simply word of mouth. Ask anyone whose judgement you respect and who has young children, if they know of a good childminder or nursery which may have vacancies. Or of a nanny who is planning to move on. Do not leave any stone unturned. Ask your friends, mother-in-law, GP, health visitor, librarian, church (if you are a member) – even local shopkeepers.

Talk to your local National Childbirth Trust (NCT) or Parents At Work group (may be known as Working Mothers Group). Although it is not their job to find childcare they tend to have their ear to the ground on such matters. (Some Working Mothers Groups even keep a nanny-share register.) If word of mouth fails to yield any results there are several other steps you can take.

Childminders Your local authority will keep a list. Ring up the Social Services Department and ask for it. Or it may well be in the local library. The National Childminding Association keep a register of their members and will have details of members in your locality. Some childminders also advertise vacancies in shop windows or local newspapers (check they are registered). Once you have the list, it is a question of selecting suitable minders – those who take under-fives, for instance, who work the days you need, who live nearby – and then ringing them up to find out which have vacancies.

Nannies For nannies, you may have little choice but to go through an agency or to advertise yourself in local papers or in specialist journals such as *The Lady* and *Nursery World*. Agencies claim that they vet candidates, but in some cases, this amounts to little more than checking that they really worked for their last employer. *Do not rely on an agency to check the nanny's suitability. Always check references yourself.*

'I gave a very specific job description to the agency,' says 'Jane', a solicitor. 'So specific that they only came up with one name. But that didn't matter to me because she was the nanny we chose and she has been excellent.'

Au pairs You may also find an agency to be a good way of selecting an au pair, using similar provisos as for nannies. However, a recommendation through friends who have au pairs can often yield dividends and can be a lot cheaper.

Nurseries Again ask your health visitor and NCT group for any recommendations, although your Social Services Department will have a full list. If you phone a nursery which only takes children of three upwards, ask if they know of any that take younger children – they often do. Once you have a list, ring the nursery and find out if they have any vacancies. In my area, the waiting list for the most popular local nursery is over two years. So if you're planning to take a few years break from work, it might be worth putting your child's name down early!

INTERVIEWING A POSSIBLE CARER

The initial contact

Once you have established the availability of a potential carer, you will want to give them an initial phone interview to weed out possible candidates. I have found that it is pretty easy, even from one phone call, to tell who is a hopeful and who is not. People who seem wholly uninterested in the child and wholly interested in pay can be weeded out, as can any who make you feel uneasy (gut instinct is very important). One woman told me that no, she hadn't had any experience of children, but had decided to work as a 'nanny' because the pay was better than what she was earning now. If you want to see how easy it is to put someone off with an initial phone call watch the hilarious Mrs Doubtfire in which Robin Williams, posing as a nanny, tries to put his wife off the other candidates by ringing up and pretending to be them.

Here are some initial questions which are worth asking:

- Where do you live?

- When will you be available?

- What is your experience with children?

- Do you smoke? (A word of warning, the answer, 'no, but I'm a social smoker' actually means yes).

- What pay do you expect?

If you are calling a childminder you might also want to know:

- Do you have a garden?

- Do you have pets?

- How many other children do you mind?

- What are their ages?

Tell the interviewee:

- The age and number of children you want cared for.

- The hours and days of work.

- The approximate rate of pay.

- That you will be working from home.

The interview itself

A word of warning here. Interviewing is difficult, but it will be much better for you if you ask all the questions you want answered, however embarrassing, now, rather than take on someone unsuitable. However, the interview is a dialogue and you will be able to tell as much about the person from the questions they ask you as from their answers. Be prepared to be specific. It is not fair to invite a nanny to an interview and then confess that you haven't thought about what sort of salary you might pay. If your husband is taking an active interest in his child, ask him to be present, for at least some of the interview (or arrange for him to see the short-list with you). This is absolutely vital for live-in nannies especially as there is no point employing Mary Poppins only to find that she and your husband fight tooth and nail.

If you plan to use a childminder, do visit during the day when the childminder has her charges with her. It will tell you as much about her as the interview itself.

Questions to your prospective carer might include:

- Why did she become a childminder/nanny/mother's help?

- What experience does she have with children?

- What do children in her care do on a typical day?

- How does she react to misbehaviour such as hitting younger children, biting, tantrums etc.?

- What sort of relationship does she have with the parents of the other children/previous employers?

- How does she expect to be paid?

- Would it be a problem if you were delayed occasionally?

- What happens if she – or you – go on holiday? Does she expect to be paid for that time?

- Would she mind if you contacted some of the other mums who are using her or have used her in the past? Can she give you their phone numbers and addresses?

Note: When you go to view a nursery for children of two and under, you might want to find out if it has a designated member of staff for each child, or if the staff take communal responsibility.

Useful addresses

Daycare Trust, Wesley House, 4 Wild Court, London WC2B 5AU. Tel: 0171 405 5617

Kids Club Network, Bellerive House, 3 Muirfield Cresc, London E14 9SZ. Tel: 0171 512 2100 (information on out of school clubs)

National Childminding Association, 8 Masons Hill, Bromley, Kent BR2 9EX. Tel: 0181 464 6164

National Childbirth Trust, Alexander House, Oldham Terrace, Acton, London W3 6NH

Parents At Work (see chapter 1)

Pre-School Learning Alliance, 69 Kings Cross Rd, London WC1X 9LL. Tel: 0171 833 0991

FIVE

The law, the taxman, NI and your business

The legal basis of your new business

There are several ways your new business can be legally constituted:

Sole trader This doesn't mean you have to trade. It just means that you work by yourself. A consultant could be a sole trader, as could a writer, craftsperson, knitter etc. This is the simplest form of business set-up. If you use your own name for the company, there will probably be no problems (but look at the section on choosing a name just in case).

Pros:

Easy to set up.

You get to run the business your way.

Cons:

You are all on your own if something goes wrong.

Your liabilities are unlimited.

Partnership Although there is no legal requirement to have a deed of partnership, it would be wise to get a solicitor to draw one up. Otherwise you may find yourself in thrall to the Partnership Act in the case of a dispute. It is also remarkably easy to become a partnership without knowing it. If two of you work together and split the profits, you are a partnership, even if you don't think of yourselves as one, unless it is clear that one of you is employed.

Your own partnership agreement should cover such things as who writes the cheques and up to what limit (to prevent either of you being taken for a ride), how profits (and losses) will be distributed, under what circumstances a partner can join or leave the partnership, and so on.

Pros:

Two heads may be better than one.

All liabilities are jointly shared.

Cons:

Even if you have a document which states who will blow whose nose in the case of a cold, there may still be scope for rabid internal politicking and disagreement – although a good partnership can give all parties a tremendous boost.

Even if one of you is a 'sleeping' partner (which means he or she is not actually working in the business) s/he will still be liable for any debts incurred for the partnership!

Limited company In order to set up a limited company, you need at least one director, at least one shareholder and a company secretary. (These could all be the same person.) Be aware, however, that if a director and/or shareholder guarantees payment of the company loan, he or she gets to pick up the tab if the company goes bust. In this situation, the shareholders may lose all that they have paid for their shares. If they did not pay the full price of their shares when they bought them, they may also have to pay the remainder.

The formalities of creating and running a company are much

greater than either method listed above. There are obligations to file annual returns to Companies Registry and to file accounts, which apply to most companies. Directors may be held responsible for the company's actions, so you may want to consider insurance against Directors liability. You also need to hold an annual shareholders' meeting.

The Company Secretary or his or her nominee (who could be a solicitor or accountant) must make sure all the forms are filled in. Making the most of a limited company generally involves some fees for accountancy advice. Incidentally, companies pay corporation tax rather than income tax and you will be treated as an employee of the company even if you are the one and only.

Pros:

> Company liabilities are limited to its share capital, so assuming there are no personal guarantees involved, you will not be liable for the full debts if the company goes under.

> There can also be tax advantages.

Cons:

> More cumbersome to set up.

> May need to pay out professional fees to make the most of the advantages.

> Won't protect you if you have given personal guarantees.

A co-operative A co–op requires at least seven members. For more details contact the Industrial Common Ownership Movement.

In practice most small businesses just starting up tend to be sole traders or partnerships, while a limited company becomes more attractive for tax and other reasons as the business grows.

Liz Davis and Diane Mutkin are partners working together in their dried flower business, Field House Design.
'I think it's actually a help that we weren't close friends before we became partners,' says Liz. 'That way if it didn't work out we had nothing to lose.'

Liz had trained with Marks & Spencer, but had given up work when her children were young. Out of interest she took a dried flower course and fell in love with the art. Diane had been working in television prior to having her children and had done a floristry course. They got together, 'literally at the school gates,' laughs Diane. 'We were asked to do a charity event, sold out and never looked back.'

The partners both work at promoting the business. 'You have to be persistent,' says Diane.' We've supplied Harrods but that only came about because we asked the buyer to see us. She said she'd give us ten minutes – but that was enough for us.'

'We're a good partnership' adds Liz, 'because our strengths merge. But we've also made sure that we've got the business side sorted out and we each know what we are supposed to be doing when. Now it's just a question of looking for new ways to expand the business. It gives us both a real buzz and it fits around the children – although it's never going to make us a fortune.'

What's in a name?

If you intend to trade under your own name as a sole trader or partnership, you should have few problems. However, do check that there isn't someone else with the same name trading in the same market in your area. For instance, if there are two 'Fred Jones, the plumber', it could cause endless confusion.

If you intend to trade under another name as a sole trader or partnership, you will still need to reveal your real name and address on your business stationery and company information. You can check that there is no one else trading under this name by calling Companies House – although this will only tell you Limited Company names. If you want to find out if there is anyone trading under this name – even if they are a sole trader or partnership, you may have to go to a private register such as Business Names Register.

It is not illegal for two companies to have the same name – but it can be illegal to try to 'pass off' yourself as someone else. For instance, if you decide to call your company the same name as a household name company, making the same product, the household name might be extremely narked and decide to sue.

How valuable is a name? If your company is called Jingle Jangle, making bracelets in Cornwall, you might not be too bothered if there is a Jingle Jangle plumbing service in the Highlands. On the other hand, if you have been trading as Jingle Jangle bracelets for five years and someone else starts making Jingle Jangle bracelets in the next street you might not be too amused.

It is illegal to use certain names – you cannot just decide that you will call your biscuits Royal Biscuits, even if the Queen's cousin did munch on one once!

Franchising – a helping hand or a drain on resources?

Franchising basically means buying into a successful business formula. You normally pay a one-off and an annual fee (which may be a percentage of profits) to the head company. In return, you get a helping hand with things like training, suppliers, use of the company name, help with actually getting going, operations manual and an exclusive operating area – but only for the franchise company in question, not its direct competitors! In the early stages you should be able to get a lot of help with day-to-day start-up problems, publicity and possibly even with legal and financial matters.

Sounds too good to be true? Maybe. While franchises do have a low failure rate, not all franchises are equal and some are downright flops, or charge exorbitant fees or give lousy support. Even if a franchise is well-established, high start-up costs might mean you could see little profit for several years.

Many franchises are run by high street names such as McDonalds, Burger King, The Body Shop. However, there are franchises which might well appeal to homeworkers. Some – such as language tuition courses – may cost as little as a couple of hundred pounds. Others, like image consultancies or children's gym clubs can costs thousands.

Before you buy a franchise, do as much research as you can. Talk to other franchisees of the company, read not just the company material but what is said about it. And get a solicitor to go through the contract with a fine tooth comb. Your bank may also have an in-house franchise advisor. He or she would be worth seeing even if you don't need to borrow from the bank. It's also worth looking at competition in the area. You may have an exclusive franchise, but that doesn't mean people who don't belong to that particular franchise network can't set up!

Franchising can be an excellent way to start a business, but careful checks increase the chances of success even further. The British Franchise Association is the umbrella body for many reputable franchise companies and has a useful information pack. A helpful book is *Taking up a Franchise* by Colin Barrow and Godfrey Golzen (Kogan Page).

BALANCING THE BOOKS – INCOME TAX, NATIONAL INSURANCE AND VAT

Getting on top of tax

When you are an employee, you pay-as-you-earn, and your tax is generally worked out by your employer. When you become self-employed, you are entirely responsible for your own tax affairs. Employees are normally on what is called Schedule E tax. The self-employed are on Schedule D.

'The biggest mistake I see, is the number of people who don't let anyone know they are becoming self-employed and then find themselves with problems later,' says one accountant who has many years experience of dealing with small businesses. 'This is not an advert for employing an accountant, but at least get some free advice. Talk to the bank manager, or ring the tax office. Ask them what you need to do at the very least.'

Indeed, as soon as you become self-employed, you should inform your local tax office (look under Inland Revenue in phone book). Even if you are still holding down a day-job, as it were, it is important to tell them because some of your tax will be for your self-employment and the rest for your day-job. If you have stopped working for an employer, you must also hand over your P45.

The *good news* about self-employed taxation is that you can claim against business expenses. That means in additional to the personal allowances given to everyone, you can get a proportion of relevant expenditure set against tax.

However, such expenses must be incurred 'wholly and exclusively' for the purposes of the business. For instance, if you use your phone for both business and private calls, you can only off-set tax against that proportion of it which is used solely for business. (An itemized phone bill will help.) Below are listed some of the things that are commonly regarded as allowable expenses. The list is by no means exhaustive, but it will give you some idea of the sort of things that you can claim for:

- Stock i.e. goods or raw material that you buy for re-sale.

- The proportion of light, heat, phone and gas bills, and water and business rates that are used wholly for pursuing the business.

- Professional fees and subscriptions incurred solely for carrying out your business e.g. membership of a professional body.

- The cost of running business transport.

- Stationery, printing stamps.

- Many professional services. (However, there are some exclusions so check with your accountant.)

- Employee wages.

- The cost of replacing worn out tools with new tools or repairing equipment.

- Business insurance (but not National insurance).

- Interest on debts incurred wholly for the business e.g. your bank loan for the business or overdraft.

- Running costs of the business e.g. the part of your heating and lighting bills, or computer costs, which are down to the business alone.

So the principle to be aware of is that you can only set off against tax that proportion of your expenses which is solely for business use. For example, if it would cost you £5 to replace your tools, and you use them 50 per cent of the time for business. You can set off £2.50 against tax.

However, there are certain expenses which are not allowable: the two that most people are surprised by is clothing and entertainment. Some forms of clothing are allowed, but only when they are used as protective clothing. (The costs of cleaning and replacing specialist clothing such as a barrister's wig or a plumber's boilersuit are allowed, but not the cost of ordinary clothes such as a suit – even if you only wear it when you see clients!)

Similarly business entertaining is not classed as allowable. This seems a bit rough if you frequently buy lunch for clients you would never dream of eating with from choice, but those are the rules. The Inland Revenue would argue that you got to eat lunch whatever company you kept!

You also cannot deduct capital costs such as the cost of buying fixed assets such as specialist equipment, or intangibles like 'good will'. However, you may be able to claim *capital allowances* on the equipment purchased for the business e.g. delivery vans, computers, office furniture, tailors' dummies, etc. New equipment (as opposed to equipment that you are replacing because it is clapped out) is subject to capital allowances. This means you cannot set off the whole amount in one chunk but over a period of several tax years.

For more details, the Inland Revenue has a whole series of free, easy-to-read booklets on all aspects of tax including *Starting in Business, How Business Profits are Taxed, Simplified Accounts* – a procedure which can be used by any business with less than £15,000 turnover. (Turnover is your earnings before you deduct the cost of business expenses such as stock, stationery etc.) The Inland Revenue is also bringing in a new way of assessing tax called *self assessment* and has a booklet on this. Get any of these from your local tax office.

Even if you intend to employ an accountant it is important to keep your books in good order. The Inland Revenue will not take it on trust that you have purchased what you say you've purchased. Just like a shop, they want to see a receipt. What's more it is now illegal not to keep records, under the new self-assessment regulations. These also mean that you will be taxed on a current year basis (the tax year ending on 31 January for most people, although you can run it from, say, the date you start trading, to a year after that). You will be liable to penalties if you are late with your return.

According to the Inland Revenue's own pamphlet *Starting in Business*, records will need to show:

● The takings.

● All items of business expenditure such as rent, rates, lighting, heating, insurance, repairs to premises, repair to fixtures and fittings, motor vehicle running expenses, purchase of goods for re-sale, wages and salaries of employees (gross, i.e. before tax and national insurance – NI – contributions), plus employer's share of NI contributions, stationery, postage, telephone etc.

● Any private money introduced into the business, giving the amount and origin (for example cashed-in national savings certificates, sums received on maturity or surrender of assurance policies, dividends on investments).

● The amount of cash taken from the business for your own or your family's use (for example weekly living expenses).

● The amount of any cheques drawn on the business bank account for private purposes and the reason (for example buying clothing, life assurance premiums).

● The market value of any goods taken from the business for your own or your family's use, if you did not pay for them in cash at the correct retail price.

● Amounts owed to you by customers at the accounting date, showing the total and the amount owed by each debtor.

● Amounts owed to you by suppliers at the accounting date, showing the total and the amount you owe to each creditor.

You can keep the books yourself – but be warned: it is time consuming. Most of the people I have spoken to who do so, set aside half a day each week. How successful you are at own book-keeping also depends on your personality type. Numerate, rational characters may find it easy to keep tabs on a business. Others, like Elana Rubenstein, a graphic designer and greetings card manufacturer, found keeping books 'the most depressing part of running the business for someone who enjoys creativity.'

You could keep an expenditure file on a week-by-week basis, with receipts carefully stashed. Or you could divide into types of expenditure, again with receipts carefully saved alongside. Even if you do plan to employ a book-keeper or accountant, keeping meticulous records will help lower their charges. Some people use accounting software. This is very useful, but still depends on you listing things in the correct boxes and taking the time to do it. Most small businesses have a separate bank account. This certainly makes it easier to keep track of what money is going where.

Finding an accountant

Personal recommendation is an excellent way to find an accountant. Ask other people who work in home based or small businesses. This is important, as you are looking for someone who is conversant with your way of life and aware of the tax benefits and pitfalls. Your professional association may also be able to recommend someone. Many accountants advertise in local papers. Some offer a first consultation free. This would be an excellent way of getting to know an accountant. You will also find accountants listed in the Yellow Pages and Thomson Directory, but picking one at random might not be the best way of finding the one who suits you.

It is important that you trust your accountant and that he or she seems to have time for you. Ask about other clients. If the rest of the clients are household names, the chances are that not only will bills be very high, but that you will always come bottom of his or her priority list. It is perfectly in order to ask a prospective accountant to estimate what keeping accounts for you will cost – provided you make it clear how much you intend to do yourself. If you stuff receipts into every available drawer and leave your accountant to hunt them down at the end of the year, you can expect to pay a great deal more than if you present her with a neatly labelled week-by-week file of expenses and impeccable sales transactions records.

Self-employed or employed?

Occasionally self-employed people find that the Inland Revenue challenges their own assessment of themselves as self-employed and says they are actually employees of a client. This is particularly likely if you do a great deal of your work for one client or spend a lot of time on one major deal. However, it is theoretically possible to be employed even for a two-day stint. So what is the difference? The Inland Revenue leaflet *Employed or Self-Employed* contains this handy little checklist:

If you can answer 'yes' to the following questions you are probably *employed*

- Do you have to do the work rather than hire someone else to do it for you?

- Can someone tell you at any time what to do, or when and how to do it?

- Are you paid by the hour, week, or month. Can you get overtime pay?

- Do you work set hours, or a given number of hours a week or month?

- Do you work at the premises of the person you work for or at a place he or she decides?

   If you can answer 'yes' to the following questions it will usually mean you are *self-employed.*

- Do you have the final say in how the business is run?

- Do you risk your own money in the business?

- Are you responsible for meeting the losses as well as taking the profits?

- Do you provide the main items of equipment you need to do your job, not just the small tools many employees provide for themselves?

- Are you free to hire other people on your own terms to do the work you have taken on? Do you pay them out of your own pocket?

- Do you have to correct unsatisfactory work in your own time and at your own expense?

National insurance

Dealing with the formalities of tax and national insurance is one of the perennial headaches of the self-employed person. As an employee, it is all done for you. As a self-employed person or even employer you have to do it all yourself – and many of the benefits you receive in turn are not the same as those of an employee.

If you are an employee you pay Class 1 contributions. If you are self-employed, sixteen and over, you pay Class 2 contributions unless you are a pensioner or you earn below a certain threshold which varies from year to year (it was £3,200 in 1995–1996). If you think you may qualify for exemptions, talk to the local Contributions Agency or Social Security office (address in phone book). They will send you the relevant forms. Class 4 contributions are paid by anyone who is self-employed and earns over a certain amount – between £6,640 and 22,880 in 1996 (the figures change every year).

If you have an accountant, she will tell you how to ensure you pay the correct contributions. Otherwise the Citizens Advice Bureau or your local Contributions Agency should be able to point you in the right direction. Do try to pay on time as you can be taken to court if you default. Many people pay by standing order or direct debit to avoid having to remember when to pay. These are only basic rules. There are plenty of exemptions and exceptions, so it is worth talking to the Social Security office or your accountant when you set up.

VAT

If your turnover is over £45,000 (1996 figure) you must register for

VAT. You must also register if you have made taxable supplies of over £45,000 or expect to do so within the next 30 days. Not to register could result in a large fine. So if you are lucky enough to find your turnover creeping that way, register immediately. You can do this through your local Customs and Excise Office. Even if you do not achieve these figures, registration may still be worth considering.

Pros:

If you have to pay a lot of VAT on supplies to your business e.g. electrical goods, word processors etc., you will be able to claim the VAT back

Charging VAT makes it look as if you are successful.

If your clients are VAT registered, they can claim your VAT charges back.

Cons:

If your clients are not VAT registered they may find your prices uncompetitive or expensive besides non-registered competition.

You need to keep detailed VAT records, with returns being filed (in the main) every three months. Can you trust yourself to do this or are you willing to pay someone else to do it for you?

Punishments can be severe if you get yourself in a mess or are late filing the quarterly returns.

If you have any problems or doubts about whether or not you need to register, talk to your local Customs and Excise Office or your accountant.

This is only a very brief guide to the taxes likely to be paid by a home based business just starting up. If you decide you do not wish to employ someone to help you with such matters as national insurance and Income tax (and plenty of businesses find it quite manageable to deal with all these hurdles themselves), do make the most of free advice available. The Inland Revenue will help you with any queries you have on income tax, the Contributions Agency with NI and Customs and Excise with VAT. The Citizens Advice Bureau could also be a very useful stopping-off point. This is particularly true if you are not earning a great deal and may be entitled to low-income benefits such as Family Credit or tax exemptions. They can also point you in the right direction for problems such as bad debts (see also chapter 6).

Useful addresses

Business Names Register, Somerset House, Temple St, Birmingham B2 5DN. Tel: 0121 643 0227.

Companies House, Crown Way, Cardiff, S. Glamorgan, CF4 3UZ. Tel: 01222 388588 (for England and Wales)

Companies House, 37 Castle Terrace, Edinburgh, EH1 2EB. Tel: 0131 535 5800 (for Scotland)

Companies House, IDB House, 64 Chichester St, Belfast BT1 4JX. Tel: 01232 234488 (for Northern Ireland)

Customs and Excise, Dorset House, Stamford St, London SE1 9PY. Tel: 0171 928 3344 (for your local Customs and Excise Office, and local tax and NI offices, look in your local phone book)

Industrial Common Ownership Movement, Vassali House, 20 Central Rd, Leeds LS1 6DE. Tel: 0121 523 6886

SIX

Hit the ground running

However skilled you are at the work you plan to do from home, your primary consideration in setting up your new business, must be to establish your market. Quite simply, that means finding your customers. In any business, whether you are a plumber, consultant or counsellor, you need customers to succeed. Tracking customers down – and holding on to them – is one of the most difficult challenges for any new business. If it is remotely possible, it is best not to leave your current job, if you have one, before you have at least one or two leads.

'I started off with several clients,' says Joel Brizman, management and computer consultant. 'I think it must be very hard to start up without that because if you have clients they tend to refer you to others.' However, your customers need not necessarily be current ones. Perhaps you made cakes for a hobby and are now turning it into a business. If so, contact friends who had previously bought your cakes, and ask them if they'd like any more – or know anyone who would.

MARKETING

Finding new customers is all down to marketing. In its widest sense, this means persuading people to buy your goods or services. *Advertising* and *public relations* are also valuable tools for letting people know that your business is there and will be included in this section. Marketing can be done on a huge or tiny scale. Donating a few of your products to a local charity raffle is marketing – but so is sponsoring an entire football team. In this section we will concentrate on some of the more cost-effective methods.

How to market yourself

Many people imagine that marketing themselves is somehow immodest and what they should be marketing – if anything at all – is their product/service. However, when you are starting off *you* are the representative for the product or service. The most effective marketing tool at your disposal – and also the least expensive – is you. Which is why you need to devote considerable thought to the best way to let people know that you are *out there*, as it were. Rosemarie Ghazaros who runs a marketing consultancy is in the sort of business where her time is money, but she freely admits that she devotes considerable time to meeting contacts, attending professional seminars and generally ensuring that she is well known in her field. That's because she recognizes that marketing yourself is invaluable.

Below I describe ten key methods of marketing yourself.

Perhaps the best marketing tool, particularly for services or specialist products, is **networking** – talking to the right people, at the right time, in the right places. This is the surest way to encourage the spread of that most precious asset: the word-of-mouth recommendation. 'I've never advertised,' says Susanna Cheal, a charity consultant. 'All my clients have come from contacts or other clients.' However, word-of-mouth recommendations don't just happen. In order for people to recommend you they need to know *what you are doing* and that you are *doing it well*. It is important to network – both with other businesses and within your own trade or professional body to ensure that potential clients know you exist.

'When I set up, I went to see a lot of GPs and told them what I was doing,' says one psychotherapist. 'That paid dividends in that they could see the sort of work I was doing. I'd also trained as a social worker and so when I told former colleagues about my work, they also kept me in mind if someone needed psychotherapy.'

'It's important to keep networking because you never know whether you'll lose a client,' says book-keeper Fiona Bradley. 'I attend my local Chamber of Commerce, I lecture at the Business Link, so I'm always in touch with what's going on in small businesses who are my core market.'

People often think of 'networking' as something that is only done at high-powered levels. Not so. Letting mothers at the school gates know about your services, swapping information with friends at the rugby club is all networking. 'I found that other mums were my best customers,' says Sarita, a beauty therapist. 'When my sons were invited to tea with their friends, they'd often mention that I ran a beauty business and I got plenty of of clients that way!'

You cannot afford to be too indirect about offering your services. On the other hand, old contacts may be put off if you continually pester them for work. It is better to engineer a meeting about another matter and then explain what you can do for them, rather than endlessly cold calling. Persistence may pay off – but it can also put people off. This is why 'forums' for networking are so important. They can take the form of training days, professional conferences, charity breakfasts, even the village fete. A person who works from home and tries to sell their own skills without belonging to some form of networking organization either has brilliant contacts already or is storing up potential trouble.

Networking does take time, but it is normally time well spent. However, you do want to beware of spending so much time networking that you neglect your business. In choosing *where* to network, you need to apply the rules of market research as stringently as for actually producing your goods or services. Networking at the local school gates is ideal for someone producing childrenswear, or offering beauty treatments – it may not be ideal for someone who is an export specialist.

Before you decide to attend a conference or meeting ask yourself:

- Who else is likely to be there? (Can you get a guest list in advance?)

- Will they be receptive to your idea/product? (Look at the agenda carefully.)

- Will there be time for informal chats and questions? (A conference where you have to keep silent all day may be useful for training purposes but not for networking.)

- How many useful contacts can you expect to make at this meeting, and how much information can you expect to gather? (Be realistic.)

When you start off, you may well find that you go to a few dud events. However, with practice you will soon learn where you are most likely to make useful contacts. What should you do if someone asks you to keep in touch, but does not offer you firm work? Here the golden rule is to find some means of establishing a closer contact. Perhaps you might ring to suggest a lunch or drink. Or perhaps you could send something of interest to them – be it a catalogue or a piece about your business in the local paper – or better still, a piece that might be relevant to their business. The important thing is to make sure they don't forget you.

You do need to beware of being too pushy. In the USA it is perfectly acceptable to pursue your quarry with unstinting zeal (it is even admired). Here, alas, we tend to fight shy of people who seem too keen – perhaps because it is easy to appear desperate. 'I think that if you have confidence, that inspires confidence in the people you meet,' says Joel Brizman, consultant. On the other hand if you are desperate, people sense that and it makes them wary.

Supplying a first class service is another excellent marketing tool. All the networking in the world will only land you a client once. If, that once, your service or craft is shoddy, they will never use you again. It is important not only to attract clients, but to retain them. Which brings us to method number three:

Caring for your clients and contacts is paramount. One of the cardinal mistakes people make when setting up is to run helter skelter after new clients forgetting that the most important source of work is actually those good old dependable clients who faithfully repeat their orders. It is important to look after your old clients for two reasons – firstly to ensure repeat business, but also because they are the most likely source of other work. 'Once a year, sometimes more, I hold a coffee morning for all my regular customers,' says Mary Ross, interior designer. 'There are always some of my items on show and the morning is in my house, which is really my showcase. It's both my way of thanking them and of reminding them that I'm still here and can do other things for them.'

If your clients are satisfied they will not only use you but will pass on your name to other friends and associates – and they may also give you a reference. Another variation on this theme is to team up with someone in a related area and offer to put work their way if they will do the same for you. For instance, a catering firm might team up with party organizers, a beauty therapist with a fitness trainer. Mary Ross, for example, frequently teams up with a carpenter, Roy. He makes hand-crafted cabinets – and she decorates them. Each supplies the other with work. 'My only rider is that the person you choose must be excellent,' says Mary. 'Or it will reflect on you. I love Roy's work and know just what a craftsman he is, so when I recommend him, it reflects on me in a very positive way.'

The Ten Commandments for keeping customers happy (and ensuring a good reference).

1   **Be reliable** Do what you say you'll do when you promised to do it. 'The client is taking a chance when they take on a small outfit,' says marketing consultant, Rosemarie Ghazaros. 'I repay their trust by making sure I get the work done on time and giving them the best service I can.'

2   **Make sure both you and your customer know what is expected**
    If your customer thinks that you are doing one thing – and you
    think you are doing another, dissatisfaction is bound to ensue.
    So be clear as to what you hope to achieve before you take the
    job.' Some people do think that counsellors will solve their
    problems for them,' says Anita Kanter, 'and I have to make it
    clear that is not my role. I am trying to help them work towards
    their own solution and they come to understand that.'

    The same applies to quotations. If you give a quotation for a
    job, it is fair for the customer to assume that she will have to pay
    that amount. She will not be impressed to be told that you failed
    to take account of an upturn in paint prices and as a result the
    room you designed for her now costs £300 more than quoted. If
    you cannot give a firm quote, say so and give an estimate. Then
    work out a quote with a realistic profit margin – customers do
    not like to find addendums to their bills because you've been
    sloppy in costing.

3   **Don't promise what you can't deliver** In the early days of
    building a business, it is easy to take on orders or customers,
    even when you cannot cope or do not have the knowledge to do
    what you have promised. However, a botched job is a worse
    advert than no job at all.

4   **Be a good communicator** To give clear explanations, be polite,
    courteous and friendly. You may be a brilliant plumber, but if
    you come across as surly and resentful you are unlikely to
    attract business.

5   **Deal with complaints promptly and politely** If the customer is
    in the right, and a product is clearly faulty, do not attempt to
    cover up or to bluster through the situation. Admit the problem
    (and resolve to find out what went wrong later), apologize and
    offer a replacement or a refund. That way the customer is likely

to see the mistake as a one-off and use you again. Forcing them to keep a clearly faulty item, apart from being illegal in the majority of cases, will only ensure that they never buy from you again – and that they tell their friends not to either. If you are up front, the chances are the client will either accept a refund (to which they are legally entitled) or even an exchange. However, goods which are sold as faulty (e.g. seconds) need not be exchanged or refunded provided the defect was bought to the attention of the buyer at the time of purchase. Nevertheless, they still have to be fit for their purpose. For example, you can sell a tea-towel with a design that is not quite as it should be, but not with a whopping great hole in it.

In the case of a service, complaints may be far harder to deal with. How do you react to the person who tells you your teaching isn't good enough? Or that your counselling has been a complete waste of time. In this case, the key is listening carefully to what is being said and trying to get to the bottom of the problem. Was it a misunderstanding or were you genuinely deficient in some respect? (We all make mistakes from time to time.) And, most importantly, can anything be done to rectify the situation?

However, do not assume that all complainants are automatically in the right. The man who's aggrieved at a counsellor for failing to save his marriage, may have been looking for a miracle worker rather than a therapist. The woman who's cross that her childminder gives the kids fish and chips now and again, may be being unreasonable – particularly if she did not ask the childminder to exclude these foods from the child's diet.

In the case of unreasonable complaints, you are perfectly entitled to stand your ground. But do so politely and calmly. If you are not sure whether a complaint is unreasonable, try to talk it over with someone else in a similar field or a professional body. Many professional associations have helplines for their members for just such eventualities.

6   **Keep learning** Even if things are going brilliantly, there are still things you can learn. I once interviewed Sophie Mirman who had started as a secretary in the typing pool and gone on to found Sock Shop and later a successful childrenswear shop, Trotters. When I told her I liked the shop, her first comment was, 'Any complaints? What could we do better?' – a sure sign of someone who was never going to be complacent. 'I always set aside time for keeping up to date and learning,' says Joel Brizman, computer and management consultant. 'It's vitally important to be completely up to date.'

7   **Return calls promptly** Keeping the customer waiting does nothing to increase your reputation – or the chance that he will employ you. If you do not have the information he requires, at least ring to tell him that although you cannot answer his query instantly, you will research it and ring him back. If you go away on holiday make sure your answer phone or message service says that you cannot be contacted until your return.

8   **Keep your clients informed** That way if there are any necessary but sudden changes, they know what is going on. 'I'm a sole practitioner and I think one of the things that clients appreciate about that is that I keep them informed,' says 'Jane', a solicitor. 'I write to them and let them know what is going on before they phone me.'

9   **Go that extra mile** Everyone appreciates that service or product which is just a little bit special. 'We always give a teas-made and have a whole host of things which people can borrow if they have forgotten to pack something,' says Belle Hepworth of The Half-Way House Guest House. 'People really notice those personal touches.'

10   **Do your best** Someone who is clearly committed to providing a professional service, a beautiful piece of work or excellent

product is bound to be more impressive than someone who isn't.

Looking the part makes all the difference. It is important to dress appropriately for your job. If, for instance, you are selling jewellery, it is a good idea to wear your own merchandise to parties, health clubs and generally out and about. Jane Gregory, who sells Cabouchon jewellery, has found this an excellent way to encourage interest. 'People say to me. "Oooh, that's nice where did you get that?" and they are really pleased that you can show them a catalogue.'

It is also important that the tools of your trade speak for you. Stationery, business cards etc., should, in general, be the best you can afford. They needn't be masterpieces of graphic design unless you are in a field such as journalism, design or PR where image is all important. But they should be clear and explain what you do and where to find you.

When I received the bill for my professionally designed stationery, I couldn't believe it could possibly be worth such a huge outlay. However, many of my editors have commented on how much they liked it and one even rang back within a day of getting my letter. 'The design made it stand out,' she told me. 'So I looked at your ideas first.'

Giving free samples reaps dividends. Sometimes, alas, it may be necessary to do something for nothing. You may, for instance, need to make up some children's clothes to show a buyer long before you've ever sold any. If you plan to sell your own home-made jam, customers at a craft fair or fete may well expect a taste before they buy. If you are an unknown author or graphic designer, editors are quite likely to expect you to submit your work on a trial basis, before acceptance. All of these things are painful for the business person who wants to be out there selling rather than giving away. But you've heard of taking a sprat to catch a mackerel.

Children's jeans designer Jennie Woodcock, had an idea for a range of up-market children's casualwear. She interested the Early Learning

Centre in her idea and they asked her to make up some samples – within two weeks over the Christmas/New Year period.' It was absolutely fraught,' Jennie recalls, 'and meant giving up most of Christmas. But I knew it would be worth it in the end if they took the clothes.' They did.

The moral is that sometimes you have to give a little to reap greater rewards later. It may not be material samples. For instance, if you are an accountant, you may choose to send out a fact-sheet on current tax law to prospective clients to show them your expertise and commitment. 'I often find I end up being generous with my advice to projects,' says Jennifer Butcher, charity consultant. 'But in this field you have to. You need to be aware that people want a lot of help and don't have huge budgets.' Giving free services (*pro bono* work, as it is known in legal jargon) to voluntary organizations can often pay dividends in contacts and recommendations as well as being useful both in making contacts, building skills and contributing to a worthwhile cause.

Offering sponsorship is a good way to get noticed. Donating a prize to the town carnival, or sponsoring a piece of equipment or event, can all raise awareness. But the sponsorship must be appropriate. It's a great idea to sponsor the barre in the local ballet school if you sell ballet shoes, not much good, though, if you are selling football boots. What sorts of event do your customers attend? What sponsorship would warm the cockles of their heart? And what would the sponsorship do for their perception of you? These are all questions to ask yourself when you are approached for sponsorship.

Advertising can be an extremely effective method of marketing. However, there are two riders: it must be targeted carefully and it must advertise the service properly. OK, so the TV ads create brand images in a beautifully elliptical and oblique way – such subtleties are fine for the big boys who can afford to pay hundreds of thousands of pounds for a campaign. You, however, are not so much looking to build brand awareness as to let people know you are out there at all. 'I advertised in my local paper, but nothing came of it,' says Simon Bacon, osteopath. 'I now think that for a service like mine, people look for recommendations.'

Christine Buckingham, on the other hand, found advertising paid dividends for her ironing service. 'I started off cheaply advertising in newsagents' windows, putting leaflets in schools, at the doctor's, mother and toddler groups – everywhere women go and would see it. Then a friend suggested advertising in the Jewish Chronicle because there's a big Jewish community round here. I was inundated with calls.'

Before you advertise ask yourself: Where do my prospective customers go, what do they read, how can I reach them? It may be cheaper to place a series of ads in a publication, but only do this if you know they will reach your target audience (e.g. in a hobby magazine). Otherwise try one advert at a time.

What to put in your advert.

The wording and lay-out of your advert is crucial. There is no point advertising in an excellent trade journal if your ad is too obscure to understand. 'A lot of people make the mistake of putting in an ad or writing a brochure which tells a lot about themselves, but nothing about what their firm can do for the customer,' says home based copywriter Brian Morris. 'What the client wants to know is how your service will help, or what your product will do.'

It is also worth getting to the point early on. Recently I saw an ad at a tennis club. The first three lines were all about the joys of tennis. It was only in the last line that the ad revealed it was for hiring evening menswear. I'd expected it to be for tenniswear and felt disappointed when it wasn't! Whether you want to get professional help in designing and writing your advert depends on your budget. It is pointless laying out £100 worth in advertising fees for an ad that is going to cost £30 in the local newspaper – unless you intend to use that ad time and time again. However, if you are competing against major agencies or services, you may need to be sure your work has that professional finish.

If you have a unique selling point – stress it. If, for instance, you can teach even the most obdurate computer illiterate to operate a PC, say so. If your rocking-horses are hand-crafted and each design is original – stress it.

Advertising need not be expensive. The simplest form is an ad in the newsagents' window, in the local press or radio, or in Yellow Pages or the Thomson Directory. Classified ads in specialist publications are often good value as well. It is perfectly possible to run a successful advertising campaign on very little money provided the ads are well targeted and well put together.

However, it has to be said that you cannot make wild claims in your advertising. For a free guide to what's allowable and what's not contact the Advertising Standards Authority.

Becoming a self-appointed PR expert is part of the job. Public relations is the art of presenting your company to the world to maximum advantage. Major corporations have whole teams of experts to work on the public face of their companies. However, for the small at-home business, PR's most direct application is in getting press, radio and, if you are very lucky, TV coverage. 'Editorial coverage is worth a great deal more than advertising,' says Belle Hepworth of the Half-Way House Guest House in Crayke, 'because it is an independent assessment of the standard of your establishment.' Mary Ross, interior designer agrees. 'Clients like to see that you've been featured and it stimulates interest too.'

How do you achieve editorial coverage? Simply sending a press release about the fact that you have set up, unless you have a highly unusual profession, won't have the desired effect. The media wants stories with an angle, which means that you need to find what is newsworthy. For instance, Paul Mitterhuber, an osteopath, has several clients who are well known locally. He plans to ask them to feature in a press release about the work he does. Their fame makes his story well worth writing about.

Judy Lever and Vivienne Pringle of the mail-order maternity wear firm, Blooming Marvellous, managed to interest a parenting magazine in featuring their clothes – a move that helped launch their success. And Verna Wilkins feels that national newspaper interest in her books, which present positive images of black children, was very helpful in establishing the company. 'I was inundated with people wanting to buy them because there was this pent-up demand and no one satisfying it.'

So before you try a blanket approach to the media, think again about your target audience is and what they are most likely to be interested in. If, for instance, you are selling hand-crafted pottery you can prompt interest from the local newspaper by revealing that you have just won a major pottery competition. You can create news stories too: helping charities, organizing competitions, giving free prizes or creating photo-opportunities can all work in your favour.

Often, publicity breeds publicity. Milliner Katherine Goodison, was featured in a law journal after she'd left her solicitor's firm to start her own business. That article was picked up by a journalist on a women's magazine. This, in turn was picked up by a TV station and national newspaper – all helping to establish her credibility and build a clientele.

Of course, an editorial is not like advertising in that you have no say over how you are presented. The article that appears may not pick up on all the features or qualities you wanted to mention. You need to accept this as the downside of PR – a minor one in comparison to the sales and benefits to be gained from good exposure. One way of avoiding the problem is to write articles yourself for relevant journals and local papers. These may attract clientele and will enhance your credibility.

If a local newspaper is buying your piece, they will generally pay very little, so make sure they print a contact number. (But think, too, of the security implications, see below.) If you are appearing in a professional journal, make sure your name and company are credited. Even if the journal will not print a phone number or address, make sure the editor has one in case of interest.

How do you find out who will be interested in your story? There are several excellent media guides including *Willings Press Guide, Benns Media Guide, Brad,* used largely by the advertising industry, and *Hollis,* which lists services for the media and communications professions. All are available in good libraries.

Holding open days, demonstrations and party-plan are all very effective marketing tools. Which is why you shouldn't pass up any opportunity to give talks to local or special interest groups. Linda Greenbury, careers counsellor, found that talking to local National Women's Register Groups gave her higher visibility as well as locating prospective clients. Sex therapist Bella found that talking to women's groups netted several clients. If you know of a local group which offers a target audience, make the first move and offer to talk about what you do. Most local groups are always on the look-out for speakers. If you have a demonstrable skill – beauty care, floristry, for example – you could give a demonstration, rather than a talk. This is particularly useful if you are shy. If, for instance, you are hoping to start a gardening business, opening your garden in aid of charity might be a good way of showcasing your expertise and could also attract press interest. However, you do need to be aware of the security implications. (See chapter 8.)

Another way of getting your wares to a wider audience is through party-plan, particularly suitable for small items such as jewellery, books, children's clothes or cosmetics. Party-plan basically involves getting friends and contacts to hold meetings to demonstrate your wares – informal 'parties' if you like, with tea and cake on offer. 'I've found this a very good way of selling my clothes,' says Kiren Darashah designer of the children's clothing range Ben Go Tig, 'because it gets the clothes to the people most likely to buy them. I have demonstrated them in offices where lots of mums work and have found that also works very well indeed.'

Cold calling and direct mailing are more demanding. We all fear rejection. We all worry that the people on the other end of the phone will be rude and that our approach won't get results. However, provided your cold calling is well targeted it often pays off. Jane Lewis of the caterers Lewis and Grant, has occasionally cold called prospective clients, if she knows they have a function coming up. 'Often it's worked,' she says. 'If not right away, then six months later when they need another party and invite us to tender.'

The golden rules of cold calling are to be polite, not to hassle uninterested clients and to follow up leads. Certain professions, such as financial advisors, have strict limitations on cold calling. Talk to your professional body if in doubt.

Direct mail is another useful way of marketing – again provided the mailing is tightly targeted. Andy Binfield, wood turner, always makes sure old clients have a leaflet telling them of the craft fairs he will be at for the rest of the season. 'A lot of people collect wooden fruit piece by piece, so they want to know where they can find you, when they can afford the next bit,' he says. 'I've found it very effective.'

Esther Kaposi is a communications consultant. She believes that successful marketing is one of the major keys to business success.
Esther had thought about becoming self-employed, but it wasn't until half her company was made redundant, that she decided to take the leap. Image is very important in consultancy and Esther felt that she 'wanted to give myself all the help I could. I regarded having a laser printer and professionally designed business stationery as tools that would enhance my image.'

Esther also did her groundwork thoroughly. She wrote to all her contacts telling them what she was doing and followed up with a phone call. 'I tried to find a reason to phone rather than just asking about work. If a client had a baby, I might phone to see how the baby was and mention what I was doing at the same time.'

Esther's organization paid off and her client list has grown steadily. However, despite this, she spends part of each week on marketing 'even when I'm very busy I still think it's important to look for new opportunities.' She also does some voluntary work. This she feels gives her an outside interest and provides useful occupation if there is a quiet patch – although it has also given her a whole new network of contacts.

As Chief Examiner for the CAM (Communications, Advertising and Marketing) Foundation exams, Esther is well aware of the importance of clarity in marketing. 'I'll never use jargon, if plain English will do. Clients are more interested in what you can do for them, than your pro-active strategy. Overall, she has been delighted with the way self-employment has worked out. 'By marketing even in the busy times you get a steady flow of work and that gives you a lot of confidence.'

How to make sure they know about you.

John Whitmore is a barrister who works from home, specializing in discrimination cases. As a former Director of the Commission for Racial Equality, he had commuted from Leicester to London for eight years and has found working at home a boon. 'I'm sure I'd earn more in chambers,' says John. 'But it's not an atmosphere I thrive in.' He also feels that his reputation helps him get work. His cases are frequently reported in both national and local newspapers and a victory can spark off a flurry of calls. He also teaches and is frequently out at court or visiting solicitors. 'Isolation isn't a problem for me,' he says. 'But there's no doubt that coverage in the newspapers attracts a lot of attention and helps your reputation. And it makes sure people remember you.'

Facts that helped a factor. Mark Dickson is a factoring broker.

He provides a service often used by small businesses with high turnover and tardy payers. Factors will collect debts for the business in return for a fee. They may also lend money against the debt, again for a fee. Mark liaises between people who want factoring facilities and the institutions that offer them. He started with just one client, but an article about him in a regional paper did wonders for his client base.

'It came just at the right time and quite a few clients got in touch with me from that. I think that the fact that it was editorial rather than an advert impressed them.'

Since then, Mark has relied largely on word of mouth. 'I find one thing tends to lead to another. I certainly don't think it matters that I work from home. All I, as a factor, need is a phone, a car – and to do the job properly.'

How to give a professional impression from a home base

Many people worry that clients will not take a home based business seriously. In fact, nowadays, it can often be an asset. 'My clients like the idea that they always get me when they pick up the phone,' says PR consultant Dana Cukier. 'That's an advantage.'

The most important thing is to take yourself seriously. Act professionally and your clients will learn to treat you with respect. In fact, you can even make a positive advantage of working from home. Tell clients you have opted to work from home to save costs – costs that mean they won't be paying for expensive premises.

However, if you are in one of the few industries where working from home is still not accepted, there are various ways around this. For instance, if you are worried about the impression your home address gives on a mailing list, give your home an inspiring name. Few would guess that Georgian House, 2 Jones Court, is actually a home rather than an office block. But do make sure the postman knows!

A separate phone line for business calls is also essential in this case, and may anyway be advisable if you have young children around. One woman told me how mortified she was when, in the middle of a major negotiation, her two-year-old began to sing nursery rhymes down the line!

Some homeworkers have all their meetings at clients' premises –
which is often a bonus for the client. 'People like the fact that I'm so
willing to go to them,' says copywriter Brian Morris. Others hold some
meetings in their own offices and homes. 'I often see clients here,' says
accountant Nick Weedon. 'They are mainly small businesses and like
the homely atmosphere.'

If you feel your home isn't up to a high-powered breakfast pow-
wow, consider joining a club or relevant professional association with
premises. The Institute of Directors, for instance, has grand central
London premises, with meeting rooms and full office facilities. A
private club might also make a good venue for meetings. Such facilities
can cost anywhere from £50–£500 a year and will be good value if you
have meetings frequently. They also enhance your image.

Five ways to build a good relationship with your suppliers

- Research suppliers thoroughly – look at trade journals, talk to
  people in the same field, make a short-list of likely candidates and
  visit them. The more research you do in finding your supplier, the
  better the chances of a successful relationship.

- Take a note of their attitude. If they treat you like an
  inconvenience or don't return calls promptly what are they saying
  to you?

- Treat them with respect and if they have queries/reservations
  about your requirements, listen to them and talk the problem
  through.

- If something isn't right tell them promptly – that way they can put
  it right next time and will also know that you are no pushover.

- Pay their bills promptly – especially important if you are one of
  their smaller clients. Prompt payment can do a lot to make up for a
  comparatively small order.

Felicity Scholes spent a year researching suppliers of beads before setting up her jewellery business, Beads by Scholes, with her husband.

'Beads are a by-product of lots of manufacturing processes, but in Britain, they don't keep them,' says Felicity Scholes. Nothing daunted, she and her husband decided to do their research on the continent, spending a great deal of time in technical libraries and contacting the trade departments of embassies to find likely suppliers. 'We then tried to combine our holidays with checking out the factories,' says Felicity. 'We wanted to be sure they understood what we wanted and could supply it.'

However, she feels the research has paid off as she now has a thriving jewellery business. 'We talk to our suppliers regularly and make sure they understand what we want – and we understand their needs too,' she says. 'That's part of building up a relationship, but I'm sure all our research must have helped.'

HELP! I'M TIED UP IN RED TAPE! – COMMON PROBLEMS FOR START-UP BUSINESSES

Licensing, registration and inspection

It is amazing how many businesses require some form of licensing, registration or inspection. Bed and breakfast establishments, for instance, may need to be inspected by fire officers, to be registered with the local authority, and may even need planning permission and official approval of their signs from local planning officers. That's before they start taking on *catering*, in which case there is another host of rules to contend with. These rules have been set up for the public good, wisely or otherwise. But many people do not know about them. Unfortunately, ignorance is no defence and you could end up being fined heavily if, for instance, your kitchen is not up to environmental health standards for a catering business, or if you are an unregistered childminder. If you make toys which do not comply with safety standards or sell clothes without the correct labelling, you could also end up in hot water.

As a general rule, it's a good idea to find out about what red tape is involved before you set up a business. Your local authority is a good place to start. Tell them what you want to do and they will put you in touch with the relevant person: the local trading standards officer for instance, if you plan to make and sell goods; the Social Services Department if you plan to run a childcare facility or nursery. The local environmental health officer if you want to run some form of catering outlet.

However, if you plan to grow produce or package it – say for instance, you have a herb garden and want to sell your dried herbs, the Ministry of Agriculture, Fisheries and Food has all the details of what you can and can't do. If you plan to set up some form of manufacturing process your local branch of the Health and Safety Executive are the people to contact. They can also be very helpful if you plan to take on employees (see chapter 7). If your local authority cannot help for any reason, then your local Business Link or TEC are also good sources of information.

Do try to follow the rules carefully when setting up. It will save you an awful lot of aggro later. And remember that if you sell goods you need to comply with the Sale of Goods Act, 1979. Again, your local trading standards officer can supply relevant details.

Bad debts

Bad debts are the nightmare of every small business. It isn't possible to avoid them, but it is possible to minimize the risk. Firstly, be sure that when you agree to sell any goods or undertake any work, you issue a very clear statement of your *terms and conditions*. This should include how much, when and by what means you are to be paid (e.g. if you expect a deposit, you should spell out its exact amount, and the amount of the balance to be paid later.) For instance, many guest houses insist on a 10 per cent deposit on booking and a 50 per cent cancellation fee, if cancellation is within a fortnight of the intended stay. Although, legally a contract can still be binding if it is made orally (e.g. over the phone), it is always best to put things in writing – a short letter confirming what has been agreed can avoid disputes later, or help to resolve them in your favour.

Many businesses require payment up front – therapists generally work on a per session basis, for instance, and most craftspeople and mail order companies will expect payment in full at the time of ordering/delivery. Although there are some businesses where payment is generally made after the services have been performed, you *must* have a clear contract before you undertake the work, or you will find all sorts of problems later on. If your customer has not sent you a contract – or if its terms are unacceptable and you have not yet agreed to them – then you should send them one. It could be as simple as a letter stating clearly what the work is to be undertaken, how it is to be done and when, what the price is, and when and how it is to be paid.

It might seem somehow 'unfriendly' to put your agreement on such an official footing and several people have expressed this reservation to me. In response, I'd say that it is not so much unfriendly as professional. Secondly, would you rather be friendly or paid?

When the cheque wasn't in the post

'Heather' a copywriter now sends a standard letter of terms and conditions, along with the agreed payment, whenever she receives a commission. That's because she had one bad experience: 'I was offered some work by a man I used to work with,' she says. 'It was all done in a very chatty way over the phone and it seemed a bit cold to confirm it in writing. Besides, he was working for a major company and I felt there would be no problems at all.'

In fact, the man was made redundant shortly after the project and his replacement denied that Heather had ever been commissioned to do the work. 'He claimed that the firm were looking at several different copywriters and that I'd just been asked to do a sample of how I'd tackle the job. Without anything in writing it was his word against mine. So I decided to drop it – even though it was several hundred pounds down the drain!' Heather has since instituted her terms and conditions letter. 'And I've never had any complaints. After all, how would an employee feel if their employer told them they couldn't pay them this month or had changed their mind about paying them at all? So why should I be treated like that just because I work for myself.'

Even so, Heather has still had plenty of tardy payers. She has even had to resort to staging a near sit-in at a client who had repeatedly delayed payment. 'When I got there, she told me that she could send the cheque that night. I told her I'd wait until it was written. Within half an hour I had my money, but it was an awful feeling.'

However, if all else (including repeated phone calls, pestering and an angry letter from your solicitor) has failed, court action may be your best bet. There are several ways to pursue this. If the claim is relatively small, you can pursue the debtor through the *small claims court*. This has a current ceiling of claims for £3000. The procedure is relatively simple and you probably will not require a solicitor to help you. Your local Citizens Advice Bureau is a good place to start for more details of the procedure. They may also be able to advise you as to your chances of getting the money back. (Difficult if your client has done a moonlight flit.) Look them up in your phone book or Thomson Directory.

If, however, your claim is for more than £3000 or the debtor claims that your service was unsatisfactory and puts in a counter claim, you will need to go to a higher court and may decide to engage a solicitor. If not, it is well worth talking to the Citizens Advice Bureau about presenting your case. You may be lucky and find that your debtor pays up once your summons (the first step in taking court action) has been issued. You should try to ensure he also pays the cost of the summons, of your solicitor and any interest that was built into the contract. Alternatively, he may fail to put in a defence or to appear in court, in which case judgment is likely to be in your favour. In the worst case scenario, he may choose to defend himself and you may have to slug it out openly in court.

Whether you feel it is worth the risk of losing your time and money (and if you are not in the small claims court of having to pay the other side's costs), as well as gaining possibly adverse publicity, is up to you. But it is well worth thinking over before making the decision.

If you are dealing with a large company, one way to embarrass them into paying up is to issue a *winding up order* which can be used for debts of over £750. Your solicitor will tell you how to go about it. If alas, the company that owes you money has gone bust, you will need to join the list of creditors. Again, a solicitor can help you do this, but your chances of recouping the whole debt are slim. Incidentally, many companies delay payment for as long as they can – i.e. until you make a fuss. Asking for your money from a reputable company shouldn't make you unpopular. Even if it does, you have to ask yourself am I prepared to work for this company for nothing and retain their goodwill and gratitude – or would I rather be paid?

It is galling to have a bad debt, but even more galling if you are expected to pay tax on it. Alas, the Inland Revenue does not accept extra-slow payment as bad debt. However, if a company which has gone bust owes you money, they may well accept that you are not going to be paid. This is one of those technical areas where advice from a solicitor or accountant who specializes in tax could be very useful.

Thinking about exporting?

This is a major step for most small businesses and requires a lot of foresight and planning. If you are a one-man band, working from home, you must expect to need some help, paid or voluntary, once you get to the point of exporting your products. You may, for instance, need to employ someone to act as a translator for you in your business dealings, or even to help you suss out suppliers or the competition abroad. You may also want to employ a local agent or advisor. The first step is to get in touch with the people who can help. This includes your regional government office. Their number can be found in the phone book and they are sited in major centres. Alternatively, you could talk to your local TEC or Business Link as many are starting to employ export advisors. Both will give you excellent advice on how to do further research into your market. The Department of Trade and Industry can also supply a great deal of help as they operate many schemes, often in conjunction with the Foreign Office. These include the chance to exhibit at trade fairs abroad, to take part in overseas marketing initiatives and to get information about trading conditions in the country you plan to export to. There is also a know-how fund for firms who want to trade in Eastern Europe. Your local Chamber of Commerce will also be able to help and you may find that the country you want to export to has its own trade association with a base over here. (Contact their embassy to find out.) Your bank may also be able to help you if they have an overseas department.

Useful addresses

Advertising Standards Authority, 2 Torrington Place, London WC1E 7HW. Tel: 0171 580 5555

British Franchise Association, Newtown Road, Henley on Thames, Oxon, RG9 1HG. Tel: 01491 578050

Association of British Factors and Discounters, 1 Northumberland Ave, Trafalgar Square, London WC2N 5BW. Tel: 0171 930 9112.

CAM (Communications, Advertising and Marketing) Foundation, Abford House, 15 Wilton Rd, London SW1 0PR. Tel: 0171 828 7506

Institute of Directors, 116 Pall Mall, London SW1Y 5ED. Tel : 0171 839 1233

Ministry of Agriculture, Fisheries and Food, Whitehall Place, London SW1A 2HH. Tel: 0171 270 3000

National Association of Citizens Advice Bureaux, 115–123 Pentonville Road, London N1 9LZ (for your local branch, see your local phone book) Tel: 0171 833 2181

SEVEN

Organizing the Home Office

There are thousands of successful businesses that started on kitchen tables. Laura Ashley, for instance, started as a 'corner of the kitchen' business and went on to make millions. However, just because a business starts on the kitchen table doesn't mean it should end there. If you intend to spend ten hours a day at work, then it makes sense to give some thought and time to the environment you work in. If you plan to entertain clients, then making sure your office is presentable is even more important.

Before you even start working from home though, do a few basic checks to ensure that you are not in breach of your mortgage or tenancy agreement (see chapters 1 and 3). Once you know you are *legally* at least on safe ground, it is time to start thinking about where to locate your office. A few sociable souls really do enjoy working in the middle of the family hubbub, but most require some peace and quiet. The ideal solution is a spare room wholly devoted to your work. Indeed, the spare bedroom is currently the most popular location.

But what if you don't have a spare bedroom. Try thinking creatively to see where you can make extra space, for instance:

● Do you have a dining room and kitchen? Could the family eat most meals in the kitchen with the dining room being reserved largely for your work and for guests?

- Do you have a living room and find that your family are out most of the day? Could you partition off part of your lounge as your working area?

- Could you install a shed at the bottom of the garden? There are several new de-luxe garden offices being developed with the homeworker in mind. Firms which make them include Home-lodge, Oakmoor Telecentres and English Heritage Buildings (see addresses list).

Alas, what is best for the homeworker isn't best for the tax bill. If you are using much of the house exclusively for business purposes you may get clobbered for the Uniform Business Rate. One homeworking employer told me the sad tale of two of his employees who both worked out of their conservatories. One had a tiny conservatory with only room enough for the knitting machine, a chair and wool storage. The other had a larger conservatory with room not only for the machine and storage but for a large dining table and chairs for summer eating. The woman with the small conservatory had to pay business rates. The woman with the large conservatory didn't.

If, however, you do want designated space and don't have a spare bedroom you could try converting the garage into an office or converting the basement or loft into an office. Before you do either of these check that you will not fall foul of planning regulations. Contact your local authority as a precaution and read the planning section of chapter 3.

Having the computer in full view in the living room can be a problem. The answer? Fit it with a drape for when it is not being used or use a purpose built unit such as Grahl's Home Office.

DECORATING AND EQUIPPING THE HOME OFFICE

If you want to be sure of creating the best impression you might decide to hire an interior designer. Alternatively, Laura Ashley charge £50 for a styling consultation for three rooms, refundable against purchases of £50 or more. At the most basic level:

- Rooms in one neutral colour, particularly white and cream look larger than their actual size.

- Blues and pastels are restful, soothing colours.

- Blacks and greys are traditionally 'trendy' – but could be depressing.

- Bright colours promote a feeling of energy – but can be distracting to work in.

- Blues, greens and greys are colours which will make a room look – and feel – cooler.

- If you want to warm up a room pinks, oranges and browns all add a feeling of heat.

- Neutral carpets hide stains, while vinyl floor covering offers easy maintenance. If you are asthmatic, you may find that vinyl is a better choice than carpet as it will cut down the number of house dust mites (and their excreta) which can trigger asthma.

It is essential to make your working area look as professional as possible, particularly if you intend seeing clients at home. A clinical air will make them feel that they are entering an office rather than your home.

A Room with a View. Linda Greenbury is a professional careers counsellor who has given a great deal of thought to her office environment.
Her company, Career Development Centre for Women, is based at her home and her office is at the top of the house. Clients are shown up there and are able to look out on a vista of fields, rivers and trees.

'I wanted to give a professional feel in my office,' says Linda. 'All my vocational books are up here, as is a desk for us both to sit at. I also like to keep it organized for both my clients and myself.' The interviewing desk is the focus of the room, but at the side is a computer table, telephone answering machine and other files. Book shelves are orderly and the decor is neutral in tone, giving a confident feel. The impression of space is increased by the fact that most of the lighting is natural, coming through the windows. Indeed, the PC has been carefully placed so that the light will not increase glare onto the screen.

'I spend a lot of time working and I want my clients to feel comfortable, so I tried to create an atmosphere that is professional but not intimidating,' says Linda. 'When I'm upstairs in the office, I'm a very different me from downstairs at home.'

Home offices differ from the standard office in that they tend to have less space and often have to blend into living rooms, dining rooms etc. There are very few firms specializing in home offices. IKEA has basic home–office furniture, while Selfridges have recently opened a whole home office department with fully trained staff. If you can afford to customize your furniture, or want to hide away the tools of your trade, Neville Johnson, Southway Interiors or Albert Plumb are also possibilities. But be warned – their furniture isn't cheap. Some companies do office furniture that fits easily into the home. Mail–order suppliers Estia fall into this category. You can also pick up good quality office furniture at second hand shops and auctions, but do be a little wary of buying computers or office chairs second hand, unless you are very sure you won't need after–sales service or the chair is extremely good. (See the section below on equipment.)

It is tempting, particularly if you are just setting up to make–do–and–mend on a spare table with a few boxes for storage. This may be necessary if you have absolutely no spare cash, but research in the USA, where there are many more homeworkers, has shown that those working in carefully thought out home offices feel more positive, more efficient, and are even more willing to take planned risks than those trying to work in difficult conditions. In some ways this is common sense: if you walk into an airy, organized office, you assume the company is efficient and the workers happy. Walk into a badly lit, ill ventilated tip of papers, and you assume the organization is on the way down.

The minimum requirements for the home office are that it is:

- Comfortable – heated when cold, cooled when hot, well-lit and equipped with furniture which minimizes back and posture problems.

- Organized – important equipment is within easy reach, and files are stored neatly and in intelligible (at least to the user) order.

- Private – enough space to work undisturbed, with somewhere for confidential files to be stored. 'Before I had my waiting room installed, I was frequently invaded by the children,' says 'Caroline Smith', optician. 'On one memorable occasion my youngest sat down and did a wee just under the patient's chair – fortunately I had enough time to clear it away before they arrived. Having a waiting room has meant that clients don't have to sit with the family and it gives a much more professional impression.'

Your chair If you lash out on one piece of equipment it should be your chair. This is because back pain caused by bad posture is exceedingly expensive in time and money, not to mention discomfort. All new chairs have to be adjustable, but if you are considering buying one second hand from a charity or junk shop, you should certainly ensure that it is.

According to back specialists you should test a chair by sitting with your hands relaxed at your sides. When lifted your elbows should sit comfortably on the desk and your feet on the floor. If you can't reach the floor in this position, buy a foot rest. Lean your back against the chair. The back of the chair should support you from the base of your spine at least up to the bottom part of your shoulder blades. It is vital that the chair swivels so that you don't strain your back. Without a swivel chair you are likely to move only the upper back, putting undue strain on the lower. A rounded seat is generally more comfortable than a square one, but this may be a matter of taste. Wheels can be useful for rolling from one area of your desk to another, but may be a liability if you have young children who would enjoy wheeling themselves into trouble if unsupervised. It's definitely worth taking some time to choose a chair – and do try it out before you take it home.

Your desk Your desk should be large enough to house all your important equipment. If you are going to be using a PC and printer, you might decide to have a computer table in addition to a desk in order to ensure that you have enough space for the PC and for all your other equipment such as phone, filing trays etc. Peter Cobden, home office buyer for Selfridges, suggests that an L-shaped unit, will maximize the chances of being able to reach your equipment.

The telephone Here the major decision is whether to have a separate business line or not. For mail-order businesses, this would certainly be a good idea if you want to be able to choose when and how to answer calls, and to be sure you are not losing business while another family member is chatting on the line. Indeed, for any business where family members are avid phone users, a business line is a good way to avoid conflict over phone priorities and ensure that customers are answered in a professional manner.

I will never forget the embarrassment I caused myself, when just starting up, when all my phone lines were on the same circuit. While I was downstairs on the phone to an eminent psychiatrist, my daughter was upstairs with her nanny. In an unguarded moment, she ran to the upstairs phone and was soon joining in the interview – singing 'baa, baa, black sheep' insistently down the line. Fortunately, my interviewee was good humoured about the interruption, but I nevertheless gave the impression that I was a 'dabbler' in journalism, rather than a professional.

Of course, a business line will cost you – both for installation and for rental – but it may be an investment worth making if your business is a heavy phone user. On the other hand, if you tend to be out and about a lot and the phone rings rarely, this may be a needless expense. There are a whole range of phone services available from both BT and Mercury, and any number of discounts for heavy users. Phone up and ask what you could be entitled to. Useful services include *call waiting* and *call divert*. Call waiting lets you know there is another call waiting for you and allows you to hold the first call while you find out who it is. Some people, however, are not too keen on this as they feel it makes the original caller feel less important than the first. Call divert can be used to divert your phone messages to another named phone number when you are out. There are charges for both of these services. If you are working in a garden shed, or are moving from room to room then you might find it useful to have a Cordless phone which can accompany you on your travels. Check, however, what the range is before you buy it. These may need to be recharged periodically, at least overnight.

If you are in a business where it is vital to get to the phone quickly you might consider not only using existing phone lines, but adding to the number of phones. Malcolm Pein who runs a mail–order chess software company has 'phones in the bathroom, bedrooms, living room, kitchen – and pads beside them all. In our business it is essential that calls are answered quickly and I can't afford to have someone hanging up because they can't get hold of me. I also have a call divert service to someone who is knowledgeable about chess because I want my customers to be able to have their questions answered when they phone. In my experience people buy from people – not answering machines.' However, if you do not feel it is essential to answer every call immediately yourself, an answering machine could come in handy. It will take messages when you are out and most have technology to enable you to call in from another phone and find out who has called in your absence. Some answering machines are combined with faxes (see below).

Mobile phones, pagers and answering services So you want to do more than just find out who's been telephoning you in your absence? If you want to be contacted wherever you are, there are a variety of methods to chose from. Mobile phones have become more popular as the price has decreased. These can receive calls almost anywhere (but not in basements or tunnels, and it's illegal to use a hand-held one in the car). It's expensive for the caller to call you and for you to make calls, but if your work is largely on an 'emergency' basis or you are on the move for a good part of the day you will probably want to invest in one.

A cheaper alternative is a pager. It can be rigged up to your answering machine to let you know whenever a call has been left. Some pagers will even show you the number that has called, allowing you to make an informed guess at the urgency of the call.

On the other hand, if you yearn for the human touch you might consider an answering service. This method is favoured by many workers who need to give the impression that their firm is bigger than it is (e.g. consultants) – or more metropolitan than it is. A 'receptionist' somewhere else answers your calls and then transfers them to you or takes messages. In some cases, this can even disguise just where you are working. Richard Nissen's company, The Virtual Office in Piccadilly, gives the example of a Manchester firm which wanted clients to believe they had a London presence. The clients were given the number of The Virtual Office and calls were re-directed through them. They were also able to arrange meetings at The Virtual Office's premises and to have mail sent there. These services are not cheap but can add prestige and self-confidence if you feel you lack it.

The fax The first question to ask is whether you really need one. If you are in a business where time is of the essence and where material is regularly faxed back and forth e.g. journalism, sales, law, marketing – the answer is probably yes. On the other hand, if you have rarely used one before and find that you require only a very occasional sortie to the local fax bureau, then it may be less essential. However, with most bureaux charging between £1–£2 to fax – or receive – a single sheet, you would need to fax only 100 sheets to make buying your own machine worthwhile. That's without considering the loss of time, petrol and queuing involved in using bureaux.

Before you buy a fax take the following considerations into account:

- How much will you use it? Do you need a separate telephone line to avoid it taking up your conversation time?

- If you have several phones in the house, what happens if you answer on the one that isn't connected to the fax? Will all your phones know how to handle a fax or will calls be interrupted by that horrible fax tone?

- Do you need a plain paper fax (that uses ordinary office paper) or will it be OK to use the cheaper thermal paper? (Thermal paper is shiny, curls up a lot and also fades with the passage of time, so is not ideal for documents that will be referred to repeatedly.)

- Do you need to transmit photos, illustrations etc.? If so, you will need a better quality resolution.

- Will the fax store information if the machine jams or you run out of paper? (A memory can be helpful in this case.)

- Do you need a machine with all the add-ons or will a simple one that merely sends and receives do just as well?

Some of the more common features of fax machines include:

- Auto re-dial – avoids having to wait for an engaged line to clear – the machine itself will keep dialling the number automatically until it gets through, and will then send the fax.

- Ability to use plain paper – useful for those who don't want their faxes to fade or curl up so they look like tangled swiss roles. Makes for better presentation, but can be expensive.

- Cutting device for thermal paper (which comes in rolls) – cutting reams of paper into manageable sheets is an almighty bore.

- Memory – so the machine retains information even if you are out of paper. A good memory also makes it faster to send messages.

- Number programming. Works in the same way that you can program your own phone to store certain numbers automatically – useful for anyone sending lots of messages to a restricted set of numbers.

- An answering machine facility is included on some models.

It is essential before you buy that you find out how much back-up you will get from the manufacturer if the machine goes wrong. This is particularly necessary as many fax problems can be sorted out over the phone – provided there is someone at the other end telling you what to do.

There is an alternative to using a specific fax machine – it is getting your computer to do the faxing for you. The advantages are that you don't need a separate space-clogging fax and you can send documents stored in your computer without printing them first. On the other hand, you can't transmit anything that isn't stored in your computer without using a scanner, and if you want to receive faxes while you are not around, you have to leave the computer on. Of course, if your computer/fax gets stolen, you are bereft of both bits of equipment simultaneously.

The Computer According to the Midland Bank, while only 25 per cent of office workers use a computer, around 70 per cent of homeworkers do so. A computer can be invaluable for helping you present and work out your accounts, keeping your office diary, for data processing, graphics, word-processing and, yes, even to play games on, in those dull moments. The more computer literate can also whizz around the Internet, gleaning information from dusty corners of the globe. 'What surprises me is how many people buy computers for their kids, but never consider what the computer can do for them,' says Richard Nissen, Director of The Virtual Office, a business centre for remote workers in central London. 'People over 35 are scared by the technology but it's the fear rather than the technology itself which is the problem.'

There are hundreds of home computers on the market, so it's easy to be dazzled – and bewildered – by the choice available. However, what you have to ask yourself is just what you intend to use your computer for: will you be doing reams of desk-top publishing – or just printing out the occasional letter? If the latter is the case, there may be no point buying a top-of-the-range model – unless you plan to use it for the children as well. You may well be satisfied with a designated word-processor. On the other hand, if you intend to foray regularly onto the Internet and make the computer do everything but dance for its supper, then you will want a superior model. Remember, though, that with computers, today's top model is tomorrow's dinosaur!

Computers also come in two sizes – the small portable computers that can be transported everywhere and the ordinary desk-top machine. The portable computer is more expensive, but can be taken on trains, out into the garden and works on batteries for a limited time. The desk-top is cheaper, easier to read but too large to schlepp. I chose a lap-top believing that I would spend lots of time typing away on trains. Alas, fears about it being stolen, as well as the fact that the batteries do not last long, means that I could have managed with a cheaper desk-top version – and saved myself a lot of eye strain.

Of course, to some extent your budget will determine your choice, as will the experience you bring to bear. If you are a computer whizz who regularly takes all the latest computer magazines, you may feel quite happy buying from a chain store. Alternatively, the less confident could try buying from a specialist dealer. Recommendations from friends, competitors and from your trade association are often the best guide to the system you are likely to be happy with. Computer magazines and consumer magazines such as *Which?* are also a good way of finding out what's going on in the market. Some manufacturers also sell direct.

Whichever way of buying you choose it is vital that you:

- Find out what is included – and what isn't. Don't assume that just because you are buying a word-processor, a printer is automatically included. Likewise, many machines do not have internal modems. ('Modems' allow your computer to 'talk' with other computers – enabling you to receive email and to join the much-hyped Internet.).

- Find out what after-sales service is offered. Who can you call on when things go wrong and what is the guarantee period? Do you have to take the computer back to the shop if it breaks down or is there on-site maintenance (i.e. will they come to you?) or at least a collect and return warranty? Test out the reliability of a proposed supplier before you buy by giving them a ring and seeing if they return your call. How helpful are sales staff? Do they appear to be knowledgeable about computers or do they think a ram is something that chews grass and dates sheep?

- Decide whether it is worth buying direct from the manufacturer – it may be cheaper, but make sure you know that they have a helpline and what it costs, if anything.

- Find out how long the make you are considering has been in business. Do you know anyone else who owns one? In general, stick to makes that are well known.

- Investigate any deals which allow you your money back within a certain period if you are not satisfied.

- Decide what technical specifications you are looking for. Read computer magazines, talk to anyone you trust in the industry about what you want your computer to do for you. And remember that today's flashiest model is quickly obsolete. At the moment, if you want to use your computer for its full range of functions, you will probably find it best to look for a pentium processor with at least 8 megabytes of RAM, although 16 megabytes of RAM is apparently the coming thing!

- If you are employed by a company and work from home only a couple of days a week, make sure the system you plan to buy is compatible with the office system. Ask the company's technical support department to check for you.

- Find out what help is available if you have software problems (i.e. you get into a muddle operating the machine). You will generally be referred back to the software manufacturer. Most of these have a certain period within which you can phone free for help – but after that they charge. The motto is to get yourself some training. 'A lot of people are sold the most expensive model in the shop by a crafty salesman,' says one computer buff. 'It can do everything but fly to the moon – trouble is the people who buy it can't drive it at all.'

If you are buying a computer the most common add-ons (apart, of course, from the various software) are: a printer (quality varies from the daisy wheel to the top class laser jet) and modem. Once you've got your computer and attendant goodies, make sure it is insured (see below) as theft is very common. What's more you can avoid business catastrophes by taking a few simple precautions such as:

- Backing up (i.e. copying) everything onto disk.

- Installing anti-virus software (if not automatically included) to avoid the whole system being contaminated.

- Storing disks in a different room from the computer to avoid them both being stolen.

- Ensuring you make it clear who can use what piece of software and disk. You don't want your kids to overwrite your work, for instance, or bring virus-infected software into the system.

- Getting yourself booked onto a basic training course if you are at loss with the technology. Courses can be taken privately or through further education colleges, TECs and private companies.

And finally, remember that if you are working with a computer, it is very important to arrange your office lighting so as to minimize strain on your eyesight. Above all, you should aim to avoid glare. That means not sitting with the light falling directly onto the PC. Blinds or curtains are also important to control the amount of light in the room and a dimmer switch and anglepoise light could come in handy.

Other home office equipment Besides the major items discussed above, you should also budget for some sort of **filing system** e.g. filing cabinets, **address book** (or **electronic organizer**), **stationery, business cards, paper clips, pens, stapler, calculator, message pad**. If ideas come to you in the middle of the night keep a spare message pad by the bed. If you do heaps of photocopying a **photocopier** may also be necessary.

Remember that, when buying any piece of equipment, there are two vital questions:

- What is the guarantee period? (If it is insufficient for your needs you may need to look again or find out if an extended guarantee is possible and at what cost.)

- What back-up will I have if things go wrong?

And with all equipment it is worth considering whether you really need to buy it. If you need it only for a very short period of time, it might be better to hire. When buying it is worth looking out for any special deals such as interest-free credit, free extended warranty and additional after-sales service. Remember too to keep all your receipts safe so that you can claim against tax. If you are not taking immediate possession of the equipment you are buying, paying by credit card will protect you in the event of the company going bust before you get your equipment as you can claim against the credit card company for purchases of over £100.

Wildlife artist Stephen Gayford works from a house on a private island in the Thames.
Stephen's pictures of swans, ducks and other animals are sold through Harrods and galleries. He chose his home because it offered him such good access to the creatures he paints. 'Being in a high-rise flat couldn't give the same sort of inspiration,' he says. In his studio, he keeps not only his easel, but natural history reference books and administrative materials. As an artist, light is very important to him. ' I wish I could live in the South of France for the light,' he says. 'But meantime, I make do with north-facing windows, so that the light is diffuse rather than harsh. In the winter, I have lightbulbs that recreate the feel of daylight.'
As Stephen's equipment is very mobile, he often works outside. He is also capable of locking himself away till the early hours of the morning, 'if work is going well'. 'I play golf when I want to switch off,' he says. 'Though even then I might see a deer or fox which will inspire a new picture. It's a round-the-clock profession, really.'

Writer and broadcaster Tobe Aleksander uses a spare bedroom as her office.
'Having a designated area as my office, makes me feel a lot more

serious than if I was having to work in the living room,' says Tobe. 'I'm in the process of upgrading my equipment too, because newer machines can do more things and there's been a lot of wear and tear on my old computer.'

Tobe feels that her main problem is having too much paper – 'continual paper-overload, really,' – so she has spent heavily on filing cabinets and tries to keep up-to-date with her filing. 'A real chore but better than not being able to find anything.'

Tobe's advice for anyone setting up is to invest heavily in their chair. 'The price of mine seemed outrageous at the time, but I knew I had back-problems and didn't want to make them worse.' Her investment has paid off. While many of the homeworkers she knows are continually complaining of back pain, Tobe has suffered very little. 'People think of home offices as cramped,' she says. 'But so are a lot of the offices that I go into in town. And at least at home, I look out on to a view of magnolia trees and plants rather than at a brick wall or dustbin!'

Making your home office work for you

As a homeworker, you will probably not have many of the support systems available to the office worker – secretaries, colleagues etc. Investing in useful equipment is one way to even the stakes. Another is to make sure you know where everything is and how you can reach it! Many people find it useful to make a list of what they need and how often they need it. Once the list is completed you can plan desk and storage space so that what you use most often is closest at hand. Other tips from homeworkers include:

- Buy the best you can afford – it makes you look professional and gives confidence.

- Use an office equipment firm to deliver your stationery etc. to prevent running out.

- Deal with each piece of paper as it arrives.

- Be ruthless. Don't file things you don't need.

- File what you do need regularly – preferably once a week.

- Create a filing system that is intelligible to others as well as yourself. Filing by subject, alphabetically, chronologically or by colour coding are all well-established methods.

- Keep tax records for six years – and keep them where you can find them if you need to!

- Store delicate materials or hard-to-replace ones out of reach of children.

- Buy in bulk. It's much cheaper.

- Keep one diary for both work and social events and know where to find it.

- Photocopy all important papers, address books and so on. Back up computer files on to disk and don't let your cups of tea get anywhere near valuable papers or disks.

- Don't overload the electrical circuits – it's very easy to do. And get the wiring checked if it hasn't been done recently.

SECURITY AND INSURANCE

Insurance is vital for all homeworkers. There is a current urban myth doing the rounds that all home office equipment is automatically covered on your home insurance policy. Alas, this is not necessarily true. It is essential to ring your insurance company and let them know that you are working from home and tell them about any additional equipment you've bought as a result. If you are using your employer's equipment don't assume that they have insured it for your use. Check and find out whether it needs to be covered on your policy. If you are using only a few pieces of equipment – say a fax and answering machine – you will probably be able to take out additional cover on your household insurance, if necessary. If your equipment is expensive, or you entertain clients or have employees, you might want a stand-alone policy.

Some companies already offer insurance packages aimed specifically at home office users. These include not only insurance for property, but other sorts of insurance which any self-employed person might need including:

Stand alone insurance for equipment – in case of fire, accidental damage or theft. However, many policies have exemptions for certain sorts of damage or if you do not take precautions to protect your equipment (particularly computers), so check for any exemptions.

Public liability insurance This is insurance which protects you against being sued by anyone who is injured as an accidental result of your business. It also offers protection against damage to their property resulting from your business activity. For instance, if you are a psychotherapist and a client falls off the couch during a therapy session and breaks their leg, they could sue you. Similarly, if a short-sighted client visits an optician and trips over the doorway, they might sue.

Professional indemnity insurance This protects you should you be sued for giving wrongful advice or treatment. Most useful for professionals such as consultants, accountants, solicitors, dentists and counsellors.

Business interruption insurance This covers you if damage to your property or equipment leads to a shortfall in your profits because you are unable to conduct business as usual.

Product liability insurance covers you if the product you make causes harm to someone e.g. if you are an aromatherapist and one of your home-made oils causes a skin reaction in your client. This may be useful too if you repair or sell possibly harmful items, though you may also be covered by public liability.

Money insurance covers you for loss or theft of money and/or cheques.

Goods in transit insurance useful if you often send goods from place to place. A craftsperson who regularly takes their goods to craft fairs might find this useful for instance.

Policies that are geared specifically to homeworkers often contain at least a couple of the above types of insurance. Companies which provide such policies include Midland Bank and Lloyds Bank insurance arms, S-Tech, Michael Pavey, Anthony Charles International, CNA and the Tolson Messenger Group. Talk to your insurance broker for specific details or contact the Association of British Insurers who are very helpful and can give you further details.

Other types of insurance to consider include:

Employer's liability insurance If you employ anyone you *must* by law take out this insurance to protect you from any claims against you as a result of your employees working for you (unless they are very close relatives).

Permanent Health Insurance This covers you in the event of you falling sick and being unable to work. Premiums will depend on your 'exemption period' i.e. how long you think you can struggle on for without income from the business. Most policies will not make up completely the amount you lose from being ill, but go some way towards it. Some will also take into account nursing fees.

Personal Accident A similar form of insurance which covers you in the case of an accident. Some policies combine elements of permanent health insurance and personal accident.

Private Medical Insurance Waiting lists mean that you could be out of action a good while awaiting an operation or treatment on the NHS. Private medical insurance could help cut that waiting time, but be warned, most insurers exclude treatment as a result of any conditions which you have when taking out the policy.

As you can see, the range of possible insurances is vast and most home based businesses can expect to pay out at least £500 a year for protection. Do make sure, though, that you are conversant with the exemptions on your policy and that your household insurers know about any other policies you have taken out. This is so that you do not have problems about who pays out when it comes to claiming. Also, many insurance policies have caveats about letting people into your home, for instance, or security precautions they want you to take – which is an additional reason for taking some basic security precautions (see below).

There are other financial considerations to take into account if you are self-employed. A private pension and some form of life assurance are just two of them. 'When you are in a firm and have all the benefits of their pension, private medical insurance and so on, you don't realize just how it adds up,' says communications consultant Kim Pickin. 'You need to earn a certain amount just to cover that.'

Taking care of your safety

If you are running a business from home, you need to feel safe. What's more your insurance company may, as I mentioned earlier, expect you to prove that you've taken safety precautions. Here are some basic security measures you should take:

- If you have equipment or stock stored at home, be very careful when you go out that you've locked doors and shut windows. A burglar alarm could also be a useful deterrent and some insurers may demand it.

- If you need to store confidential papers or valuables, a lockable storage cabinet or safe is a must.

- Make sure your home is well lit at night.

- Protect your privacy with net curtains, hedges, fences. Research in the USA has shown that these sorts of subtle 'keep out' signals act as psychological – as well as physical – deterrents to would-be burglars. However, it is essential that you can see over the hedges.

- If the law requires you to put your mailing address, rather than a PO Box number on your catalogues, then put a disclaimer saying something like 'please, no callers in person'.

- If your profession requires you to have visitors in your home – e.g. if you run a bed and breakfast, or are a counsellor, optician, chiropodist etc. – try to find out something about them before they come. Take a note of their address and telephone number and confirm the appointment by ringing. Make sure someone else knows that they are coming and, even better, try to have someone else in the house when you are seeing them. Some counsellors work in pairs for this reason.

- Make sure clients have appointments. Install a peephole so you can see who is at the door before you answer it.

- Try to make your office look professional. Keep the doors to the rest of the house closed.

- Have your seat nearer to the door than the client's.

- Have a personal alarm.

- Ann Howell, Crime Prevention Officer, says that if a client does become heated it is essential to calm the situation. 'Don't answer aggression with aggression. Make an excuse and leave the room – offer them a cup of tea perhaps. Talk calmly and quietly and try to persuade them to calm down. If they are becoming agitated it may be necessary to leave the house altogether.' She also suggests that if you are suspicious of someone, 'follow your instinct and don't let them in. You might even say bluntly that you can't help them.'

- Pets can be a mixed security blessing. Dodo the Doberman might well protect you from a burglar, but you don't want her biting your best customer. In general, keep pets out of your office. This is because:

They might eat your papers

Your clients may be allergic to them

It doesn't sound terribly professional to have frantic mewing in the background when you are making an important call.

Christa is a remedial masseur. Her practice includes sports stars, dancers and people with back injuries. For her, security is a major issue.

'The problem is that in this country massage has certain connotations,' she says. 'If you look at some of the adverts, it's all "massage for discreet gentlemen". It put me off starting my training for six months I was so affected by it!'

Christa has found the best way to avoid misunderstanding is to avoid advertising. 'At first clients came to me through friends and then I had a write-up in a magazine which emphasized the clinical side of massage and that attracted the right sort of people.' Even so, Christa was careful when taking on a new male client, always making sure her partner was in and that he answered the door and waited with them, until Christa was ready. She also made sure that a male voice answered the phone. 'I'd advise anyone starting off to do the same. One way to attract custom is to talk about what you do to the local paper, making it clear that it is a health treatment.' She also feels it can be very useful to court local hairdressers. 'A good relationship will guarantee a steady string of lady clients.'

Christa also makes sure her consulting room 'is hygienic and not too personal. I have a wooden floor, plants and my diploma as well as a poster for London Contemporary Dance, but that's it.' She has only had one client who came with the wrong idea. 'I thought he was just testing my nerves, but when the second time he came he still talked on and on about sex, I was rude to him. But he's the only one.'

Christa says that homeworkers are often a good source of work. 'It's the computer screen that does it. People get absorbed in it and their neck muscles tense and their faces scrunch up. They lean forward and create all sorts of potential back problems. I can always tell when a client has spent a long time at their computer!'

What to wear to work

It may seem bizarre to think about what to wear round the house, but the fact is that clothes can help or hinder your working ability. There are some souls who can work perfectly well all day in their dressing gown. But most people find that actually getting dressed acts as a motivator to start work. You may not want to wear a full suit and jewellery, but looking presentable will help your confidence and self-esteem. However, if you do go out to work, remember that you need to dress up to normal 'office standard', and possibly above, since there is a tendency to think homeworkers slop around all day in their slippers. 'I have made the mistake in the past of coming into town in T-shirt and skirt and have seen the disparaging looks,' says copywriter Heather. 'Since then, I've bought two designer-type suits and wear them to meetings. I can see that people view me very differently then. One even mentioned how well I was doing – before I said anything at all!'

TAKING ON AN EMPLOYEE

The home office can become a little crowded if you start to take on employees. Indeed, this is one of the major reasons many people decide to move to an office. If you only need occasional help, a full-time employee could be a drain on your resources. So ask yourself what function the employee will fulfil.

If it's to tide you over the busy times, it could be worth hiring a temp through an employment agency or sub-contracting. This means giving specific tasks to specialists who remain self-employed, that is, they are free to work for anyone else they choose. However, if you are looking for someone who will work for you and you alone, then they are likely to be employed, even if they are a part-timer. (See chapter 5 for more details on employed and self-employed status.)

If you lack secretarial support, an independent word-processing service or, for a wider range of tasks, an office bureau could be the answer. If you need someone to answer your phones, consider an answering service (see p.160). If you need someone to work for the business on a regular, committed basis and to gain some knowledge of it – you are looking for an employee.

Interviewing and choosing an employee can be difficult. It can be tempting to pick on a friend, but be careful. Friendship (or even being a family member) does not guarantee job suitability and can lead to soured relationships if things don't go right. Recommendation is a safer bet, as is advertising. But do check out *all* references thoroughly. In the main, written references are not a good enough testimonial. Phoning up previous employers is likely to lead to a more truthful assessment.

Taking on an employee commits you to a variety of obligations (unless they are close family). These include:

- To take out employer's liability insurance (see above – this may not be necessary for very close relatives. Talk to your insurer).

- To give a period of notice, which varies with length of service.

- To pay statutory sick pay and statutory maternity pay and to giving any pregnant employee 14 weeks maternity leave. (Some employees are entitled to more, but not necessarily if you employ less than five people.)

- To deduct the employee's tax and national insurance contributions – as well as pay employer's national insurance. The Inland Revenue has a video about employing people which you can get from your local tax office. They will also send you a New Employer's Starter Pack.

- To ensure the employee's health and safety while at work. If you are doing an office-type job, contact the local Environmental Health Department, which is generally responsible for the health and safety of office employees. They will send you a form to fill in and possibly a booklet on making the office safe. If, however, you are planning to do manufacturing of some sort contact the local Health and Safety Executive which is responsible for safety for employees in more dangerous concerns.

In the main, home offices are not high up the priority list for inspection by either body, unless they involve working with dangerous materials. However, it is still worth taking the precautions required of you. If you are inspected, the inspectors will normally give you some time to get any problems right – unless they are extremely serious. 'The common problems we see are screens giving off glare, files obstructing exits, trailing flexes,' says one environmental health officer. However, be warned, failure to comply with advice from either office is serious. You can be imprisoned or given an unlimited fine for dangerous breaches of safety legislation. It's up to you to establish the safety of your employees – not just for their benefit but for your own!

Giving an employee the right to a written statement of terms and conditions to be given within thirteen weeks, (unless employed for less than sixteen hours a week). This should include:

1 Name of employer and employee.

2 Date when employment began.

3 Rate of pay, how calculated, and whether it is to be paid weekly or monthly. This section should include what happens in the case of out-of-hours working, overtime etc.

4 Hours of work.

5 Entitlement to holidays (legally, you do not have to give an employee any holiday at all, but virtually all employers do) – and whether holidays are to be paid for and how this relates to normal pay.

6 Any sick pay provisions (although you must pay statutory sick pay), pension rights.

7 Length of notice or of contract for both employer and employee.

8 Job title.

9 Definition of offences and disciplinary procedures.

The Department of Trade and Industry has several booklets which give a more detailed breakdown of how to prepare a contract, as has ACAS. Both should be able to help you with any potential problems. It might also be worth talking to your professional body or the Small Business Federation if you are a member.

Although, it might sound daunting to take on an employee, few of the people I spoke to who had done so had any regrets. 'I'd go mad here if I was all by myself,' says potter Michael Levy. 'The people who work for me are not just good at their job but company too.' Lisa Denning, who runs her own PR company and has several employees says that 'there's no way you can expand if you don't take staff on. I've found having staff not just a way to grow the business, but an excellent source of ideas and enthusiasm.'

Elana who runs her own greetings card company has found getting the right staff more problematic. 'Even though this is an office atmosphere, you feel that you need to be extra sure you can trust your staff.' Her business has peaks and troughs of demand and she has found taking on students a good way to cope with this and has also employed some outworkers through a charity. 'I find it good to have people around,' she says. 'When I first started I'd often spend too long chatting on the phone to clients, simply because I felt a bit alone. Now, with my staff and getting out to clients a lot more, it's a better balance.'

Nick Rustige who sells second hand computer equipment would agree – but then his staff is his mother. 'At least if she's working for the business, she won't complain when the place is full of computers!' he jokes.

Useful addresses

ACAS (have a selection of reasonably priced leaflets on employee/employer relations) Reader Ltd, PO Box 16, Earlshiton, Leicester LE9 8ZZ. Tel: 01455 852225

Albert Plumb, 31 Whyke Lane, Chichester, West Sussex. Tel: 01243 789100

Association of British Insurers, 51 Gresham St, London EC2V 7HQ. Tel: 0171 600 3333

BT (for business equipment) Tel: 152; (for listing in Yellow Pages) Tel: 0800 671 444

English Heritage Buildings, Cold Harbour Farm Estate, Dallington, East Sussex TN21 9LQ. Tel: 01424 838400

ESTIA, 5–7 Tottenham Court Road, London W1 9PB. Tel: 0171 636 5957

Federation of Small Businesses (see chapter 1)

Grahl, Tel: 01494 792601

Homelodge Buildings, Kinswell Point, Crawley, Winchester SO21 2PU. Tel: 01962 881480

IKEA (look in your phone book for the nearest branch; or ring the head office) Tel: 0181 208 5600

Mercury Communications (for business services) Tel: 0500 700 101

Neville Johnson Offices Ltd, Broad Oak Business Park, Ashburton Road West, Trafford Park, Manchester M17 1RW. Tel: 0161 873 8333

Oakmoor Telecentres, Talewater Works, Talaton, Exeter, Devon EX5 2RT. Tel: 01404 850977

Selfridges, 400 Oxford St, London W1. Tel: 0171 629 1234

Southway Interiors, Southway House, 964 North Circular Road, London NW2 7JR

Thomson Directories, Tel: 01252 516111

EIGHT

Getting the balance right

One of the perceived advantages of working at home is that you get a better quality of life. If you are self-employed, so the theory goes, you have far greater control over how and when and how much you work. If you are employed, then you at least dispense with those dreadful, demoralizing, time-wasting commuter journeys. What's more, you are blissfully free of all the time wasted on office politics, manoeuvrings and so on.

Well, yes. Up to a point. But there are plenty of people who spend every hour that they would have been commuting working their butts off – and then work on late into the night and in the early morning as well. 'My family are dreadfully unhelpful,' moaned one homeworking business woman to me. However, what she meant by their being unhelpful was that they were fed up with her working through weekends, evenings and even refusing to go on her annual holiday, 'because the clients might not be here when I get back'.

Working from home *can* give you greater freedom, flexibility and a better quality of life. It can mean being there for your children and can even save marriages But only if you let it. Below are some of the pitfalls to watch out for – and how to avoid them.

DISTRESS SIGNALS

Over and over again the people I talked to for this book agreed that an inability to switch off is one of the major problems of working from home. 'Sometimes I'm just passing my workroom and I can't stop myself going in,' says Katharine Goodison, a milliner. 'Switch off? Sometimes I think I never do?' says management consultant Joel Brizman.

There are two major problems:

- Being self-employed means you are likely to be more emotionally involved in the business, since your status, livelihood and feeling of self-esteem may be intricately linked with your business.

- Even if you are not self-employed, working at home often means that you cannot separate yourself from your work – it is always just around the corner or literally in the next room. Many employees use their car or train journey to separate themselves mentally from the office. That's not an option open to homeworkers.

You might think that it doesn't matter that you are always involved with business and rarely take a day off – if that's what you like. But there are potential problems if you become overloaded and do not build any breaks into your life, both from your own point of view and also from your family's, if you have one. However much you earn, your family may well become resentful if your job means that you never have time for them. Warning signs include:

- Thinking of work all the time – even when you are with your family or supposed to be enjoying yourself.

- Feeling unable to take a holiday.

- Weepiness, continual irritability, mood swings and other stress symptoms (see below).

- Never taking a day or evening off.

- Your family complains all the time that you never have enough time for them.

- Generally feeling stressed.

Stress is a much misunderstood word. Some stress in our lives is good – it helps us to perform better, even gets us up in the morning. The trouble starts when a healthy degree of stress becomes unhealthy – due to work pressures, financial worries and so on.

But what is stress? It is where the body prepares itself for flight, just as it did thousands of years ago when confronted by a woolly mammoth. Except these days, it's more likely to be stash of bills or an irate client that you are confronting. The heart beats faster, lactic acid builds up and adrenalin pumps. Trouble is, that if you don't physically flee – or relax afterwards – the after-effects remain. You know it could be work is stressing you out if you suffer several of the symptoms below and there is no medical cause suggested by your GP:

- Headaches

- Stomach aches

- Mood swings

- Irritability

- Weepiness

- Feeling out of control

- Asthma attacks

- Drinking excessively

- Feeling Depressed.

SURVIVAL STRATEGIES

Taking short breaks in the day

It can be just as important to have a ritual for switching off from your work as to have one for switching on. Even going to make a cup of coffee, walking round the block or – at the end of the day – changing your clothes can have significant psychological impact. For instance, 'Bella' a sex therapist leaves her counselling room between clients and takes a stroll around her garden – something which never fails to soothe. Mary Montague a theatre designer likes to take a long, hot bath when feeling overstretched. Lucy Daniels, Director of Parents At Work, works partly at the office and partly at home. She finds she concentrates better at home – so much so that she has to set an alarm clock to alert her that it's time to have a break. When the alarm goes off she knows it is time to have a coffee or just walk around to give herself a short respite. Nick Weedon, an accountant, closes the office door firmly behind him when he wants to switch off.

Coping with your computer

If you are working at a computer screen all day, it is essential to take short breaks. Working continuously can lead to a whole host of problems including back-pain, eye strain and even RSI (Repetitive Strain Injury) a debilitating joint condition. You can even exercise at your desk by circling your shoulders, one at a time and then both together or letting your neck circle slowly from side to side. However, getting up for a walk around is just as good and possibly better.

Visual Display Screens have been the subject of much controversy. However the latest research shows that:

It is **FALSE** that VDUs cause eye disease.

It is **TRUE** that badly positioned flickering screens or staring too long at the screen can cause eye fatigue and accentuate any previous eye defects.

It is **TRUE** that VDUs can cause headaches – often a result of glare, poor image quality or posture.

It is **FALSE** that they cause radiation sickness.

It is **TRUE** that employees have the right to have the risks of eye strain and headaches minimized by correct siting of the VDU. They must also be offered eye tests paid for by the employer.

It is **FALSE** that VDUs cause miscarriages.

Taking regular exercise

Exercising is an excellent way to unwind – and helps promote general well-being. To maintain a reasonable level of fitness, experts suggest you take mildly aerobic exercise three times a week for at least twenty minutes. This means doing exercise that leaves you mildly out of breath – it could be hill walking, using gym equipment, swimming, or squash, for example. The important thing is that you do it.

Paul Curitz, a consultant, enjoys cycling, often training for sponsored cycle rides, as a way of keeping fit in a largely sedentary job. Verna Wilkins, a publisher, likes to go to the gym three times a week 'to rest my brain and work my body. People in offices take lunch breaks, why shouldn't I do something I enjoy with the time?' Jenny Hulme, a writer, also enjoys her health club membership. 'It means that you did something more with that day than just work. It's another interest as well as keeping fit.'

Exercising needn't be expensive. You can join a state-of-the-art gym if you want to, but most communities have local exercise classes, often held in church calls or community centres. Tennis clubs and courts in public parks abound and there are plenty of swimming pools, both council and private. Yoga classes are also very relaxing, although they may not be aerobic.

Even if you are not keen on exercise, look on it as an investment. If you are unfit you are more likely to fall sick or have a back problem – both of which could mean weeks or months off work. You invest in your business – why not invest in your body?

Eating sensibly

One result of stress rarely mentioned in the official tables, but a real *bête noire* for people working at home is the proximity of the fridge. At work, there is lunchtime and, if you are lucky, coffee breaks. At home there is unadulterated opportunity for noshing. If you have just been turned down for a job, if the kids didn't eat your lovingly cooked dinner or if you are just feeling peckish, it can be all too easy to comfort eat/finish up leftovers/have a snack that turns into a three course meal.

To prevent a snack-attack:

- Keep anything you'd rather you didn't eat out of reach.

- Eat a sandwich or other food at lunchtime rather than working through and pigging out later.

- Ask yourself why you are eating what you are eating.

- Treat yourself when things are going well rather than badly.

- Try to keep the fruit bowl full and use it to relieve snack-pangs.

Singing after your supper.

'It's taken me a long time to realize that I actually need something that's just for me, not for my work or my family,' says training consultant Bridget Seddon. Bridget is a keen singer and attends classes. She feels that singing gives her relief from the intensity of her business life. Not only does she work at home, but she also works with her partner and employs her mother. 'And sometimes that means my partner and I can see almost too much of each other. You need fresh input, something outside work and the family.'

Bridget finds that her singing is an ideal way to switch off as it is totally unrelated to work. 'Don't get me wrong, I enjoy my work very much,' she says. 'But everyone needs a break or things can get out of perspective.'

Taking time out to relax

Having an absorbing hobby can be an excellent way to relax. It doesn't matter if it's gardening or watching football, provided you feel refreshed at the end of it. If this isn't enough you might consider services aimed to make you feel relaxed. Many complementary therapies can be used to aid relaxation including aromatherapy, acupuncture and yoga. Your doctor can also show you simple breathing exercises that can help to relax you if tension is becoming a problem.

Taking stock

If you are feeling stressed it helps to look at what is stressing you. It may be obvious – an unpaid bill, cash-flow problems, an irate client – in which case you may be able to resolve this short-term stress with some lateral thinking or advice from any of the agencies mentioned in the 'How to get good advice' section of chapter 3.

On the other hand, if you are feeling generally low and miserable, you may need to reconsider your priorities. Judy Tame, a life-planning consultant and former financial whizz kid, reassessed her life after failing to hit her financial target one year. The impact of that failure, albeit small to the company, was enough to make her question why she was doing the job at all. She now counsels many small business people, 'who feel the fun has gone out of the business. Sometimes because it has grown into something different from what they enjoyed, or sometimes because they feel they are heading for trouble.'

If you have an underlying feeling of disquiet about your working life, it is important to assess just what your priorities are – and how your current business is satisfying them. Ask yourself *why am I working*? Below are some answers you might give for yourself:

- Because I'm the major breadwinner and need to earn enough to keep my family?

- Because without my income our standard of living would drop?

- Because I want to have money that is my own?

- Because I love what I am doing?

- Because I enjoy the status my work gives me?

- Because I need a break from the kids?

- Because my spouse expects it?

Then ask: *why am I working at home?*

- Because it's cheaper than hiring an office.

- Because the company made me.

- Because it cuts down on commuting.

- Because it allows me to spend more time with my family.

- Because it allows me to spend time on other interests.

- Because I like being at home.

- Because my family likes it.

    Then ask:

- Have my priorities changed since I started working from home?

- How would I like them to change?

- Can I do anything to get my priorities closer to what I want them to be?

This questionnaire might provide you with some very interesting answers as to why you feel disconnected, or that life is out of synch. However, sometimes it takes a major life event to cause a reassessment. 'Lizzy' is a conference organizer, who had cancer diagnosed two years ago. Although she is now in remission, the experience caused a total reassessment of her priorities. 'I'd already started my own firm from home because I wanted to spend more time with the children, but I realized that I'd been spending more and more time working and not as much as I wanted with the kids. I discussed it with my husband and decided that I'd rather take a cut in salary and spend more time with them.' 'Jonathan', a craftsman, thought working from home would be an ideal way to save money – but it proved a disaster. 'Financially, it made sense to work at home, but I just felt very isolated, and at the same time my wife felt that I was always under her feet. The work space was cramped and I found it hard to get down to the bits of the job that I don't enjoy – the book-work particularly. I now share a workshop with several other craftsmen and women. Financially, it's not a wise move, but I do feel a lot better for it.'

Several of the people I spoke to during the course of this book had similar feelings about taking part in pilot teleworking schemes. Often the pilot was the brainchild of one particular manager who pushed it hard – but had been unable to get support systems into place. One man told me. 'I thought I didn't like my colleagues – until I didn't see any of them day in and day out.'

Matching your priorities to what you are actually doing can be a great way of relieving stress. You may discover that working from home is not for you, or that you need to make subtle adjustments in your lifestyle to get yourself back on to an even keel.

STATUS AND THE HOMEWORKER

Let's face it. To some people, working from home has the same status as driving a Reliant Robin! This is partly because when you mention that you work at home, many people think of traditional homeworking with its low rates of pay and cowed workforce. It is also, however, that there is an innate resistance to anything that is new. In the USA, homeworkers are seen as in the vanguard of future employment patterns, environmentally friendly and extra-efficient. In Britain they are seen as *different*. If you work in an office, factory or shop, people can immediately 'place' you, not only by your job title, but by your accessories – the executive desk, or lack of one, a sales till of your own, or not. However, it is hard to place people who work at home as easily and the tendency is to assume that they spend all day watching daytime TV and not really doing anything constructive. This particular assumption is generally made by those who, if they were working at home, would spend their time idling!

Many homeworkers don't care about their status. They care about the money they are making (generally more than if they were having to pay the overheads of a workshop or office). Or they like the work they do. Or the quality of life that working from home gives them. But for those who do care about how other people regard their employment, homeworking can be frustrating.

Helen Maloney, a successful dressmaker, often feels frustrated when people talk in awed tones of a friend who is a shop manager. 'They always tell me how well she's doing, but they don't seem to regard the fact that I've run a business which pays the mortgage and gives me a decent income as being successful because I work at home. If I moved into premises in town then suddenly I'd be seen as being successful – even if I was losing a lot of money from overheads.'

Difficult although it may seem, the answer is to *have confidence in what you are doing.* Do you enjoy what you do? Does it seem to be working? Has it improved your quality of life? If the answers are yes, then you need to discount the sceptics. Use any tools that can help you. Plaster any professional certificates/awards/letters from satisfied customers over your walls. When people ask what you do, talk it up. Dr Johnson once observed that it was a foolish person who denigrated themselves because people would take them at their own evaluation. Telling people you 'just do a bit of work at home for Company X' gives quite a different impression from saying 'I'm one of the first part-time teleworkers employed by Company X.'

Modesty in Britain is generally regarded as a virtue. That may be fine if you are Richard Branson or a captain of industry. It won't help people working from home feel good about themselves or attract possible clients. 'I call it the Val Doonican syndrome,' says furniture specifier Maggie Hall. 'I walk tall and look the world right in the eye. To be honest, I think a lot of people who make jibes about working from home are jealous.'

'I make it a selling point,' says PR consultant Dana Cukier. 'I think people take you a lot at your own estimation. I point out to my clients that because I'm a small business, they get a lot of experience for their money without the overheads. It's not as if I'm going to pass any of their work down to a junior and they understand that.' Joel Brizman, consultant, agrees. 'I think as long as you can do the work, the client doesn't care. I've even solved problems from the hotel telephone while I've been on holiday!'

In other words, status is, to some extent, something you confer upon yourself. When I left my full-time well-paid job I felt an enormous loss of status. However, many of my friends regarded what I was doing as having more status since they now saw my by-line far more frequently than before. Jennifer Butcher, a charity consultant, was previously director of a major charity. When she decided to work for herself, she found it quite a culture shock. 'I did miss the feeling of going into work, being part of a team, the buzz of getting a huge project done.' However, she feels she has learnt a lot from the many small charities she works with. 'I think that not being cushioned by a large organization does make you realize what is really important and worth doing. My work now has given me an extra dimension.'

For women, there may be an additional problem – an overload of domestic responsibilities. 'When you are at home it's easy to become the one who does the housework, arranges the diary, does the gardening – but it takes a lot of time,' says communications consultant Kim Pickin.

Adam Sisman was previously a senior editor for a large publishing house. He is now an author, journalist and copywriter.
'The odd thing is that even though I earn more than I did before, there is a certain loss of status,' says Adam. 'I think it's also a prejudice

against people who don't live in central London. There is this editor's view that if you don't have a central London telephone number that you can't be doing that well. So when you move to the country you feel that.'

Adam believes that it's important to have confidence in yourself – and to remember that your work is equally valid wherever you do it. However, he also adds that he found it helpful to get together with other people in a similar situation. 'When I was writing a biography of A.J.P. Taylor, I started a biographers' lunch where we could swap information and gossip and just share our experiences.'

He feels that for women, the change from high-powered career woman to homeworker can be even more difficult. 'I think there's an instant assumption that a woman who's working from home is somehow not working. I think, too, that a lot of women get dumped with all the household tasks because there is an instant assumption that since a woman is at home, she'll do them. I think it's something that women have to fight against – and men don't.'

DEALING WITH REJECTION

One of the problems of starting up a small business – whether at home or elsewhere – is that you may come up against an awful lot of rejection – especially in the early years. Once you are well-known for your hand-embroidered cushions, your brilliant consultancy or your ability to train even the most untrainable, then you will experience less rejection because you've built up a reliable client base and have a steady stream of work. But in the initial stages, rejection can feature as prominently as success. It can be heartbreaking to observe everyone walking past your hand-embroidered cushion stall as they go straight to the hand-embroidered bib stall. It can be incredibly demoralizing as another letter thuds on the mat, saying that Mixed Up Management Incorporated do not need any consultancy at the moment thank you.

However, there are lessons to be learnt from such situations:

- Every successful business has some failures as well as some successes. It's just that bigger businesses hide their failures from general view. You are not alone.

- Rejection is part and parcel of success. 'At first, the rejections hit you hard,' says financial consultant Caroline Loman. 'But after a while you get used to it. It'd be quite amazing if every lead resulted in business.' Jane Gregory who sells Cabouchon jewellery agrees. 'You have to learn to develop a thick skin,' she says. 'And if people are unpleasant when they don't want to buy anything, I always tell myself it's their problem not mine.'

- If you don't get a particular job or contract – ask the firm why they rejected you. You may learn something that will be useful for future bids – or you may learn that your work was in no way at fault, but that internal politics decided the deal.

- Rejection is part and parcel of marketing yourself successfully. 'I'm an object lesson in how not to work from home,' says Avadon Carol, a writer. 'I find it very hard to market myself – to put myself up, in case I get shot down. People generally like the work I do, but I'm not very good at getting it.'

- Persistence pays off. It may not turn a no to a yes, but it can certainly turn a maybe into a positive. 'We thought our dried flower arrangements would do well in Harrods,' says Liz Davis of Field House Design. 'But we had to keep pestering the buyer. She was out, or not available. In the end she said she'd give us ten minutes – we took some arrangements and ten minutes later, we were supplying Harrods!'

     That's not to say it's easy to be persistent. Even as a journalist, a profession famed for its tenacity, I find it hard to repeatedly phone people who don't answer my calls, who are never there or who can't talk now. However, when you do get hold of them you do at least usually get an answer to your questions – even if it's just flat rejection.

Everyone has the right to be turned down. Getting no response at all is much worse than rejection because it gives you false hope.

- When things are not going well generally, it is well worth assessing the reason. If your competition is suffering similarly or there is a clear cause (you sell rainwear and it's a dry, hot summer) you may need to go with the flow. If you do not know the reason, it may be worth taking a long, hard look at what you are doing and asking yourself if you need to adapt. In a world where the pace of change is speeding up, you need to be able to think on your feet and alter your product when necessary. There is no point being attached to a great idea that just doesn't sell. Visionaries may be lauded after their death, but there is not much fun in being the man or woman who was too far ahead of their time, just as there is not much mileage in being behind the times. If, for instance, your firm has decided to try teleworking, but you are not enjoying the experience, work out what it is that you don't like. If this cannot be changed then consider asking to go back to the office. Homeworking is a success for 80 per cent of the people who try it – but that leaves one in five for whom it fails.

Adaptability: the key to success?

Jill Swinney ran a highly successful dried flower business from her home in Northumberland. What's more she grew the flowers for drying in her own garden. This added to her success as it kept costs down and meant she could grow what she used.

When Jill's marriage broke down, she had to leave her house – and her beautiful garden. 'It was a blow at a time when I had other problems,' she recalls. Jill didn't feel she could make her dried flower business work without using her own flowers. But she knew she wanted to run a business – and her passion was gardening. So she sat down and thought about possible products she'd like to grow as a gardener.

She'd always been interested in topiary and the idea of creating small frames to house topiary sculptures occurred to her. Market research established that there was little competition in the area and she soon started a new business – Topiarese – which has gone from strength to strength. 'There are busy times and quiet times, but it is growing steadily,' says Jill. 'In some ways, it has got me through the bad times, because it is such fun and so absorbing. And each success is my success. I've got several agents now and am even exporting!'

Jill feels that being adaptable was the key to starting a second, now equally successful business. 'I think that if one avenue closes, you've got to start looking for new ones,' she says.

YOUR FAMILY AND YOUR WORK

Theoretically, people working from home should have a much better quality of family life than office workers. Not only are they on the spot, they are also not arriving stressed and exhausted after a hard day's commuting.

If only things were so simple. During the course of writing this book, I have spoken to many people who previously worked at home and who have now gone back into an office – as well as those for whom homeworking is proving more pain than paradise. There are a variety of reasons why working from home does not suit everyone (see chapter 1), but I often came across people who claimed that their families were sabotaging their efforts. Their argument generally ran something like this: 'Here I am, working my butt off to keep a roof over their heads and are they grateful? Are they hell.' The indignant homeworker would then go on to list the number of unreasonable demands their spouses and children were making – demands like taking time off for the school play, to spend some time with the kids at the weekend, even to wash the dishes occasionally.

To my ears, these 'demands' sounded eminently reasonable – more like duties, even, than demands. What's more the disgruntled homeworkers seemed never to have asked themselves one vital question: Do I need to work this hard, or would my family be satisfied with a lower standard of living and a bigger share of my energy? Sally Wilkins, who makes the Wilkinet Baby Carrier, summed it up for me when she said 'I'd stress to anyone that you have to watch that it doesn't take over your life completely. Because what have you got if you alienate your family? You've got a desk in a building and a product. That's all. But that's not what it's all about.'

Even if you want to look at the work–family equation in purely business terms, there is little doubt that people's working life suffers when they have emotional problems. 'People who work at home don't have colleagues with whom they can share their emotional life,' says Donu Kogbara, a broadcaster and journalist. 'That means they often find that when they do have emotional problems, they sit there with them going round and round in their heads, unable to concentrate at all.'

I once interviewed employees of a company which specialized in providing counselling in the workplace. They had just been taken on by a major corporation which was in the throes of radical change. The directors of the corporation expected that people would use the counselling service to help resolve problems at work. In fact, over 60 per cent of the problems people wanted to talk about were personal ones – unruly teenagers, troubled marriages, difficult divorces. The motto of the story is very clear: it's hard to have a happy working life if your personal life is in turmoil.

Of course, on the other side, there are plenty of people who don't get homeworking off the ground simply because they can't tear themselves away from their children/husband/mother and start work. This problem is rarer simply because most people have to earn a certain amount of money to live, and they use that as a means of disciplining themselves. Nevertheless, if this is a problem it's as well to set yourself distinct work and play times – and stick to them.

Below I describe ten key strategies for smoothing work-family relationships.

Consult the family This is especially important if you are considering working from home and have not yet talked to your family about their feelings about having you around all the time. Do not assume that they'll automatically be thrilled at the prospect. Talk through the implications – the fact that you will need some undisturbed time, that you may see more of each other – even that you might need to fill the house up with stock. 'My mother's been a real help in the business,' says Tim Rustige, who sells second hand computers from his home. 'She can't be too thrilled about having computers everywhere, but I've always told her what I'm doing and she's always been right behind me.'

Draw boundaries Once you are working at home, it's important that you draw boundaries between work time and play time. And between what areas children (and spouses) are welcomed into – and what are reserved strictly for work. This may not be easy if you have a toddler and at-home childcare, but it is certainly worth trying. After all, having your five-year-old answer the phone to your most important client may not enhance your professional image.

'When I'm working, I'm working,' says consultant Paul Curitz. 'If I need to get a cup of coffee, I'll happily walk past a pile of dirty dishes to get it. The children have grown up with knowing they mustn't disturb Daddy when he's working and they accept that because it's what they've always had to do.' 'When I'm with the children, they have my full attention and when I'm working I have my full attention on the job in hand,' says marketing expert Rosemarie Ghazaros.

Make time for your family One of the great advantages of working from home is that you can schedule family time, be it to attend special events, go for a walk together, or take the children for a swim. Scheduling time with your family will not only help you switch off, it will stop family members becoming resentful of your work and of you.

Learn to switch off See section one in this chapter.

Get away from the house Working at home can be claustrophobic and isolating. If your partner is the only person you see, week in week out, that forces them to become the sole provider of all your entertainment, social stimulation and camaraderie. Attending meetings, joining committees, going to the gym, are all ways of extending your social life – and thus relieving the pressure on your partner. It will also prevent you from becoming boring.

Get away from each other this is particularly vital if you both work at home or in the same business. Having different interests outside work can stop the atmosphere becoming too intense, or your relationship turning entirely into that of business partners.

Keep your family informed Every so often, the local papers report a familiar story: the sad case of the businessman who, having had money worries, commits suicide. The grieving family, who have been kept in the dark, are left not only to cope with the death of a loved one, but the horrendous mess he's left them in. These stories always amaze me. Whom did the suicide think he was protecting by his actions?

Keeping your family informed in the good times as well as the bad is not only a way of sharing the burden, but a way of showing respect to them. It is a cliché, but true nevertheless, that a trouble shared is a trouble halved. What's more, by having a different perspective your family members may be able to suggest a way of out a pickle that you hadn't thought of.

Accept the lows as well as the highs Just because homeworking is a more conducive way to work doesn't mean that every day you'll wake up feeling as if you've already arrived in paradise. If you are running a business, there are bound to be days when you don't get prospective clients or make sales or when the book-work seems overwhelming. If you are working for an employer, there will be days when you feel dumped on by your boss – or wonder why you are always the last to hear office gossip. Working from home has more advantages than disadvantages, but that doesn't mean it's going to be perfect.

Share tasks All too often the partner who works at home finds that they are doing more and more of the daily tasks simply because they are the nearest at hand. But this needn't necessarily be the case. If you are working and taking on an unfair share of the domestic burden as well, reallocate it – not only to your partner but to your children. In many developing countries children are expected to contribute to the household economy by the time they are five – so it's not too much for them to lay the table or make their own bed!

Enjoy yourself Working from home *is* a way of achieving greater independence, family involvement and a better quality of life. So make the most of it!

> **Robert Hedges is a market gardener. His family also work in the business and the market garden is attached to their home.**
> 'The good thing about working at home is that if anything happens, I'm there to sort it out,' says Robert. 'In fact, the whole family can pull together really quickly.'
>
> However, the down side is that sharing the same home and the same occupation can become difficult. Both Robert's father and brother take an active role in the business. 'It could be a bit much if we didn't have other interests,' says Robert. 'And I think it's vital that if you work together you make sure you do have different things to do

outside work.' Robert is interested in politics, while his father prefers aerobics and swimming, so they spend their leisure hours apart. 'It would be boring if it was all work,' says Robert. 'But having outside interests does stop you going round in circles about things.'

Kerstin Wright has been teaching at home for over thirty years, working with language students first for other companies and latterly for her own.
'For me, it has been an excellent way to work,' says Kerstin. 'I was around when the children were small, so they were never latch-key kids, and I've run my own business too.'

Kerstin believes the secret of successful homeworking is discipline – 'the discipline to make yourself work when it needs to be done, but also the discipline to stop. It can be hard to make time to swim or teach keep-fit when I'm under pressure, but I know that doing those things will re-charge my batteries. It can't all be work.'

Kerstin also feels that family support is essential. 'My children grew up with it, but my husband was tremendously supportive and that is so important.' Kerstin feels that working at home shouldn't mean being isolated or lacking prestige. In fact, she is Chair of the Business Women's Club Wales, and has also been given an award by the King of Sweden for her work with Swedish students. 'I think that now, working at home is much more common than when I started,' says Kerstin. 'It has really come into its own at last.'

NINE

Twenty ideas for making serious money from home

Running An Agency

An agent often has showbiz connotations, the Mr Ten-per-cents fixing up deals for their stars. In fact, an agent is merely a middle-person supplying services to those who want them and haven't the time – or resources – to do their own finding.

What qualities do I need?

To be a natural fixer, to enjoy wheeling and dealing, and diplomacy are all vital qualities. It also helps to be thorough and good at research.

What qualifications do I need?

No formal qualifications are required, but it helps to have some experience in the field you are hoping to enter. For instance, if you plan to run an employment agency, it helps to have used one. If you want to run a cleaning or nanny agency, it might be helpful either to have been a nanny or cleaner, or to have employed one, just so you have an idea of the pitfalls.

However, there are all sorts of other agencies that you might consider – from home-finding to supplying companions. One word of warning, though – check out the competition by looking in Yellow Pages, at least. There is no point in setting up a nanny agency if there are already ten operating within a mile of each other – unless yours has a unique selling point (such as specialising in help for children over five!).

How do I set up?

You used to need a licence from the Department of Employment to set up an employment agency. Now you don't, although there are still restrictions for nursing and midwifery agencies. You may need a licence from the local authority, however. It is illegal to charge potential employees for finding them work. But you can charge your employer clients as much as you think reasonable (and they are prepared to pay). Look at other agencies for a good idea of rates.

   You then need to find potential employers – and employees. Word of mouth is one way of attracting custom – but it is something that tends to grow after you have a few satisfied customers. Advertising, both for employers and employees may be a surer way at first. You could try local papers, leafleting or a specialist press.

   If you plan to interview potential candidates in your own home, be very careful. Make sure someone else is about or check out their references first. In fact, as an agent it is part of your duty to ensure that people you put forward for a job are suitable – that means checking references thoroughly and not just relying on written ones. On the other hand, you should also check out potential clients as you do not want to find that either you or the employees do not get paid. Dating agencies require even more care and it is probably wise to suggest clients meet in a public place at least initially. For this reason too, it may be advisable not to run a dating agency from home if you are going to be a sole trader.

How much will I make?

Impossible to predict. Your major costs will be phone bills, advertising and administration, but it may take quite some time for your client base to build and you will also need to do a lot of leg work before you actually get any fees in, so cash flow may be a problem. However, successful agencies can produce profits into the millions.

Pros:

Flexible, varied people-orientated work.

Relatively low start-up cost.

Cons:

Much of your work may be done in evening when employees are free to talk.

Heavy competition with much of the employment market dominated by larger firms.

Many small agencies go under.

Sheila Hill started Nexus Nannies after she'd tried to find a nanny for her daughter.

Sheila had been ill during her second pregnancy and was confined to bed. That meant finding a nanny for her five-and-a half-year-old. She contacted local agencies and was disappointed with their standard of service. 'Some never phoned back, others had nannies phone me who hadn't a clue what I wanted. One sent a nanny who ran off to Holland with her boyfriend – and it took me months to get my money back.'

When Sheila at last found a good nanny, she heard that the nannies themselves were equally disillusioned. So she decided to set up her own agency. At first, she worked from an office, but found working at home meant she had more time with her children – and it was cheaper! 'I started by leafleting in the neighbourhood, not only for nannies but domestic help,' she recalls. 'The phone didn't stop ringing both with clients and prospective employees.' After that initial leaflet drop Sheila has relied largely on word of mouth as well as advertising in *Nursery World*, a magazine for professional nannies. 'My clients know I check references thoroughly,' she says. 'It can be quite frightening sometimes – girls who've written their references themselves or claim to have qualifications they haven't – I've seen plenty of that.'

Sheila believes that clients must be able to trust an agency and that keeping them informed is vital. She also says it's important to stay on top of the paperwork. 'And there is a lot of it.' However, she finds the job extremely rewarding. 'Not only does it provide a living, but it gives me a real thrill to match people up – and I'm able to see my kids grow up too.'

BEAUTY THERAPY

What qualities do I need?
It is essential to be interested in health and your own personal appearance. If you would never have a beauty treatment yourself, you are unlikely to make a good therapist. You also need to like people, be patient, energetic and have a sympathetic manner.

What qualifications do I need?
This depends largely on which branch of beauty therapy you choose to specialize in. A beautician specializes in skin care, make-up, facials, waxing and manicures. A beauty therapist does similar work, but also does body treatments and toning. You can also get qualifications to enable you to use electrolysis to remove unwanted hair, while aromatherapists specialize in aromatherapy (see Complementary Therapy).

There are several recognized qualifications including NVQs (National Vocational Qualifications, administered by CIBTAC), BTECs and City & Guilds examinations. Your local further education college is likely to have a recognized course. If not, your careers office (look them up in Yellow Pages) can point you in the right direction.

It is also possible to complete your qualifications through certain private salons and health farms. Courses take around 300 hours, normally over one year full-time or two to three years part-time. Mature students will find there is normally an element of home study in the course. Aromatherapy courses take around 100 hours. Costs vary enormously. Some further education colleges charge around £1,000, while some of the swankier schools charge nearly £3,000.

How do I set up?

Your course should give you some advice on this. However, before starting up you will need to do some basic spadework. This should include setting aside a room in your home for your beauty treatments. You may be able to get away with working in a bedroom if you are only offering manicures and pedicures, but for other treatments you will almost certainly need more space than this.

You will also need a basic beauty kit including treatment couch (from £200–£2,000), towels, waxing pots and wax, manicure and pedicure tools plus nail varnishes, oils for massage etc. It's also useful to have running water in the room you use. You will also need a professional insurance policy, somewhere to store your kit and perhaps an answering machine. A budget for advertising in local newsagents, through leaflet drops and local press is a good idea too – although word of mouth is likely to be your most valuable marketing tool.

If you plan to practise by visiting your clients in their homes then your own transport is essential as public transport may be too unreliable. Altogether you can expect to spend somewhere between £500–£3,000 on setting up depending on what equipment you need. Beware of buying expensive machinery whose worth cannot be guaranteed. Remember it may well take you up to six months to really 'grow' your clientele.

If you plan to practise ear piercing and electrolysis you may well need a licence from your local authority, phone them up and talk to the public health department. This is because there is a risk of passing on infection through equipment that is not properly sterilized.

How much will I make?

This depends on a number of factors, namely: the area you are working in, the number of clients you see and how many hours you work .You may be able to charge £40 an hour for a massage in central London, but it is unlikely that you would be able to charge that in the provinces. Look at the prices charged by local beauty salons and set yours accordingly, (preferably a little lower to attract clientele).

Pros:

Very flexible and enjoyable work with a wide variety of clients.

Can give a reasonable income of between £10,000– £15,000 a year.

Cons:

Success may depend on where you live. If there are too many therapists already practising in your area – or everyone is hard-up – it may be difficult to get established.

Can also be insecure as the number of clientele may drop or soar. Your earnings as a beauty therapist are, alas, unlikely to put you in the super-tax league.

Related professions

Hairdressing can also be done at home if you have the space for dryers etc. Qualifications can be achieved through training at salons and hairdressing schools. However, the on-the-job element of training may discourage women with children and wages can be very low.

'Anita' Johnson, 43, is a beauty therapist. She has been practising at home for over ten years.

'I started working from home when I was having difficulty getting pregnant. I thought that working from home might be less stressful and help me have a baby. I built it up slowly, with a few clients from the salon who then passed their friends on to me. I've been lucky in that I've not really needed to advertise. I think that if you do, it's important to have an answerphone, because beauty therapists always get dirty phone calls. A lot of my clients came through the schools my children went to.

'At first, I worked just to earn a bit extra. Now, like so many people. I work to live. Sometimes my family grumble, but I tell my boys that if they want a new pair of trainers, this is the way I have to earn it.

'The nice thing about working from home is that your clients are more than clients. They feel relaxed and able to share problems with you and they are always really pleased and happy when they go out. The drawback is that people feel free to muck you around, more than if they were in a salon – and you have to put up with it if you want to keep the client. However, if people consistently miss appointments I do charge and they seem to get the message.

'Beauty is a luxury trade which means that it's the first thing to suffer in a recession, so it's worth taking a good hard look at the area you live in before you set up. You should also check how many other therapists there are – too many and you can't make very much. I also keep my prices as low as I can, much lower than the salons, certainly, because that is one of my selling points. I also try to keep appointments together to make it time-efficient. It's frustrating to have a gap of half an hour between clients because it's hard to do anything with that time.

'It's also important to get out because you don't get the social life you do at a salon. My husband jokes that I must take myself out for my office Christmas party. I've done an evening class, voluntary work, even taken a very part-time job just to get some company!

'Overall, though, beauty therapy has enabled me to have an enjoyable career, earn money and still be there for my kids when they need me!'

Useful addresses

CIBTAC, Parabola House, Parabola Rd, Cheltenham, Gloucestershire GL50 3AH

City & Guilds Head Office, 76 Portland Place, London W1N 4AA

International Federation of Health and Beauty Therapists, International Council of Health, Fitness and Sports Therapists and Federation of Holistic Therapists, 38a Portsmouth Road, Woolston, Southampton, Hampshire. Tel: 01703 422 695

RUNNING A B & B, OR HAVING PAYING GUESTS

It's a common dream. The idea that one day you will sell up, move to the country and open up your own guest house. Or if you love your house, but are strapped for cash, that you will put a sign outside and the guests will be flooding in solving all your money problems at a stroke. The reality, alas, is somewhat different.

Running a B & B can be intensely rewarding, but it is also hard work and it can be expensive – cripplingly so if you don't get enough guests. You can make a success of B & B, but you need to do a lot of hard work *before* you open the door. A less expensive alternative, but equally satisfying for someone who enjoys mixing with different people is to take in a paying guest. Language schools, universities and even conference venues are often on the look-out for comfortable, clean homes in which to billet students and business people. Talk to your local university and language schools (addresses in Yellow Pages) for more details.

What qualities do I need?

Organizational skills, a genuine liking for people, an interest in domesticity and stamina are all prerequisites.

What qualifications do I need?

None – although you can take qualifications through City & Guilds or conventional hotel management qualifications. If you plan to open a B & B you should take a basic food hygiene course (talk to your local environmental health officer to find out where you can take one locally). You may also find a small business course run by the local TEC extremely useful in helping you market the business and understand the red tape involved in setting up. If you plan to take students as paying guests, tolerance, good humour and a willingness to communicate will be more useful than any qualifications you possess!

How do I set up?

For paying guests it is merely a question of getting on the books of a language agency or of contacting local universities who might have students in need of accommodation. In both cases, you are likely, quite rightly, to be subject to some vetting.

However, if you plan to start a B & B the first thing is to establish that there is likely to be a market for accommodation in your area. That doesn't mean you need to be in the most picturesque area in Britain – often these have too many guest houses for the population, but that there is some reason why visitors might want to stay with you. Perhaps you are near a major conference venue, a hospital or a museum. The Rural Development Commission, your regional tourist board and local council may be able to give you good pointers. Looking at how many guest houses are listed in the Yellow Pages could also be a useful indicator.

Think too about how you intend to open – will it be just during the season? Will you take a long-term lodger? Will you be offering basic facilities, or en suite bathrooms in every room plus teasmades? Doing market research as to who your clientele is likely to be may make that decision for you.

If you plan to make major changes to your home, you may well need planning permission. However, if it is going to remain essentially residential in character and you plan merely to add a washbasin in each room you are unlikely to need it. Nevertheless, it is worth calling your local planning officer, *before* you do anything, just to be on the safe side. Your local planning officer may also be able to help you on such issues as car parking.

You will also need to satisfy the requirements of the Fire Precautions Act, particularly if you intend to sleep more than six people (including staff and guests and children). If any letting bedrooms are above the first floor or below the ground floor, you will also need a certificate. In any case, you will want to ensure that your guests are not subjected to unnecessary risks, so a visit by the Fire Prevention Officer would be advisable. On top of that there is the cost of public liability insurance, the possibility of paying the uniform business rate, the expense of employing staff, the possibility of getting a liquor licence, hygiene regulations to satisfy and the requirement that any illuminated sign you display outside your home should comply with local authority rules.

All this expense and cost means you should look long and hard at the viability of your business before you set up, although it has to be said that a small business (perhaps with only one or two guest bedrooms and no alterations needed to either the interior or exterior of the house) is likely to be easier and cheaper to set up than a large one. Remember too, that you may need to claw back the cost of alterations in your price list. If this means that you will be most expensive guest house in the area by a large margin, you may want to think again.

Once you are up and running, you will need to advertise to attract your clientele. However, it is important to maximize the use of your advertising budget by selecting locations very carefully. Why advertise in the local paper if you expect most of your customers to come from three hundred miles away? On the other hand, if you have a local sports centre which hosts plenty of fixtures, a simple card on their bulletin board telling of your services might attract interest from people looking for rooms for their opponents. Make sure the local tourist board knows about you too. If you are lucky, satisfied clients may recommend you to some of the many non-paying guides and you may then be visited by an inspector (likely to be anonymous) and written up.

Above all, you need to make your guests want to come back. So a clean, comfortable establishment and a friendly welcome are vital. Few guests relish being treated as mere commodities to pay off the mortgage, but those who have had a thoroughly enjoyable stay will be likely to pass on your name to any friend planning to visit the area.

How much will I make?

Not a lot in the first year, is the most likely answer, particularly if you have to make alterations to your home (see below). On the other hand, if you are planning to start in a very small way, perhaps with accommodation for only two to four guests and need to spend very little on adjustments, you might go into profit quite quickly. Bear in mind, though, that there are all sorts of hidden costs involved in B & B. It's not just insurance and business rates (for over six guests). There is the cost of your guests hogging the showers, turning the central heating up and eating a big enough breakfast for a dozen.

If you are to make a profit your prices must be realistic – and yet not exceed local rates. It is hard to charge less than £10 per person per night and only the poshest places will be able to charge more than £40. How much you make out of that depends on how much work you've had done, how often you get guests through the door and how high your occupancy rate is. For those taking in paying guests, rates can vary between £7–£15 a night.

Pros:

A useful way to make your house pay, particularly if it is too large for your needs.

A good way to enjoy the hospitality industry and work for yourself.

Sociable, varied work.

Cons:

Lots of red tape to navigate.

May be a heavy initial outlay with no guaranteed return.

It takes time to build a reputation and clientele.

Belle and Pete Hepworth have been B & B owners for eight years. They currently run Half-Way House in Crayke, York, taking a maximum of six visitors.

'It all started when we bought Crayke Castle,' Belle recalls. 'It was a fifteenth-century Grade One listed building which needed a lot of work doing and we thought B & B might be one way to pay for that. I'd seen a brochure for Wolsey Lodges, which is a group offering hospitality to people as if they are in a home-from-home, and I fancied that.

'We found out about most of the red tape by accident when we applied for a licence from the local authority. The police come and check you out and then the fire officers, so we learnt all the requirements when they came. It's an expensive business. We had bathrooms fitted and providing all the little home comforts we like to offer adds up – the tea and coffee making facilities, TV and all the little things that you are likely to leave at home – spare toothbrushes and the like.

'Getting custom can be difficult at first. I asked other B & B owners to send their overflow to us and paid to be in various guide books. Advertising helps too, but it's a matter of trial and error. I now appreciate that editorial coverage in magazines is worth a lot more. A write-up in *Country Living* did a lot for us when we first opened. When the recession came though, we had to sell up and moved here. By this time though, a lot of people came to us through recommendation.

You really need to like people, to be a friendly type, to do this job. It can feel a bit strange at first having guests in your home all the time

– you feel you are on call all the time and it can niggle if you are just watching the last five minutes of a film and a guest suddenly needs something. But then that's the price you pay for keeping up a standard and it's worth it when guests tell you just how much they've enjoyed it.

'It's very hard work – particularly if you provide dinners. I think that you'd find it hard to do if you had young children around because making dinners is so time consuming. My two were 10 and 15 when I started, but I did sometimes feel odd when I was giving them a hamburger supper in front of the telly while preparing fillet mignon for the guests. Still, at least this way you can have them near you while you work, as opposed to having to leave them totally. And I love it. I wouldn't – couldn't do it – otherwise.'

Useful addresses

The English Tourist Board (publishes a very useful guide: *Starting a Bed and Breakfast Business*, price £10) Thames Tower, Black's Road, London W6 9EL. Tel: 0181 846 9000

British Federation of Hotel, Guest House and Self Catering Association, 5 Sandicroft Road, Blackpool, Lancashire FY1 2RY. Tel: 01253 352683 (has a reasonably priced information pack on legal requirements)

Your local branch of the **Rural Development Commission** will be in the phone book, as will your regional **Tourist Board**

BOOK-KEEPING

What qualities do I need?
It is essential to be numerate, and tidy, organized and practical. It will help build your client base if you are also confident and persistent.

What qualifications do I need?
Strictly speaking none, although if you are doing the books for a limited company or a partnership, they will have to be signed off by a qualified

accountant. However, in order to have any real idea of what you are doing, it is necessary to take some form of course in basic book-keeping or accounting. Your local college may hold such a course and you can also take O and A levels in accounting. There are also courses leading to qualifications run by the Royal Society of Arts and NVQs which can lead to a licence from the Association of Accounting Technicians, a rather more senior qualification. Most book-keeping courses can be done on a part-time or evening class basis and there are also several distance learning courses.

How do I set up?

Once you have learnt how to keep a company's books, including cash records, receipts, sales day book, payments, VAT records and tax, you are ready to set up in business. The main aim is to get small businesses to agree to have their books done by you. You may find an ad in the local paper extremely effective, particularly if you stress competitive rates and the fact that paperwork will be well taken care of by you. An entry in Yellow Pages could also be fruitful.

It may also be worthwhile to make appointments with local accountants who may be able to sub-contract some work to you. To ensure that you have a constant stream of clients it is important to network in places where small business people are likely to congregate – through the local Training and Enterprise Council, the Rotary Club and business centres. Once you have a few clients, hopefully your reliability, efficiency and cost-consciousness will encourage them to recommend you to their associates and friends.

Professional liability insurance is essential, in case of mistakes, as is having somewhere where clients' files can be stored with guaranteed confidentiality. The books of a business are not coffee table reading!

How much will I make?

This largely depends on the number of clients you are able to attract and the amount of work you are prepared to do. Some book-keepers charge by the hour with rates around £10–£15 an hour. Others charge by the job. Accounting technicians may charge more. Incomes can vary from around £5,000 a year, working part-time and in the early years, to £35,000 a year and beyond for a well established and well qualified book-keeper.

Pros:

As more and more people become self-employed book-keepers are likely to be in growing demand as they are, in general, cheaper than accountants.

Book-keeping is flexible with the potential to earn a good living.

Cons:

It may take time to build a good client base and it is necessary to devote some time to marketing yourself.

Book-keeping involves keeping meticulous records and mistakes can have serious consequences – make sure you are insured.

Can be isolating.

Not suitable for anyone who finds attention to detail a difficult area.

Related fields

Many chartered accountants, particularly those working for themselves, work at least some of the time from home.

Nick Weedon is a chartered accountant who works from home.
'I was made redundant at the height of the recession and after looking for jobs for a while decided to set up on my own.' Nick recalls. His first lucky break came when another accountancy firm sub-

contracted some work to him, followed by a friend introducing him to a trade association whose members were often in need of accountancy advice. 'It took about six months for me to start motoring,' says Nick. 'But now, I've really built up a practice. 'Some clients visit at home – they like the homely atmosphere,' but Nick also goes to the clients' premises. 'I think in this field clients just want you to do the job well and are not too bothered about where it's done. Some people wouldn't suit self-employment or working from home. You do need to be disciplined and deal with administration that might be outside what you hoped to do – although you can always get professional advice from someone like me! But there is freedom too – which I find a great bonus.'

Useful addresses

Institute of Chartered Accountants, C A Hall, Moorgate Place, London EC2. Tel: 0171 920 8100

Chartered Association of Certified Accountants, 29 Lincoln's Inn Fields, London WC2. Tel: 0171 242 6855

Association of Accounting Technicians, 154 Clerkenwell Road, London EC1R 5DU. Tel: 0171 837 8600

International Association of Book-keepers, 44 London Road, Sevenoaks, Kent TN13 1AS. Tel: 01732 458080

CATERING

Thousands of people who love cooking regularly daydream about leaving the day job behind and setting up their own restaurant, tea room or catering business, or even selling their home baked cookies. In fact, while the range of careers in catering is enormously wide – from running directors' cordon bleu lunches to making speciality cakes or setting up a local sandwich round – it is also often an over-subscribed area and requires a great deal of hard work. That said, it can be enormous fun, but it is well worth doing your market research (see chapter 3) before you start up.

What qualities do I need?
A love of food and an ability to cook, organizational skills, a calm manner and good communication skills (for dealing with clients). It is also helpful to be outgoing and to have stamina if you intend to market the business by yourself.

What qualifications do I need?
None at all (bar a basic certificate in food hygiene). Clients are more likely to judge you by the quality of your food and presentation than by the number of letters after your name. That's not to say that qualifications won't help. A Cordon Bleu certificate adds prestige and other qualifications such as an NVQ, City & Guilds, BTEC or a degree in catering will enhance your credibility and improve your knowledge. Many of these courses can be done part-time at further education colleges or private schools. However, all the qualifications in the world won't help you succeed unless you can cook. If you are interested in taking a qualification, your local further education college may have a course. Otherwise your local careers office can tell you what is available.

How do I set up?
Catering is a business beset by red tape. Much of this red tape serves a useful function (i.e. protecting clients from eating contaminated, unfit or old food and being subsequently made ill by it), but when you are starting up, the lists of do's and don'ts can seem very off putting.

The first step is to register your business with the local authority, who will tell you of any local requirements. Next, consult your local environmental health officer (look in the phone book), who will give you guidance as to how to prepare food in accordance with current regulations. This may well involve adapting your kitchen and the way you currently store food. He will, for instance, require you to have a separate sink for hand-washing near to the kitchen, and provision for food for catering to be stored separately from food for the family. Any advice must be followed – even if it is costly – as failure to do so could result in a hefty fine or even having your business closed down. The environmental health officer will also be able to advise you as to where you can take a basic food hygiene course.

If you intend to use your home as a base, but to work in premises such as community halls, dining rooms etc., it is worth checking that they are registered so that there will be no problems. However, if you use your premises for less than five days in every five weeks for commercial cooking, you do not have to register with the environmental health officer. Making home produce (such as jam) which carries a low risk of food poisoning, may also be subject to slightly different regulations. Once your kitchen has been kitted up to fit the guidelines, you will also need to remember that any description of what you are selling must be accurate. If you say that fresh orange juice will be supplied with the meal, then that is what you must supply. Orange squash is not the same thing at all.

Finding good suppliers is important, but exactly who they are will depend on your clientele. You may choose to buy from the local cash-and-carry or from someone who supplies all the top hotels locally. However, do shop around, as much of your profit will depend on making a decent mark-up on the cost of 'raw' goods. If you are selling foods, e.g. home-made jam, gourmet frozen foods, your own pickles, then you will need to label all the ingredients and give any necessary directions as to storage and preparation. You can, however, make the label a part of your selling strategy by emphasizing any home-made aspects of the product. However, if you are in doubt as to what to put on your label, contact the local trading standards officer who will be only too happy to help.

If you intend to change part of your home into a tea room or restaurant, you may come slap bang up against planning regulations – see chapter 3 for more details.

Once all the red tape is sorted out, you are now ready to start your business. It is important, however, that you don't over-buy – or make – before you establish demand for your product. Word of mouth, advertising and cold calling can all work for a catering operation. If you are making speciality foods, you may want to advertise in relevant publications or sell through local shops and craft fairs. If you are successful, you may find it difficult to 'stagger' your work and may need to take on staff to cope at peak times. If you do take on employees, remember that they too must observe hygiene regulations. There is no point you keeping a scrupulously clean kitchen if your assistant regularly drops fag-ash in the jam! If you are going to do outside catering, remember that you may well need to buy a van that is equipped to keep food chilled. This can cost as much as £14,000 new.

How much will I make?

It depends on what field of catering you are in. Making sandwiches for local offices will earn less than making slap-up parties for companies. If you specialize in cake decoration how much you earn may well depend on how quickly you can work. Earnings can generally be anywhere from £5,000 a year to £35,000 depending on the scale of your venture. However, do not expect to make a great deal in the first year when you will have to lay out for equipment etc.

Pros:

	Enjoyable, varied, flexible work with a high degree of customer satisfaction.
	Earnings can be good if the business is successful.

Cons:

Catering is a notably risky area (one in three restaurants fail in the first year).

The market can be over-subscribed and there is a risk of being left with large surpluses of food if you do not make the right calculations.

Red tape can be tricky to navigate.

You may find that it is too expensive to modify your kitchen to make it fit for commercial use.

Catering can require long hours spent on your feet.

Jane Lewis and Heather Grant run Lewis and Grant, a catering company based in South London.

Jane, 40, and Heather, 38, set up their catering company after the shop they were running was forced to close because of the recession. Jane had a young family and Heather was about to start one, so they wanted something that could be done flexibly. Jane had a background in sales, while Heather had worked in the food industry and even written recipes. 'We worked from home because we didn't want to have the worry of meeting the bills on expensive premises,' says Heather. Jane's kitchen has been modified to meet the environmental health regulations and they meet there to prepare food or discuss menus.

The company has now been going for five years. In the first year, business tended to come from people the couple knew personally – friends or business contacts. 'Word of mouth is our best friend,' says Heather. 'If we are doing a function and someone asks for our card, we make sure we phone them up if we haven't heard from them.' The partners also occasionally cold call companies, although they make sure that the company is likely to be interested. 'We take trade journals and read the business pages, so we can see if a company has anything coming up it is likely to want celebrating,' says Jane. 'Sometimes they are not interested, but quite often we'll get asked to quote – even if it's a year after we've sent the letter. The trouble is that sometimes we are so busy it is hard to market. And yet marketing is absolutely vital. The one thing we've found a waste of time is having expensive brochures made because our clients tend to want menus that are just for them.'

Jane and Heather believe that it's very important to price your services properly. 'We provide an up-market service, with fresh produce, beautifully served on china and our prices are reasonable – but if someone wants us to provide that at rock-bottom rates, we have to say no.'

They both believe that a calm head is vitally important – particularly as catering is liable to unexpected disasters. 'There was the time when we were doing outside catering and the oven broke down,' recalls Heather. 'Fortunately, we persuaded a local restaurant to let us use their ovens in return for cooking their deserts for the evening. Then there was the time that we were catering for a party and there was a bomb scare. And the time twice as many guests turned up as we'd been told to cater for. Keeping your wits about you and being able to handle emergencies like that is really important.'

Despite such hiccups, both women thoroughly love their jobs. 'Each party is like a one-off performance of a play, with food and wine and ambience all being orchestrated,' says Heather. And there's nothing to beat the smile on the face of the host or hostesses when they can see just how well it's going.'

Carola Brassey runs her own cake decorating business in Liverpool.

'I've had a varied career. I worked as a TV production assistant and then in PR in Manchester. The trouble with that was the travelling. I had to get to Manchester, might have to give a talk in the evening and would then have to get back to Liverpool. I'd been making and decorating cakes as a hobby for a long time for friends, but I realized there was business potential because so many people asked me to make one for them.

'I started doing them professionally while I studied for a City & Guilds in cake decoration and did a sugercraft certificate. I did the courses because although my cakes were successful, I knew there must be a better way to do things. I have also got an advanced certificate in food hygiene and I now have my own studio which cost around £1,400 to set up. I love making my cakes – I make people in marzipan to put on them and am always doing interesting designs. But it's not a profession for those who want to make serious money. I make a contribution to the household, but there's no way I could be a breadwinner because when it comes down to it, there's only a certain amount people are prepared to pay, however skilled your art.'

Useful addresses

The British Hospitality Association, 40 Duke Street, London W1M 6HR. Tel: 0171 499 6641 (provide a useful booklet on starting up a small catering business or restaurant)

The Hotel, Catering and Training Company, International House, High Street Ealing, London W5 5DB. Tel: 0181 57 9 2400 (can give details of courses available for would-be caterers)

Catering and Food Association, 1 Victoria Parade, 331 Sandycombe Road, Richmond, Surrey TW9 3NB. Tel: 0181 948 3870

CHILD-MINDING

What qualities do I need?

You really need to like children in general, not just your own. A good child-minder is loving, patient, firm, but fair towards the children –

and the mums – in her care. She also needs plenty of stamina and the ability to do at least three things at once, something most mums manage without even thinking about it. It is also vital that your own family is supportive. Jealous older children or a resentful husband can sabotage the most organized minder. Discuss it thoroughly with your family before taking the plunge.

What qualifications do I need?

None. Most child-minders are mothers with their own children, and experience with children is the pre-requisite of the job. A childcare qualification such as the NNEB or PPA is useful, but certainly not essential.

How do I set up?

It is compulsory to be registered by Social Services if you want to become a child-minder. Contact your local office (they are in the phone book) and tell them that you would like to register. They will then do a social services and police check on every member of your household over 16, to ensure there is no reason why you shouldn't become a child-minder. This is followed by an inspection of your home. This costs around £10. The social services inspector will look at such things as:

- Are your sockets covered?

- Are there dangerous flexes and wires in the house?

- Do you have safety gates?

- Are fires properly guarded and poisons, such as bleach, kept out of reach?

- Is your house warm and does it have sufficient toilet facilities?

- Do you have enough toys for the children?

- Do they give positive multi-cultural images?

Some local authorities will loan child-minders toys and safety equipment. Others hold courses for child-minders who want to register, giving the basics of childcare and safety. A child-minding certificate costs £7.50 and is renewable each year. If you are planning to drive children in your car, you will also need to be insured for them.

Once you are registered you can start looking for custom. Female employment is increasing and childcare facilities are not keeping pace, so, in the main, finding clients (i.e. parents) will not be too difficult. You will automatically be added to the social services register (available from them and often at libraries). Word of mouth is a particularly effective sales tool. If you belong to a church, mother and toddlers group, or the National Childbirth Trust, let the local chairperson know that you are looking for customers, or advertise in their local newsletter. An advert in the local newsagent is also useful. You will probably have more clients than places, so be sure to pick children – and parents – who you think will fit into the family. A disturbed child or horrible parent can make your life – as well as the children's – a misery.

It is important to draw up a contract between you and the parents so that everyone knows where they stand. This will include such things as:

- Hours of work, rate of pay and charges for overtime.

- What happens in case of illness (yours or the child's), holiday and sick pay.

- Length of notice.

- What you will supply – and what the parents will supply.

- When and how you are to be paid.

You will need to pay tax on a self-employed basis and will need public liability insurance, but do remember that toys, equipment (such as a first aid box) and outings are legitimate tax-deductible expenses. You can also claim for extra heating and lighting.

How much will I make?

Difficult to predict. Some child-minders charge by the week, (with £50 per child per week being the latest average cost). More commonly, child-minders charge by the hour, but the cost varies from as little as £1.50 to £4.00 per hour depending on the area. A child-minder can only look after three children under five, including her own, and only one of these can be under one year old. However, you can look after five under eight years and even more over this age (exact numbers are set by the local authority).

A typical child-minder might have two under fives in the day (including one of her own) and then a further two children after school. At a rate of £2.50 an hour, this would net her a maximum weekly income of around £150 a week. Child-minding will never enable you to retire to Monte Carlo, but it can make the difference between worrying over every penny and a reasonable lifestyle.

Pros:

Ideal for someone who wants to stay at home and look after her children, but who needs to earn money.

A good means of getting to know other mums in the community and building up a relationship with the children in your care.

Cons:

Very hard work.

Low status.

Can be isolating if you are new to an area.

Ashlyn Webster has been a child-minder for fifteen years.

'I started when my son was small. He was an only child and I didn't want him to get spoiled. A friend was going back to college and asked me to have her child and that's how I started.' Now Ashlyn has six children in her care, the oldest is eight and the youngest sixteen weeks. On a typical day she'll get up at 6.30 to clean up before the children arrive. By 8 a.m. the first children are at her door. Ashlyn takes the older ones to school and then spends the day with the younger ones. 'We go to toddler group, swimming, all sorts of activities. We have lunch and pick the older ones up. They have tea, tell me about their day and then all play together doing cooking, dressing up, that sort of thing. By 6.30 they've all gone.'

It's a fifty five hour week and exhausting, but Ashlyn is devoted to the job. 'It's just lovely to watch the children grow up and feel you've had some input. I need to earn a living and it's a great way to do that. The hardest thing is not interfering if you think the parents are getting it wrong. You have to remember that they are the primary carer and you're their support.

'I'd say to anyone wanting to take it up, that you really need to be the sort of person who doesn't mind wee on the carpet and mud on the settee. A sense of humour and flexibility are important too.' Ashlyn feels it's equally important to get on with the parents. She feels having a contract which sets out hours, money, what you provide, what you can and can't do with the kids, all helps. 'The disadvantage of being at home is that you can't escape your work. The child-locks are on after the kids go home. But I like my home and enjoy spending time in it, so that more than compensates!'

Useful addresses

The National Child-Minding Association (provides a pack on child-minding, with everything you need to know and can also put you in touch with other minders), 8 Masons Hill, Bromley, Kent BR2 9EY. Tel: 081 464 6164

MAKING MONEY WITH YOUR COMPUTER: WORD-PROCESSING, DESK-TOP PUBLISHING AND DATA ENTRY

There are a whole host of ways to make money from personal computers. These range from designing computer software to offering computer support for small businesses or selling second hand computers. A book has even been written on the subject called *Personal Computing for Profit* by David Bowles (Datacraft Publications). This covers everything from running your own desk-top publishing firm to becoming a systems consultant. However, it has to be said that if you do plan yourself up as a computer problem solver, guru or trainer, you must be very proficient in the area you plan to work in. For many people, offering a word-processing service – perhaps with accompanying secretarial support, or a desk-top publishing service – may be a serious option.

What qualities do I need?
Apart from knowledge of how to operate the relevant computer package (e.g. word-processing software), you need communication skills, organizational skills and the ability to work by yourself.

What qualifications do I need?
None. But you do need to be proficient on the computer you are working on and to have keyboard skills. A fast typing speed (60 words plus) is useful for a word-processing operator.

How do I set up?
If you plan to offer data input, word-processing or desk-top publishing services, the first thing is to feel confident that you can make the computer do what you want. Practice and training courses should make it clear whether you have an aptitude for this sort of work. A good computer is vital too (see chapter 6). Advertise in newsagents' windows, at social clubs, local mothers groups, or at the local Business Link –

basically at anyone who might need typing or a newsletter putting together but who doesn't have the time, energy or knowledge to do it themselves, Joining a local business club, the Rotary Club or other organization might also be useful. The key is to get regular clients, so reliability and good presentation of the work is very important. Your major equipment has to be your computer. Make sure you have a service contract for it in case of problems.

How much will I make?

It depends on the field you are in. Word-processors charge around £5 an hour. If you are keeping mailing lists, designing brochures etc. you may well charge between £10–£30 an hour. The best way to establish your price is to talk to others in similar situations, or your professional association.

Pros:

Flexible and varied work.

Low start-up costs for those with computers.

Cons:

Work may be unreliable.

May be too isolating for gregarious types doing work without high client contact.

Mick Charlsworth runs his own desk-top publishing, data in-put and printing firm.

'It was a heart attack that started it,' says Mick. Previously he was a lorry driver driving dangerous loads, but had to quit after his illness. 'I couldn't sit and do nothing so I bought a computer and started playing with it. Then I thought I'd better make it pay for itself!'

Mick started by producing a local school newsletter and so impressed were the parents that one lent him £400 for software and a good quality printer. He finds that most of his work comes through customers seeing other newsletters and through people passing on his name. 'It's great when it's busy, but it's hard to adapt to the peaks and troughs,' he says. 'But some things you do on the computer are almost addictive, so it's very absorbing. The down side of that is that you have to make sure you spend time with the family because it's easy to work over the weekend, evenings and so on.' His advice to anyone thinking of starting a computing related business is 'to go for it – but to remember that you can be in for a shock once your free banking period runs out!'

Useful addresses

British Computer Society, PO Box 1454, Station Road, Swindon SN1 1TG. Tel: 01793 480269

COMPLEMENTARY THERAPY

'Complementary therapies' cover every form of medicine that is not strictly conventional although some are more established than others. GPs, for instance, will frequently refer patients on to osteopaths or may even practise acupuncture themselves. Herbalism, homeopathy, the Alexander Technique, yoga, shiatsu and chiropractic are all well-established in this country. Naturopathy and pulsing on the other hand, are less common.

Becoming a complementary therapist is not something to be entered into lightly. Although, legally, you can start up without any sort of qualification, this is not advisable and could be downright dangerous. Quacks and untrained loose cannon have given complementary therapists an undeservedly bad name and those who are well established are very keen to protect their reputations.

What qualities do I need?

An interest in people, a good bedside manner and a certain maturity as complementary therapists treat the 'whole person' rather than just their symptoms. A willingness to study and to learn a great deal about the human body and anatomy are also vital.

What qualifications do I need?

Legally none (unless you are an osteopath). However, if you are to be taken seriously and – most importantly – do not want to do any of your patients a great deal of damage, it is vital that you study your subject in depth. Each branch of complementary medicine seems to have spawned a whole host of qualifications and schools of differing standards. However, there are several umbrella bodies such as the Institute of Complementary Medicine. If you know which branch of complementary therapy you want to undertake, they can supply you with a list of courses. If you are unsure about what you would like to do it is well worth reading *The Complementary Medicine Careers Handbook*, by Jane Foulkes (available in most good libraries).

How do I set up?

As you approach graduation from your subject, you will start to practice under supervision, much as conventional doctors do. However, once you have qualified it is up to you to build your own clientele.

It is vital to have a room set aside for your surgery and to ensure that you have all the necessary equipment (a sterilizing machine for acupuncture needles for instance). You might find a GP who is interested in complementary therapies and willing to refer to you, or you may need to advertise in local health clubs, health food shops or through local mailings and newspapers. Your best advert for yourself is the success of your treatments. Clients who feel they have benefited by your treatments and have been impressed by your professional approach are likely to recommend friends. Your professional body may also keep a list of practitioners for anyone wanting to find one in your area. Building clientele is one of the hardest parts of being a complementary practitioner – but also one of the most satisfying as you see people recover from their ailments. However, in cases where you suspect a serious illness such as cancer, it is important to give the patient the chance to mix both conventional and alternative medicine. However, it has to be said that many patients turn to complementary medicine when more conventional methods of treating back pain, migraine, eczema etc. have failed.

How much will I make?

Most practitioners of complementary therapies charge per consultation and prices tend to be between £15 at the lower end of the scale to £50 or even higher for well-known therapists. However, the biggest variable is the size of your clientele. If you treat one patient a day you are unlikely to do very well. If you treat six and have a loyal following you can expect to earn £30,000 plus. However, you may not make much profit in the first year as you may well need to recoup training and setting up costs. It is common practice to charge more for an initial consultation than for subsequent treatments.

Pros:

Demand for complementary therapists is growing all the time. If you are a skilled practitioner you can expect to have a large clientele and earn a good salary.

Fascinating and worthwhile work for someone with an interest in their subject and clients.

Cons:

Training can be very expensive – up to £20,000 for osteopathy and rarely less than £1,000 for disciplines such as therapeutic massage.

You need to be sure of your skill – mistakes could leave someone more ill than when they came to you.

Medical practitioners may also be sceptical about your skills.

Simon Baron is an osteopath. He practises from his home.
'I'd thought of doing medicine as a student, but then a friend who I met through martial arts classes began to interest me in alternative medicine,' says Simon. He was impressed by the idea of treating the whole person rather than the symptoms. Watching his friend, an acupuncturist, at work also persuaded him to look into complementary therapies in detail. 'I decided to look at osteopathy as it is the most accepted of the alternative therapies. I looked up as much as I could about it at the library and decided to study at the British College of Naturopathy and Osteopathy,' he recalls. Many of his colleagues were mature students.

Simon studied full-time for four years, although there are a few part-time courses. He got a grant from his local authority, but many fellow students were not so lucky. 'They took on all sorts of odd jobs to pay for the course which shows dedication,' he says. At the end of the course, Simon decided to set up at home because it was the cheapest way to do it. 'There are drawbacks though – the house isn't always as quiet as I would like when I'm seeing a patient and I find it very hard to leave work behind, to not think about patients and what I could be doing workwise, when I'm meant to be having time off.'

Simon needed to pay for equipment, so took an overdraft with his family's bank, having presented a detailed business plan. 'The first six months were rather slow. I advertised in the local press which was the least effective way of getting custom. Meeting up with local GPs and talking to them about what I was doing was much more effective in that they gave me referrals. I also talked to other osteopaths in the area about their businesses and got some good advice. If I have a problem which I'm uncertain about I'll either talk to a colleague or GP.'

Simon has been practising three years now and sees between 30–40 people a week.' It's hard physical work and can be emotionally draining as you spend a lot of time talking through the problem with the patient and trying to give your all to each one. It also makes me a bit upset when a few doctors regard osteopaths as quacks.'

However, he finds work is immensely satisfying and adds that he also has a lot of back-up from his professional association, 'So I never feel alone, although I love the fact that I don't have a boss and can manage my practice as I want. I feel I've made an excellent career choice.'

Useful addresses

Institute for Complementary Medicine, Unit 4, Tavern Quay, London SE16. Tel: 0171 237 5165 (umbrella body for all the complementary therapies and a good starting point; all the disciplines have their own body – or often several, so talk to the ICM first)

British Complementary Medicine Association, 39 Prestbury Road, Cheltenham, Gloucester GL25 2PT. Tel: 01242 226770.

CONSULTANCY

Consultancy basically means being paid to give advice on a subject area in which you have specialist knowledge. You can become a consultant in almost anything – from home economics to computing to management. Consultants tend to be pulled in by companies for either a one-off, or series of projects, where they do not have the expertise in-house.

What qualities do I need?

The ability to communicate well with your clients is vital as you will be passing on your knowledge and expertise, much as a teacher does. You need to have a business brain, and be good at marketing yourself as you will need to drum up the clients. The ability to do market research accurately in order to target your clientele is also invaluable. Nerves of steel and the ability to take rejection could also come in useful.

What qualifications do I need?

No formal qualifications are necessary, but you do need to have considerable knowledge about the field you intend to become a consultant in. There is no point, for instance, advertising yourself as a media consultant if your knowledge of the media is confined to watching Coronation Street! In the main people tend to become consultants in an area they have previously been working in – or in a related area where they have spotted a gap in the market. What you need above all is expertise that people are willing to pay for.

How do I set up?

The best source of work – at first anyway – is likely to be the people you've worked with in the past such as former clients, old contacts, or people on the other side of a deal who were impressed by your expertise. You need to make sure that people know not just that you are offering a service, but what it could do for them. You may also need to cold call prospective clients. Here the secret of success is to ensure that you have done plenty of market research about the company, know their problems – and how you can help.

Consultants need to project an air of authority – an impression that they are worth listening to. For this reason you will need good quality stationery (unless you are in a field where such niceties are considered not politically correct), such as notepaper and business cards which say exactly what you do.

Starting as a consultant is difficult. Clients will want to see references from satisfied former clients before they take you on. You can't get a reference without having clients and it's hard to get clients without references. If this is your situation, try to get at least some form of reference about particular projects you have been involved with, either from your previous employer or, at worst, from some consultancy you may have done on a voluntary basis.

In consultancy, your work is your best advertising tool. If you provide a service which gives companies something they wouldn't otherwise have had – whether it's added value, cost savings or knowledge – word will spread of your talents. Writing articles and letters in specialist journals or becoming a member of a professional body can all help to establish your reputation as the consultant to talk to on, say, organic duck rearing. As a consultant it is absolutely essential to have an air of professionalism. This means that your home office needs to be well equipped with either an answering machine, or a guarantee that the phone will be answered in a professional manner. A piping six-year-old can sound very sweet on the phone, but he could cost you a contract if it makes a client feel uneasy. Consultancy is one of those areas where success begets success and it's important to try to appear successful even when you are just starting out.

How much will I make?
This is impossible to calculate. A successful management or workplace consultant called in by large firms may earn over £50,000 a year. On the other hand, someone working very intermittently for small businesses may earn less than £5,000 a year. Rates vary too. Some consultants charge as little as £100 a day. Others charge nearer £1,000. The secret of success is to find a niche area where you have expertise – and where there are few competitors.

Pros:
Low initial outlay.

High rewards possible.

Intellectually challenging and interesting work.

Cons:

Severe competition in many areas.

High level of expertise needed.

Earnings highly variable.

Clients can be demanding.

Joel Brizman is a computer and management consultant.
'I've had a lot of experience in both industries which was a major asset when setting up. I was fortunate in that I started up with several clients whom I'd had contact with through my previous employment. That was important because it gave me confidence and confidence is crucial in this line of work. You need technical expertise, but you also need to convey that. Of course, self-employment is generally thought of as more risky than employment, though no job is safe nowadays, but I've tried to avoid most of the insecurity by looking for a broad base of clients rather than specializing entirely in one field. I find that most of my clients have come through other clients and that a job done well speaks volumes. In fact, I think clients actually like to employ someone like me rather than take on a larger consultancy, because they know that I will do the work and that they can always get hold of me. I will handle an emergency on holiday if necessary and I always check my answering machine to make sure I haven't missed anything urgent. I always say I have a mobile phone rather than guilt.

'Expertise is vital in this field, but you also have to be a diplomat. Making employees feel uncomfortable is a bad move if you want a continuing relationship. For instance, I was once called in on a problem which had baffled a technical team for a couple of weeks. I knew what the problem was instantly, but to show them that I'd solved it in ten minutes would have done nothing for their egos. What is more, I'd allocated a full day on the basis that it would be more complex than it was. However, I didn't want to charge for work not done. So I made out that there had been a large element of luck in finding out what went wrong. I also explained to them that I'd allocated a day to the project on the basis that if it baffled them it would probably baffle me a good while. They, of course, were thrilled that I'd solved the problem without making them feel small and told me to charge the full day. Those sorts of management techniques are vital.'

Useful addresses

Institute of Management Consultants, 5th Floor, 32–33 Hatton Garden, London EC1N 8DL. Tel: 0171 242 2140

COUNSELLING AND PSYCHOTHERAPY

What qualities do I need?
Counsellors and psychotherapists offer a wide variety of interpersonal skills and you may need rather different skills as a sex therapist, than as a bereavement counsellor. However, most counselling jobs require you to be a good listener, open-minded, non judgemental, sympathetic and good at communicating with a wide variety of people. If you have very pronounced opinions or find yourself easily becoming impatient with people then counselling is not for you.

What qualifications do I need?
Theoretically, absolutely none. It is scandalous, but perfectly legal that anyone can set themselves up as a counsellor without having had even a few days training. This is particularly worrying as counsellors spend their time helping vulnerable people resolve emotional difficulties in

their lives. For this reason, a counsellor not only needs to be sensitive but trained in the art of counselling. The British Association for Counselling, is the professional body for trained counsellors. It acknowledges three main ways in which people first get into counselling.

1 Experience in a related caring profession, such as medicine, nursing, social work, teaching or youth and community work would be useful, as would some form of voluntary counselling.

2 Several voluntary organizations, such as RELATE run their own counselling courses. Training is free provided that the prospective counsellors give some of their time gratis back to RELATE.

3 If you have no experience of counselling, a taster course could tell you whether you would be suitable for it. These courses are normally spread over eight to ten weeks with sessions lasting about an hour and a half a week. They cost between £50 and £60, and take place at many further education colleges or local universities.

Once you have decided that you definitely want to train as a counsellor, there are two routes. The first is to train with a voluntary organization whose training is recognized by the BAC. The other is to take a one-year full-time or three-year part-time course in counselling skills. This will normally cost around £3000 to £4000 and may include supervision and counselling for you. If not this can add another £1,000 to your bill. In the last year you will be allowed to take on clients at a reduced rate and under close supervision. After completing the course you can apply for BAC recognition.

Psychotherapy is similar to counselling, but psychotherapists go into problems in a different way than most counsellors and the stress is on the individual. Psychotherapists have their own UK association, the British Association of Psychotherapists. It takes longer to train – and qualify – as a psychotherapist – with five years being about the average time. It is also even more expensive than training as a counsellor and there is the added cost of undergoing your own intensive analysis. However, many psychotherapists combine working in a related profession with part-time training. Most of them say that they love their work and are dedicated to it.

How do I set up?

If you intend to work at home it is essential that you have a room which can be put aside for counselling. It should be comfortable, informal and quiet. You will also need an answering machine to ensure that you are not disturbed during counselling, and it is equally important that any children or guests know that you cannot be disturbed while working.

Professional indemnity insurance is vital. BAC has its own scheme and accredited counsellors can use it. You will also need to arrange supervision for yourself in order to ensure you are supported in your work. You can contact BAC to find out names of counsellors in your area willing to act as supervisors. It is also essential to establish a relationship with a psychiatrist or similar medical professional so that you can refer work onwards or ask them medically related questions. Some counsellors refuse to take clients on unless the client has the backing of their GP.

Security is an issue for counsellors as you may get very disturbed potential clients wishing to see you. This is especially true if you advertise in Yellow Pages or do a leaflet drop locally. It is therefore vital that you tell the client that the first interview is for assessment and that you will not be able to decided whether to offer counselling until after the interview. You can also point out that they are free to reject you as a counsellor after the initial interview. It is also extremely important to arrange this interview for a time when you know there will be other people in the house. A panic button and phone nearby are also very useful. Indeed, BAC recommends that you should only see any client when you have someone within calling distance. This may not be feasible with all clients, but is certainly important in the early stages of the relationship.

Many of your clients will come to you through word of mouth, others may come through GP referral or advertisement. Professional counsellors are increasingly in demand and you are likely to find that demand increases with your experience.

How much will I make?
The amount counsellors make varies hugely according to their experience, location and the workload they take on. A counsellor in Harley Street might well charge £80 a session. On the other hand, some counsellors charge according to what they think the client can afford – and that can be as little as £2 a session. The average at the moment is £15 to £35. The BAC recommends seeing no more than 16 to 20 clients in a 36-hour week. This would leave you with a weekly maximum income of around £500. However, most counsellors, especially those working part-time will see fewer clients than this. The £5,000 required for training also means that you may make little profit in your first year.

Pros:

Fascinating, people-based work.

Extremely flexible hours.

Great job satisfaction for a caring personality.

Cons:

Training is expensive, time-consuming and demanding.

The career itself is as much a vocation as a job.

Can be depressing.

Anita Kanter is a counsellor who practises from home.
'I became interested in counselling in the seventies and was hooked from the first session,' says Anita who originally trained as a nursery

nurse and then lectured on nursery nursing. She then took a range of counselling courses and started to counsel from home, when she returned from a stay in Israel. 'We'd thought of emigrating there, but it didn't work out. So when I came back, I was quite down and wanted to start slowly,' Anita recalls. ' I started off with four or five clients, all recommended by people who'd worked with me in the past, and built it up from there.'

Anita believes it is extra important to give a professional impression when working from home. Her counselling room is the quietest in the house 'and I'm never disturbed when counselling. I don't have family photos in that room, although I do have a lot of my books.

'There are two things which are difficult about working from home – one is pacing yourself and the other is dealing with loneliness,' says Anita. ' I've never advertised because I'd be wary of the sort of people who might come. My client base has built up through word of mouth and it is very rewarding when former clients recommend someone else.'

As counselling is confidential, Anita doesn't discuss cases with her family. For this reason, she finds that her supervisor is important in helping her establish a perspective on cases and stopping her from feeling isolated. 'I make sure that I keep in touch with what's going on professionally by attending courses,' she adds. 'I also make time for outside interests, because otherwise you can get too wrapped up in your own little world.'

Anita believes it takes maturity to work successfully at home. 'I couldn't have worked like this when I first started work because when you are younger a lot of the fun is going out to work and meeting people. Now, however, I really enjoy being at home. Of course, it is a business and you have to learn not to be embarrassed asking for money, but it's also a service and very rewarding.'

Useful addresses _____

The British Association for Counselling (helps with enquires from people wishing to be counsellors as well as those already counselling), 1 Regent Place, Rugby, Warwickshire, CV21 2PJ.

RELATE (trains counsellors who want to work in couples counselling), Head Office, Herbert Gray College, Little Church St, Rugby CV21 3AP (or contact your local branch by looking them up in the phone book)

The British Association of Psychotherapists, 37 Mapesbury Rd, London NW2 4HJ

CRAFTWORK

This can be one of the most rewarding of all businesses, combining creativity with earning money. There is a growing interest – and demand for – crafts and some of the crafts organizations also give loans and grants to help budding craftspeople set up. Crafts range from popular ones such as making jewellery, wood turning, pottery and needlework, to more esoteric areas such as hand-painted furniture, millinery or designer teddies.

What qualities do I need?

An ability to come up with an inspired idea for your craft, be it a new line in hand-painted occasion cards or pots shaped like robots. However, creativity must be accompanied by business sense – which includes the ability to conduct your own market research and market yourself. An optimistic temperament, realism and perseverance are also useful. You may be the greatest artist since Van Gogh, but that won't help you make sales if you don't have a commercial mind-set (Van Gogh sold few paintings in his lifetime. Those that were sold, were sold by his brother!).

What qualifications do I need?

Absolutely none. It is far more important to be able to turn out your craftwork – be it jewellery, paintings, furniture, knitwear, pottery or woodwork – speedily and well, than to have any number of qualifications. That doesn't mean that you won't find it useful to attend a course in your chosen area, particularly if you don't already have a lot of experience in the field. You can find craft courses in most local colleges, through evening classes and at summer schools. The Craft Council also have a list of some of the many courses on offer (for England and Wales).

How do I set up?

The majority of craftspeople started doing their craft as a hobby and found it turning into a business almost by accident. Perhaps you make a beautiful piece of jewellery, a friend asks for one just like it, her friend asks for one. You charge her, word spreads that you are making these objects and soon you have the kernel of a very small business. However, before you decide to expand, it is worth knowing that making crafts commercially is not the same as making them occasionally as a favour for friends.

If you plan to sell your work on the open-market, it must be priced *realistically*, i.e. high enough to ensure a profit, but not so high that there are no takers – see the pricing section in chapter 3. You must learn to work efficiently (it's no good spending 15 hours on a beautiful pot and charging £7.50 for it) and you must find a market for your work.

Most small craftspeople sell through a variety of sources – through local shops, mail shots to likely clients, word of mouth, mail order or at craft fairs, although the quality of these is extremely variable. They are also not an ideal way of selling for a mother with young children as they are always at the weekends.

One word of warning: do not give up your regular job *before* you are absolutely sure your craft is sufficiently in demand. Do your craftwork in addition to your employment at first.

It is worth noting that there are regulations concerning the manufacture of certain crafts, particularly toys and clothing. Toys have to be safe for children, and to give guidance as to the age they are suited for, or – if they are toys really designed with adults in mind – e.g. antique reproduction dolls – be labelled clearly as not being a toy. Before you start making your craft commercially it is well worth phoning your local trading standards officer to find out what – if any – regulations you need to comply with. The Women's Institute also runs markets which can be a good testing ground.

How much will I make?

Impossible to predict. However, it is fair to say that the larger the item you are making, the more you can charge for it. Someone selling hand-painted chests at £400 a time is likely to earn more than someone selling hand-made birthday cards at £1.50 a time – provided they are selling enough of them. The keys to earning a decent living from craftwork are to cost your product correctly (not so little that you end up earning £1 an hour, but not so much that only five people wish to buy your product), to market it efficiently (that means ensuring it is seen in the places your buyers are likely to be) and to ensure it is sufficiently original to create a demand. It is also helpful if your raw materials are cheap as their cost must be included in your pricing structure.

Having said this, most craftspeople earn in the region of £4–£10 an hour for their labours. Only the fortunate few who have found a craft which can be done quickly, with cheap raw materials, yet charged at a premium can expect to earn more than this – unless they sign a deal with a major retailer. The Crafts Council in England and Wales (and similar bodies in Scotland and Northern Ireland) may give grants to craftspeople to enable them to set up their first workshop.

Pros:

Immensely satisfying for someone who is turning a hobby into a business.

Potential for a reasonable living.

A growing demand.

Lots of customer contact.

Cons:

Can be an overcrowded and competitive market place. Dried flower arranging, wood turning and jewellery-making are particularly oversubscribed areas.

If you misjudge your pricing you may end up working long hours for peanuts or failing to make any money at all.

You need to have business acumen as well as a creative streak.

Andy Binfield is a wood turner making beautiful wooden fruit and pots.

'I'd always done wood turning as a hobby, while working as a fishmonger. When the town got a hypermarket with a fish counter, it did for my business in the high street. I started investigating whether I could make a living from wood turning. I went to a few craft shows and talked to local shops. I only supply those who will pay for my goods outright. Working on a sale or return business is too dicey.

'It's important to research your craft fairs well. There are so many of them and some of them are not worth going to. I talked a lot to other craftspeople in the early days – and then discounted some of what they said. I also kept a firm eye on what sold and what didn't. If apples sold well, then I made lots of apples. However, now I know it doesn't quite work like that. Some places they'll love apples and in others they want pots. It's difficult to tell. However, I always make sure my customers know at which fairs they can find me, because a lot of people collect wooden fruit a piece at a time and will come back and back again.

'There's good and bad in being a craftsperson. I hate the first day of a fair where you set off in the middle of the night, arrive at 5 a.m. and then get very stressed trying to ensure the stall is up in time. But the second day – when you can chat with the customers and see them admiring your work – is good. I love making things out of wood too. When it was a hobby, I'd disappear into the sheds for an hour at a time – now it's ten or twelve hours at a time. I've been established for a while, but I think it is hard for newer people – unless they've got an original idea. Originality always sells.'

Frank and Elizabeth Lord run Timber and Thread, making hand-carved rocking horses, appliquéd cot and bed covers and traditional dressed teddy bears. They were both headteachers before starting the business.

'After I had an injury I had to give up work and was confined to a wheelchair for a while,' says Elizabeth. 'I'd always loved doing embroidery and it gave me something to do. Friends greatly admired my work and asked me to take a stand at a charity fair – which I did and sold out. At the same time, one of my friends took some work, unbeknown to me, to the shop of the Guild of Applied Arts and they promptly ordered some.

'I wasn't a very good invalid – very grumpy in fact – and Frank decided to give up work to look after me. That meant that instead of facing a comfortable retirement, we had to make our small business pay. Frank had always loved woodwork so decided to make wooden rocking horses at the top end of the market. He did a lot of research on the making of rocking horses, while I contacted the trading standards authority and a society which researches into cot death to make sure that all my nursery goods were as safe as it is possible to be.

'We had to approach the bank for finance. They took our life policies as security and we also had to take out a mortgage on our property which we had paid off. Fortunately, we have done reasonably well and the business has stayed afloat. We could grow it even more by going to more trade shows, but I will only take on what I can handle so we sell to a few retailers, go to a few select craft fairs and also have an agent in Switzerland. That came about because we were asked to do a trade show in France on the best of British crafts.

'I think any novice should ask other craftspeople about which shows are worth doing – some of them are a waste of time and you can't afford to make too many mistakes. Once you are at a show, you need something which catches the eye – we always sell our door-wedge teddies which are dressed up in all sorts of costumes. One chap who was an anaesthetist even asked for one to be dressed in theatre greens and we've sold plenty of barrister teds. I always smile at customers and chat. Some of them come back year after year, showing us pictures of grandchildren wrapped in our linen or the latest addition to the family. We both love our work. Sometimes I'm so absorbed in what I'm making that when I'm interrupted – even when it's by my family whom I love dearly – I feel a bit sad I have to stop.'

Useful addresses

The Crafts Council, 44a Pentonville Road, Islington, London N1 9BY. Tel: 0171 278 7700

The Design Council, 28 Haymarket, London SW1Y 4SU. Tel: 0171 839 8000

Women's Institute Markets Department, 104 New Kings Road, London SW6 4LY

Giftware Association, 10 Vyse St, Birmingham BL18 6LT. Tel: 0121 236 2657

DIRECT SELLING AND NETWORK MARKETING

Direct selling, at its most basic, means selling products direct to the customer without using a shop. At the moment it accounts for around 2 per cent of all products sold, but that seems set to grow as there are increasing numbers of elderly people, unable to go out, and as more customers turn away from the anonymity of large shopping complexes.

There are three basic types of direct selling:

1   **Selling your own stock**   This means selling a small stock of goods from home or to your customer direct without using a bigger organization. A lot of people do this with second hand goods, or things they have made themselves (see also crafts). Often the goods appeal to a specialist market prepared to travel to buy.

2   **Becoming a 'distributor'**   Here you operate by leaving a catalogue or demonstrating goods at your prospective customers' homes. It is up to you to collect the orders, deliver the goods and collect payment (either direct to you or to your 'sponsor' company). Some companies work on the party-plan method of selling. This is where the distributor organizes a party to sell the goods, for instance, Anne Summers sex aids, or Avon cosmetics. This is often an enjoyable way of selling for both customers and sellers.

Network marketing involves not only selling the goods yourself but recruiting others to the network and taking a commission on their sales. Some top distributors sell very little – but make a large profit by recruiting hundreds of other people, on whose sales they then earn commission. Many of the established direct-selling companies such as Cabouchon, Anne Summers, Tupperware and Amway use a mixture of these methods.

3   **Becoming an agent for a company**   This involves you acting as the middleman between supplier and customer. Very experienced sales people might be interested in becoming an agent for a

major manufacturer. If you are, contact the Manufacturers Agents Association (address below). However, this sort of work is best suited to those with plenty of sales experience. Alternatively, you could make a direct approach to a manufacturer whose work interests you or to embassies in this country. At the other end of the scale, many catalogue companies look for people to act as agents for their catalogues, persuading other people to buy.

What qualities do I need?
You need to be outgoing, a good communicator, persistent, able to take rejection and willing to work hard. It helps to have a wide social circle as friends and community groups will be your first market.

What qualifications do I need?
None. It is more important that your product is suitable for the market you are trying to sell to. Before you decide what you are going to sell you should ask yourself:

- Would I buy this?

- Would I use this?

- Can I sell this?

How do I set up?
First choose your product carefully – which means not only choosing a product you like (and preferably one you'd use yourself) but that the company is bona fide. Although direct selling has cleaned up its act since the 1970s when people were sold huge amounts of stock they couldn't then shift, there is still the occasional cowboy operator. Many reputable firms belong to The Direct Selling Association whose members are covered by a code of conduct (see below).

You should also take into account what your prospective customers will like and can afford. If there are high levels of unemployment in your neighbourhood, expensive costume jewellery is unlikely to go down a storm, but low-cost cosmetics might. Check, too, that your area is not already awash with distributors of similar products. One friend of mine signed up with a lingerie company and was then saddened to find that everyone she asked to her party, had already been to at least one lingerie party within the last few months!

It is illegal for a company to ask you to shell out more than £75 on stock or goods for demonstration in the first week. However, you would be wise not to buy more than this, even after that, until you've established that it sells. Be wary of companies who want you to buy van loads of stock rather than showing the catalogue – particularly if they won't refund you for any unwanted stock. You could be left with a hefty bill and lots of unwanted goods. If the company you are interested in is arousing your suspicion, talk to your local trading standards officer about what is good practice. Normally you will be paid a profit margin on the goods you sell and may also be given an extra commission/ greater profit margin if you reach certain sales targets.

Once you've got your stock/catalogue, you need to think of ways to attract customers. If you are selling Anne Summers sexy underwear or Avon cosmetics, a party is more likely to induce impulse buying than merely dropping the catalogue through the door. On the other hand, if you are selling cleaning equipment, customers either need it – or they don't. And would you go to a bleach party? Think of other outlets for your products too. Schools might buy books for instance, a local catering firm might need Tupperware. Many of the larger direct selling firms hold training days or foster a network of sponsor/distributor relationships. These can be very beneficial in giving you tips as to how to sell or present the product better.

Once you've established a core market it is up to you to keep plugging away at finding new buyers, distributors and outlets. There is a fine line between being a good salesperson and being pushy, and only time will tell just which side of the line you are on. However, be warned, if you are shy, find it difficult to sell tickets for the school raffle or cannot take rejection, direct selling is not for you.

If you are selling direct from your home on a solo basis you will need to add an advertising/publicity budget into your calculations in order to ensure everyone knows about what you are selling. You will also need extra insurance to cover the cost of stock and, if you have a mortgage, you may have change of use problems with your building society if you turn half the house into a warehouse.

Virtually all direct sellers are classified as self-employed – that means it's up to you to keep accurate records, fill in your tax return and arrange any necessary insurance. Check with your company for any specific requirements.

How much will I make?

Despite adverts promising fortunes, few direct sellers hit the millionaire bracket. In order to do so, you need to be one of the earliest recruits locally to a network marketing scheme (as the more people in a locality selling the goods, the less profit there is for each of them) and to have a great sales gift. The average sales per direct seller is £1,400 per year and you may make as little as £10 profit from a poorly attended party. On the other hand, if your product is not available locally and is much in demand you could make £100 from just one party. Part-time direct sellers can expect to earn anywhere from £1,000 to £10,000 a year. Full-time sellers who really work at it, have chosen their market well, and have a product that's in demand can expect to make much more.

Pros:

> Extremely flexible.

> No previous experience required.

> Good for sociable people.

Cons:

> Requires large base of contacts.

May make very little if unsuccessful.

Can be time-consuming.

Not for retiring violets.

Debbie Clothier sells Dorling Kindersley Family Library Books.

'I started off by going to a party myself,' Debbie recalls. 'I really liked the books and decided to do a bit of market research as to whether they would sell. At first I wondered if people would buy from me, but then I learnt that only 20 per cent of people ever set foot in a bookshop, so I realized there was a lot of potential.'

Debbie lives in a village and has a lively social circle which provided her first customers. She was a member of the Parent Teachers Association and various local charity committees which also helped spread the word. 'I find that one party leads to another one – you'll find someone at the party who is quite happy to host another party in return for getting a nice book.' says Debbie. 'If people ask me what I do when I'm at dinner parties then I tell them – but I'm not the hard sell type. I'd hate to have everyone cross the street to avoid me.'

Debbie also sells to local schools – a task she found daunting at first. 'But knowing that I believed in the quality of the product really helped.' She has also built up a team of distributors whom she helps train and support. In return she receives commission on their sales. The better they do, the better she does.'

'I work about thirty hours a week, but I fit it around my lifestyle and children, who are both at school, rather than trying to fit myself around it,' says Debbie who estimates her earnings at over £1,000 a month. 'But I have to say that it's something that's grown gradually, rather than all at once. Which suits me fine.'

Useful addresses _____

Direct Selling Association, 29 Floral St, London WC2E 9DP. Tel: 0171 497 1234

Manufacturers Agents Association, 1 Somers Road, Reigate Surrey RH2 9DU. Tel: 01737 241025

DRESSMAKING

What qualities do I need?

The ability to sew extremely well, an eye for detail, a flair for design and communication skills are all vital.

What qualifications do I need?

None. Although a qualification in fashion or needlecraft may be desirable.

How do I set up?

A sewing machine – and somewhere to sew are basic. But you will also need cutting table, dummy, shears, pins, patterns and mirror. It's also vital to have some work to show. Perhaps you have made clothes for yourself, or made cushion covers or done repairs for friends. Most dressmakers find the bulk of their work comes from people who are either a 'difficult' size – perhaps people who are unusually large, short or tall – or people who have a special event in mind. It is relatively common to have bridal dresses made or dresses and suits for a special occasion. Some people specialize in sewing for the home – perhaps making cushion covers, curtains or re-upholstery for furniture.

Whichever you choose, where you place your advertising is important. Local press, shops and specialist magazines may be one way of attracting custom. Or it might be worth talking to relevant local shops about whether they have an alterations/curtain making facility for customers and offering your services if not. Once you've got a name for yourself word of mouth will also help. If you plan to enter the bridal market, it may be a good idea to exhibit at local wedding exhibitions and make contact with local caterers, florists etc., who may be asked for recommendations.

Once you are up and running it is important to make things to clients' specifications – even if you don't agree with them. You might try to persuade them (and a lot will ask your advice) to try a certain look, but ultimately, the decision is up to them.

How much will I make?
This depends entirely on your volume of trade and the sort of work you do. Clearly you can charge more for bridal wear than for alterations and repairs to ordinary garments. However, your materials and labour costs will also be higher.

Helen Maloney is a dressmaker.
Helen decided to become a dressmaker after she couldn't get a job she wanted in the fashion industry. However, she also adds that 'I've always enjoyed dressmaking. I find it creative and it's enjoyable to have all sorts of different clients wanting different things.' Helen feels it's important to be versatile and not to be too fussy about the work you do. 'One client brings me a lot of work and once her mother came with her and asked me to darn some stockings. I could have said no, but it would have caused a lot of resentment. It's worth swallowing your pride to keep a client happy. I didn't charge either.'

Helen feels that the major problems with her job are 'pressure of work – you can suddenly become very busy from being very quiet,' and also dealing with isolation. 'There's no doubt it's a lonely job. Sometimes my husband tells me about all the things which have happened in his office and I don't have a lot to say about what I've been doing. But I do find listening to the radio helps.'

She also gets a great deal of job satisfaction. 'When you see your

> customer trying something on and looking terrific, with that smile on
> their face that says they know it too – that's great!'

Useful addresses

The Knitting and Stitching Show, Creative Exhibitions, Lewisham Park,
London SE13. 6QZ. Tel: 0181 690 1200

IMAGE CONSULTANT

What qualities do I need?
An interest in fashion, a sense of style, creativity and communication
skills are all vital, as is a friendly manner.

What qualifications do I need?
No formal qualifications are required, although a qualification in a
related area, such as fashion, design or art might come in useful.
However, a business background would give you a good network of
contacts. Many colour consultants are affiliated to a particular
company or buy a franchise. In these cases, training is given by the
company concerned. If you want to work independently there are a
whole host of courses, ranging from six weeks to three months. There is
also a City & Guilds course and some further education colleges may
hold evening classes. Costs of franchising or becoming a consultant for
a company are around £3,000–£5,000. Look in the Yellow Pages for
details of local consultants.

How do I set up?
If you want to become an agent for an established company, contact
their head office. Well-known companies include: The House of
Colour and Color-Me-Beautiful, and there may also be local firms

listed in the Yellow Pages. Buying a franchise is expensive, so first do your market research to establish that there is a demand in your area.

In the eighties, image and colour consultancy were all the rage. Now they are still popular, but lack of disposable income means you may need to work harder to persuade women (and it is still mainly women who want these services) to part with their cash. However, everyone likes to look good and corporate clients, including men, are a growing market.

You will probably attract your clients through one of two ways – personal contacts or marketing. Health clubs, local beauty salons and boutiques would all be good places to site an advert. Or you might be able to get some coverage in a local newspaper. Alternatively, find out which local workplaces have high proportions of female employees and arrange a lunchtime or evening demonstration. Women of 30 plus are more likely to buy your service, partly because they have more disposable income, partly because they may feel more in need of a change of style. Talk to any small local businesses which require good presentation of their employees (salespeople, perhaps, or PR agencies). Remember, you will need to look your best, as you are the best advert for your own advice. Giving talks at women's groups could also be advantageous in attracting clientele.

Not only will your looks be important, but the atmosphere you create in your consulting room – so tasteful decor is vital. You will also need to have a good range of swatches, make-up and books which feature fashion styles. If you work for a major company, they may well furnish you with a catalogue of products, clothing and make-up which you will encourage your client to purchase or at least browse through – although it is important to offer objective advice.

To set up you will need to budget not only for your swatches and make-up but for quite a heavy initial advertising budget to include promotion in Yellow Pages, stationery, leaflets etc. Prices vary according to whether you are working with a group or as an individual. Color-Me-Beautiful, for instance, charges £55 for a colour analysis and £55 for a style class.

How much will I make?

It takes time to grow an image consultancy business, but a successful full-timer could expect to earn up to £20,000. On the other hand, if you are in the early stages and have had to lay out for training, or you work part-time, you might earn £5,000.

Pros:

> Creative, interesting work for those with a passion for fashion and looking good.

> Opportunity to mix with many types of people who are grateful for your help.

Cons:

> Could be hard to get established if there is plenty of competition locally or in areas of low income.

> Earnings are variable.

Elaine Crighton is a colour consultant in Aberdeenshire.

'I started off as a client. I went with some friends to a class and it made such a huge difference to the way I looked and felt about myself that I decided this is what I wanted to do.' At the time Elaine was working as a personnel officer in the family business. She investigated further and decided to get a franchise, taking out a business loan to pay for it. 'The training was in Watford, so I not only had to pay for that but for my accommodation and fares,' says Elaine.

Elaine had done copious market research before setting up. She had handed out questionnaires to various groups including accountants and mother and toddler groups, getting one person to be responsible for gathering them in. 'Out of 150 I had 120 back, so I knew there was a market. Then I held a demonstration and got a lot of clients from that.'

However, Elaine feels that she made one mistake when starting off – marketing only when in need of clients, rather than continuously. 'It meant I had big peaks and troughs. Times when I had too much work and times when I had none. Now I market myself steadily which is much better. I do an event once a month, which I advertise, and I find that pays off.'

She also feels that demonstrations are a better way to drum up business than leaflets. 'People can see just how well it works in a demo and they can't in a leaflet,' she says. 'I really enjoy it because it's amazing the difference you can make,' says Elaine. 'However, the one thing I'd say about working at home is that the only person who can really make things happen is you.'

Useful addresses

House of Colour Ltd, The Avenue, Watford. Tel: 01923 211188
Color-Me-Beautiful, 49 Greencoat Place, London SW1P 1DS. Tel: 0171 627 5511

INTERIOR DESIGNER

This is one of the most coveted jobs out. The chance to design someone else's house beautifully is not just a fulfilling way to earn money, it's a positive treat. However, do remember if you want to become an interior designer, that people pay you to design their house in a way that appeals to their taste – rather than your own. Recessionary times and falling house prices make it a competitive market for interior designers, but there are still many who are doing well.

What qualities do I need?
Creativity, imagination, taste, diplomacy, negotiating skills and organizational skills are all important.

What qualifications do I need?

Legally speaking, none, but if you are planning to do major re-designing of homes and have little design experience, you might want to do one of the many courses available in interior design. Some courses can be done by correspondence which suits many people. The Design Council sells a book on design courses, available from their book shop, but also in good reference libraries. Those who have been designing for at least three years may be able to join the Interior Decorators and Designers Association. A knowledge of plumbing, heating, lighting and ventilation is also useful.

However, many specialist designers such as specialist painters, stencillers or furniture decorators are largely self-taught. In this case, membership of a professional body is often possible – provided you have sufficient experience and can show a good standard of work The professional associations often have training days and seminars for those who are already working as interior designers.

How do I set up?

Getting the first job is the most difficult. Most clients want to see a portfolio of work and references, but if you have just started off you may find it hard to supply them. Personal contacts are very useful, as is using your own home as a showcase. You might also contact local pubs and offices to find out if any of them are looking for a refit. Publicity in a magazine for the home decor market is also invaluable, so it's a good idea to take photographs of any previous work to submit to them. A listing in Yellow Pages could also be useful.

Another good source of work could be to meet up with people in related professions e.g. carpenters, or even plumbers, who may be asked for recommendations. Joining a professional association, such as those listed below will also give you access to their directories and contacts.

You may need a fair amount of outlay to start with, for items such as paints, swatches, samples and an advertising budget. However, you should aim to buy wholesale and sell retail to your customers. Once you are established you will find you can spend less on advertising and promotion and rely more on word of mouth.

How much will I make?
Variable. Top designers may charge as much as £75 an hour. Others as little as £20. Many charge by the job, a practice which is becoming increasingly popular. At the top end of the scale, an annual income of £40,000 plus is possible.

Pros:

> Creative, flexible, well-paid work for those with a flair and good contacts.

Cons:

> Interior design is affected by downturns in the economy.

> Can be hard to establish yourself.

> Plenty of outlay before profits appear.

> Your own home must become your showcase.

Mary Ross has been running her interior design business for eight years. She specializes in hand-painted furniture and murals.
'I fell into this business really. I was heavily pregnant with my second child and having a room re-designed which was running above budget. I complained to a friend who told me to learn paint finishes and do it myself! So I did. From that, I then decorated just one small wardrobe. People said how much they liked it and business just grew from there. My first year was just before the recession and I had work coming out of my ears. I did one flat completely and a lot of work came from that. Then the recession came and work dried up. So I came up with an idea for hand-painted tissue boxes and wrote off to various country houses suggesting they buy one. Many of them did

including the Waterside Inn which is very well known. Those boxes kept me going for a while and then things picked up again.

'I also learned that one good way to encourage business is to have a coffee morning to show your work to friends and previous clients. It reminds those who've used you before that you are still around and encourages a lot of business. I've had a hundred people coming through here at one time! I look upon my own home as a showcase. It took me almost two years to do completely, and it has been featured in a magazine. I also work with a carpenter and he puts work my way, and I his. I love working with him because his stuff is so exquisite.

'Overall, I consider myself very lucky because my hobby has become my business and I love working, and I love the lulls because then I can spend more time with my children. There are no real disadvantages – apart from learning to price properly. I still make mistakes about that, quoting for two coats of paint when the job ends up taking five, that sort of thing. I've learnt now to think very carefully before I quote. It is important.'

Useful addresses

Chartered Society of Designers, 29 Bedford Square, London WC1B 3EG. Tel: 0171 631 1510

Interior Decorators and Designers Association, Chelsea Harbour Design Centre, Lots Road, London SW10 0XE. Tel: 0171 349 0800

The Design Council, 28 Haymarket, London SW1Y 4SP. Tel: 0171 839 8000

MAIL ORDER

What qualities do I need?

Salesmanship, attention to detail, organizational skills, and the ability to work alone.

What qualifications do I need?
Absolutely none – although a background in some form of business or specialist field might come in useful.

How do I set up?
Before you set up you need to ask yourself some hard questions:

1 **Who is this product aimed at and how will my prospective buyers find me?** The answer to this question might be fairly easy if you are selling to a specialist area. Suppose, for instance, you want to sell books on sub-aqua diving. You know (or should do) that many of your audience will be members of sub-aqua clubs and will read diving magazines. On the other hand, if you plan to sell hand-carved Indian crafts your market is potentially much wider and it may be difficult to pin it down without careful research. Some ideas to start with could however include those people who have already travelled to India, (travel agents specializing in the area might help), those who have already bought exotic crafts (craft magazines, shops specializing in crafts from the area etc.).

2 **Why should anyone buy this product mail order rather than through the shops?** The short answer is that it has either a scarcity factor, i.e. it isn't obtainable through many – if any – shops, or perhaps your target audience is in rural areas and can't go to relevant shops very often – if ever. For instance, maternity clothes are often sold by mail order. That's because there are few shops that sell them, the range of styles in those shops is limited and it is hard for people who live out of town centres and are heavily pregnant to make a special trip in particularly if they have a toddler in tow. Alternatively, there may be a convenience factor, for example, gift catalogues may contain a wide range of goods that would otherwise be found only by visiting scores of different shops. From these criteria you can see that selling baked beans mail-order is likely to be a futile enterprise!

3 **Will it go through the post?** Those beautiful earrings may sell well, but can you be sure you can deliver the most delicate ones in good order and still make a profit? That brass elephant statue might be absolutely gorgeous, but will it really go through anyone's letter box – even if it doesn't cost a fortune to wrap. Mail-order goods need to be easy to wrap, easy to post, easy to receive and, alas, easy to send back. Investigate this area carefully, with the help of the post office. Both Parcel Force and The Royal Mail have the necessary information. In general, smaller goods may be more saleable because they are more easily posted through the letter box.

4 **How much stock will I need to buy before I get any orders?** Some people think that you can start up with no stock at all and then just get it as orders arrive. This might be OK if you can be sure there will be absolutely no time delay. However, reputable newspapers and magazines want to know you can meet a reasonable demand before they take your advert. In any case, you would never get any repeat orders if you can't supply first time. You need to start with a realistic level of stock – research will tell you what this is. One formula suggests that you rarely get a response worth more than six times the cost of the ad – but this may not work for you.

Designing your catalogue is also very important. It must be attractive and interesting, and easy to understand, so spend time on it, or get professional advice. Both the selling and advertising of goods are covered by a hefty net of regulations, designed quite rightly, to protect the consumer. So talk to your local trading standards officer and get the Advertising Standards Authority guidelines (see chapter 6).

Remember, too, that in general mail-order customers expect to be able to return goods they don't like within a certain period, so it is best to describe the product accurately or it will come whizzing back. Make sure you have also been clear as to the period they can return the goods in. You don't want to receive a mouldy cheese back, three months after it arrived at the buyer's home.

MOPS (Mail Order Protection Scheme) is the code of conduct

operated by national newspapers and includes rigorous checks on your credit worthiness and stock. Some magazines abide by the mail-order rules of their trade association the Periodical Publishers Association. Local newspapers and trade magazines aren't covered by these rules, nor are perishable products (such as cheese, or flowers) or services.

Apart from advertising, the other way to reach customers is to either buy, or rent an established list of names and addresses. If, for instance, you think your customers are likely to be the sort of people who give to animal charities, you may choose to rent the list of a relevant animal charity. You can rent lists from a list broker. You can find these through library reference directories such as BRAD Direct Marketing or Benn Direct Marketing Services. Both should be available from reference libraries. If it is too costly to use a broker, but you know exactly what group you are aiming at, you can normally buy a list direct from the relevant trade association or with the help of a directory like Kompass. Local lists may be provided by your Business Link, TEC or Chamber of Commerce. Most directories will be willing to search their records and tailor-make a list for you – at a price.

Prices tend to be charged per 1,000 names and costs can vary from £40–£400 depending on the information sought. Some organizations refuse to rent lists but may let you put in a mailing with their newsletter at a cost. So if you see an organization which you know is likely to attract the sort of people you want to reach, talk to them. Even if they won't rent a list, perhaps you can put in a mail shot or advertising with their next publication. The secret of not spending too much on lists is to know exactly who you aim to appeal to before you start. That way you will attract the maximum return. In any case, with judicious advertising you should be able to build up your own list quite quickly.

If you keep your client list on computer you need to register with the Data Protection Registrar. There is a fee for this. Don't put anything down you wouldn't wish your customers to read as they have the right to check what is written about them.

Basically, most of the work in setting up a mail order business should be done before you set up. That way you will have a good idea of how viable the business is and where the market is. Once it has started you must offer your customers a *reliable* service. You will not get much repeat business if you send out goods three months late, or have no satisfactory policy for dealing with returns.

If you can afford it, a specialist solicitor and accountant would help you, both in sticking to the right side of the law in your advertisements and product descriptions, and in setting up realistic contracts and terms for the return of goods, bounced cheques, goods broken in the post etc. An insurance policy for such liabilities is, of course, a must. Mail order is quite a complex business, so it is worth reading some specialist guides. Malcolm Breckman's *Running Your Own Mail Order Business* (Kogan Page) is very accessible. A trade periodical such as *Precision Marketing* may also be a useful reference point.

How much will I make?

Depends entirely on how well the business goes. The sky is the limit. But bankruptcy is also a real possibility if you don't do your research.

Pros:

A chance to sell direct to the public without paying for the rent of a shop.

Possible to start the business while still doing your existing job.

Chance to specialize in an area which interests you.

Excellent prospects for good ideas well executed.

Cons:

Need to buy stock before business is completely established – even if doing so on a just-in-time basis.

May be very hit and miss in the early days.

Lots of regulations to comply with.

Could be stiff competition.

Administration is time consuming and can be boring.

Malcolm Pein sells computer software by mail-order from home. His business has been running for eight years.

'I'm an International Master in chess, so I like to be up-to-date with new trends in the game. When I heard about chess computer software I knew it was a brilliant idea, so I asked the agent if I could sell some for them,' says Malcolm. Eventually, the agent decided to sell the licence for the software to Malcolm and he gave up his computing day job. 'I never considered selling anywhere other than from home,' says Malcolm. 'What's the point in laying yourself open to large overheads?'

Malcolm found it easy to target his audience. 'There are two major chess magazines and I advertised in them. In fact, when one started to fold, I bought it rather than lose that chance. I also used to demonstrate the software at first, but don't need to do that now.'

Malcolm feels the secret of successful mail-order selling is to find a niche market, 'with low volume sales, but relatively high prices. If I make six sales a day that's fine.'

He also points out that it is essential to man the phone day or night. 'When my new baby had just been born, the phone went at 7.30 a.m. I just couldn't face answering it. I rang back at 10.00 a.m. – but he'd already bought the stuff elsewhere. People don't buy on an answering machine. They like to talk to someone and someone knowledgeable at that!' This is why Malcolm has found someone in Glasgow to whom phone calls are re-routed if necessary. 'We keep pads everywhere,' he says. 'It is an interruption, but the beauty is that you can be earning money sitting out in the garden, in the bath, watching TV. How many people can say that?'

Useful addresses

MOPS (for national newspapers), 16 Tooks Court, London EC4A 1LB. 0171 405 6806

Periodical Publishers Association, 15–19 Kingsway, London WC2B 6UN. Tel: 0171 379 6268

Parcel Force Tel: 0800 2244566

ORGANIZER

The range of things which require organization is colossal – everything from weddings, parties and conferences to exhibitions, product launches, gala dinners. In the USA there are even personal organizers, who come to your home and re-organize your working space, diary and life. A brilliant idea which seems not to have caught on over here – yet!

What qualities do I need?

It almost goes without saying that the major requirement is to be able to organize effectively. An aptitude for administration, efficiency, meticulous attention to detail, the ability to marshall staff to your bidding and nerves of steel are all essential. If you are disorganized yourself, forget it.

What qualifications do I need?

No formal qualifications are required, although good contacts in a particular sector of the market are vital as these contacts are likely to be the people who will first bring business to you.

How do I set up?

First decide what you are going to do. In certain areas, such as exhibition organizing, previous experience – or knowledge of a specialist field – would be a distinct advantage, for instance, having worked in the banqueting department of a large hotel, for a well-established conference company or having organized exhibitions and conferences in-house. In other areas, such as party organizing, good contacts could be all you need. It's also a good idea to get to know those people who are often involved with other aspects of organizing events – local caterers or companies who hire out meetings rooms, for instance. You could also try cold calling organizations which you think might be in need of your help. Advertising in local press or glossy magazines might be effective for some forms of organization such as party organizing. For conference and exhibition organizing, advertising through the local chamber of commerce newsletter could be useful. However, it has to be said that in this field, personal contacts from a previous life are likely to be your best bet.

Once you have a client, it is vital to pay attention to exactly what he or she wants – both in terms of venue, entertainment, speakers and – just as important – budget. It is vital that you do not exceed this or you will not be popular, however faultless your organization may otherwise have been. It is also important that both parties sign a contract outlining terms and conditions under which the work is undertaken and specifying your duties. This will prevent misunderstandings, e.g. they thought you were choosing the caterers, and you thought they'd already selected them. It's also vital to know, just how not only your fee, but the budget for organizing the wedding, or other event, is likely to be paid. It is important not to end up footing the bill, but few clients will trust you enough – wisely – to hand over all their money up front.

Organizing takes time and considerable attention to detail. However, even best laid plans have a habit of going wrong and it's important to have nerves of steel – and contingency plans up your sleeve. Once you have had a few satisfied clients, word of mouth and good references will help you get others. However, getting started is likely to be tough. The only consolation is that you are unlikely to incur too many costs – apart from advertising – until you have clients.

How much will I make?

Extremely variable depending on the sector and type of organizing you are offering. Clearly, someone organizing children's parties will earn less than someone organizing conferences for major retailers. However, some conference holders are now asking organizers to perform on a contingency fee basis (i.e. by how many heads they get through the door). This makes conference organizing a risky business. What will happen to your fee, for instance, if a major flood prevents people attending who'd planned to come? Think very carefully before you take on anything on a contingency fee basis.

Pros:

Varied and interesting work.

Lots of client contact.

Potential for high rewards.

Cons:

Hard to get established.

Plenty of potential for crises and disasters.

High risk of failure.

Caroline Roney has been organizing medical conferences for over twenty years.

Caroline, a nurse by training started in conference organizing by answering an advert for an organizer for a medical conference. 'I'd been looking to become self-employed and after doing that conference, I realized this could be a way to do it.' Caroline finds working from home very suited to conference organizing. 'I have local staff and can work all the hours I need, without any inconvenience.'

She feels that a cool-head is a pre-requisite for this type of work for, despite careful planning, there is always an unforeseen problem. A recent conference, for instance, was beset by industrial problems which she had to sort out. She also feels that numeracy, a good understanding of geography and attention to detail are paramount. 'You are only as good as your last conference and that is quite a pressure.'

Caroline organizes conferences which run to thousands of delegates and has to start planning three years in advance. 'It means I've always got something on the go. I must admit that when a conference is over, it gives me a tremendous sense of relief to know that it all went off well.'

Joan Friedenthal organizes all the flowers for weddings and celebrations at a local church.

Joan's career started almost by accident. Previously a stay-at-home mother, she'd done a flower arranging course and had exhibited at local shows, winning prizes for her arrangements. A neighbour, who was also a verger, heard of her prowess and asked to talk to her about organizing the flowers for the church both for normal services and for special events such as weddings.

Joan talked through her ideas with him – and landed the job. She stresses it is not just a question of arranging the flowers, but of planning her budget, consulting with clients and making sure that every arrangement is in place and on time on the day. 'It's a combination of organizational and creative skills,' says Joan. 'I love working with flowers, but I love working with people too and I make sure I know exactly what is needed. It can be pressurised – say in June when there are a lot of weddings – but it's fulfilling too.'

Joan also uses her skills in organizing flowers for a local hospice on a voluntary basis.' If an arrangement makes a patient's day then it makes mine too,' she says.

Useful addresses _____

Association of Exhibition Organizers, 26 Chapter St, London SW1 4ND.
   Tel: 0171 932 0252
Association of British Professional Conference Organizers, 54 Church
   St, Tisbury, Salisbury, Wilts SP3 6NH. Tel: 01747 870 490

PUBLIC RELATIONS CONSULTANT

PR is a much maligned profession. Jennifer Saunders in *Absolutely
Fabulous* may have been hilarious, but she gave the impression that PR
consultants spend all their time lunching. In fact PR is a very serious
business. It is all about how a company is presented to the public. PR is
responsible for the public face of that company and for managing press
coverage of that company. Poor PR leads to public hostility – which in
turn can translate into poor sales.

   Good PR, at the very least, lets the public know about what a
company produces. An enhanced public perception can increase sales
enormously. PR consultants may well be asked to help identify markets
for the company they are representing, as well as carrying out research
into how the company is perceived and how that perception can be
improved. Most people think of PR as something that is projected out
of a company, but PR people are often expected to do internal
presentations of company policy.

What qualities do I need?
You need to be a good communicator, to be interested in people, an
able administrator, organized, good at reconciling contradictory
demands with a keen appreciation of the way the media works.

What qualifications do I need?
None. Although it is possible to get qualifications in PR, it is not
essential. However, if you plan to set up on your own, previous

experience in PR would be helpful, as would experience in either journalism, broadcasting, marketing or sales, as these are all areas which relate well to PR skills. Qualifications which could prove helpful if you have no previous relevant experience include the Communication Advertising and Marketing (CAM) certificate or a diploma in public relations. You can also take a BA degree in public relations and there are relevant post-graduate courses too.

How do I set up?

Before you set up, you need one important ingredient – clients. If you have already worked for a PR agency, you may already have personal clients. If not, you need to locate some. You could try looking for local companies which you know could utilize your area of expertise. Many TECS have social meetings for new businesses which may be profitable, or you might join the local chamber of commerce, or other societies where business people are likely to congregate. Sending a personalized mail shot explaining what you can offer may also work.

Once you have a couple of clients, it will be much easier to attract other work, as you will have references and a track record – provided you handle the work well. Remember, doing the PR for a small company is not just about writing press releases and making phone calls, but also guiding their strategy. It is important not to overstretch yourself or you may end up giving poor service to old clients while you try to attract new ones.

How much will I make?

Depends how well-established you are. A PR consultant with a good track record in the industry, working full-time for major clients could earn as much as £50,000 a year. On the other hand, someone without experience, starting with very small clients would earn considerably less. Methods of charging vary. Some companies pay a monthly fee in advance, plus expenses (such as the cost of printing a brochure or photography). Others work on a project by project basis. Over half of

PR consultants earn more than £20,000. Eleven per cent earn over £40,000.

Pros:

> Varied work with high degree of customer and media contact.

> Good earnings potential

Cons:

> Clients may not realise why their new type of widget is not front page news.

> Contacts are essential.

> Not for the retiring.

Michael Dawson and his wife Amanda run their own PR company.
'Mike started the business,' says Amanda. 'He was working for one company and a competitor said to him that if he ever set up on his own they'd be very interested. So when he decided to go it alone, he wrote to them and they snapped him up.' The client was so pleased with the work that Mike did, that they recommended him to other firms. Indeed, most clients have come through word of mouth, although the Dawsons have also pitched for accounts.

'Our selling point is the fact that we are a small outfit which means that the client gets us doing their work, rather than some junior. In fact, we've recently had to turn work away because taking it on would have meant lowering our standards for existing clients.'

Amanda and Michael enjoy their work which involves both writing reports, communicating with journalists and planning strategy. Michael works full-time and Amanda part-time and they have occasionally hosted meetings in their home. 'Which is a bit nerve-wracking,' Amanda admits, 'but it also gives the occasion an informal feel which the clients like.'

For Amanda the only problems arise when she has to answer the phone on a day she is looking after her son. Dividing her attention between the client and a child about to do something he shouldn't can be stressful. 'That's only a minor problem, though. Overall I think this way of working helps you get a much better relationship with your client – you go and see them more, and it's a lot more flexible too.'

Useful addresses

Institute of Public Relations, The Old Trading House, 15 Northburgh St, London EC1V OPR. Tel: 0171 253 5151

The CAM Foundation, Abford House, 15 Wilton Road, London SW1V 1NJ. Tel: 0171 828 7506

TEACHING

There are dozens of ways to earn money from your teaching skills. Some types of teachers, such as music teachers, traditionally work from home, but you can also adapt teaching skills gained in any classroom to home tuition. If you have creative skills, such as cake decorating, flower arranging, painting etc., you might also consider holding workshops at home to pass on your knowledge to students. Some teachers use their home as a base, but work in other people's homes or community centres (popular with those setting up a toddler music or dance classes.)

What qualities do I need?
An interest in teaching, the ability to communicate your subject with enthusiasm and patience, a willingness to learn, and the ability to market yourself.

What qualifications do I need?

It depends what you are teaching and the age of the students you plan to teach. If you are a bilingual German speaker and plan to teach German to adults, you may have no formal qualifications at all. However, if you aim to provide home tuition for public examination students, it would certainly help to have a degree and preferably a teaching qualification. If you plan to teach foreign students, a Teaching English As a Foreign Language qualification (TEFL) could be necessary. You can study for such qualifications at local further education colleges and universities. The British Council has a guide to TEFL qualifications and where they can be studied. Some franchise teaching operations such as Kumon mathematics, provide their own training. Music teachers also have their own recognized qualifications.

How do I set up?

First you have to decide exactly what you plan to do. Do you like to work with infants or even pre-schoolers? If this is the case, you might want to run a toddler class in music, gymnastics or dance. You can set up on your own. But if you would like the support of a franchise there are several language teaching classes for children, such as La Jolie Ronde or Club Français. If you are interested in physical skills you could take out a Tumbletots franchise for instance – but it will take considerably more financial outlay (see the section on franchising in chapter 5).

If you want to offer home tuition to older children – perhaps the pre-teens and teenagers, you can either go it alone or, for certain subjects, sign up with a franchise. Kumon Mathematics is one of the best known. If you plan to coach children for common entrance, make sure you are qualified to do so. The same applies if you are coaching for GCSE or A-levels. Many teachers prefer teaching adults. However, certain subjects are more in demand than others. A class in computing will probably be better attended than one in medieval Icelandic history, so make sure your skills fit the market!

Once you have decided what to do, the next step is to get a good supply of materials and to market yourself. If you plan to teach young children, you could advertise in local playgroups, nurseries, schools, shops and the local paper. For older ones, tell schools about your services. If you plan to take foreign students, it could be a good idea to sign up with an agency – again local schools and the Yellow Pages should have some good leads.

Once you are established, word of-mouth will be your best source of work. That's why it is important to be honest with parents about their children's capabilities. They may hope they have the next Nigel Kennedy on their hands, but it is up to you to be realistic about the child who has three left thumbs. False hopes only lead to disappointment. If you plan to teach children, contact your social services department just to ensure that you won't fall foul of the Children Act.

How much will I make?

It depends on what you are teaching and how many you teach. Also on the cost of a franchise if you take that route. A franchise with La Jolie Ronde, for instance costs only £300. A Tumbletots franchise on the other hand is £15,000. For pre-school activities expect to charge around £2.50–£5 per session depending on the area. For older children, tuition fees can be anywhere between £10–£20. Unions such as the National Union of Teachers and the Association of Tutors may also have useful guidelines. Remember, too, that although you charge per hour of tuition, you will have spent a great deal more time on preparation and probably interviewing the student beforehand.

Pros:

Fulfilling work which can be fitted around other commitments.

Opportunity to use teaching skills outside the classroom.

Reasonable rewards can be expected.

Cons:

No support from colleagues.

You may be put under pressure by parents.

Earnings potential is limited.

Elizabeth Newport a former English teacher, now teaches from home.

'I guess I've got the original portfolio career. Since leaving full-time teaching, I've done a whole host of things, ranging from home tuition to taking foreign students into my home for residential teaching of English as a foreign language, and I do some distance learning tuition too. It's terrific fun, although not as well-paid as when I was at work. But my husband who is a pilot is delighted. It means we actually get to see each other now!

I went on a Women Into Self Employment Course which was wonderful. My confidence was at a low ebb, but this brought it back and also gave me an insight into life outside the teaching world – things like marketing, tax – all of that.

I advertised for pupils on my local post office. But a lot of referrals came through word of mouth or former colleagues. It was a former colleague who was running the agency for foreign language students that I now help out with. However, you do need to be a certain sort of person to have students at home with you, because it is a 24-hour commitment. I like having people around, though, and it's always interesting. You can earn upwards of £250 a week taking a student for residential tuition although that's not all profit. You have to provide meals, accommodation, tuition and it's vital to have somewhere they can be taught undisturbed. I'm thoroughly enjoying myself at the moment and looking at other plans too.'

Useful addresses

Association of Tutors, Sunnycroft, 63 King Edward Rd, Northampton
    NN1 5LY. Tel: 01604 24171 (provides a legal helpline and several
    different insurance packages for members)
British Council, Information Development Unit, Medlock St, Manchester,
    M15 4AA (for information about TEFL courses).
Companies offering franchises include:
Tumbletots, Blue Bird Park, Bromsgrove Rd, Hunnington, W. Midlands
    B62 0JW. Tel: 0121 585 7003
Kumon Mathematics, Ground Floor, Elscot House, Arcadia Av, London
    N3 2JU. Tel: 0181 343 330
La Jolie Ronde, 33 Long Acre, Bingham, Nottinghamshire, NG13 8AF. Tel:
    01949 839715
Le Club Français, 18–19 High St, Twyford, Winchester, Hampshire SO21
    1RF. Tel: 01962 714036
Incorporated Society of Musicians, 10 Stratford Place, London W1N
    9AE. Tel: 0171 629 4413

FREELANCE WRITER

There are literally thousands of people making a living from their
writing skills. However, the people you see writing in national
newspapers, magazines or in the top ten bestseller list are only the tip of
the iceberg. Many more people work for trade publications, in
specialist areas, or write newsletters and brochures for commercial
companies. Most writers will do a mix of all of the above.

What qualities do I need?
A talent for writing, a strongly creative bent, lots of ideas, persistence
and the ability to bounce back after rejection are all assets.

What qualifications do I need?

None – although, it is useful to have a specialist area which will give you an entree in a particular market sector. However, a short course in journalism could help you identify markets and get a better idea of the type of material required. There are hundreds of media studies and creative writing courses up and down the country, many of which offer study on a part-time or evening basis. Writers' circles also give a great deal of support to aspiring writers and there are also residential courses which may be both useful and inspiring. *The Writer's and Artist's Yearbook* (A. & C. Black), gives details of these and is generally useful. *Willings Press Guide*, available in most libraries, is another must-see publication.

How do I set up?

Writers need relatively few tools – a word-processor and a telephone are the most important. After that, it is a matter of selling your ideas to editors. Look carefully at the publications in the market you wish to penetrate and then approach the editor of those publications with an idea. If she is interested she may then ask to see the piece on spec which means that you will get paid only if your piece is published. If you have no reputation in the field, you may well have to write several articles on spec before you have sufficient rapport with that publication for them to commission you. However, once you have a rapport with an editor it is very important to make the most of it and develop your relationship, as journalism is to some extent as much about the contacts you make as about writing talent.

If you wish to write a non-fiction book, you may well have to apply a similar technique, although this time, you may be asked to supply a synopsis and sample chapter. First-time novelists, alas, will generally be expected to supply their complete opus.

Obtaining an agent is very helpful in the book publishing world. (there is a list of them in the *Writers and Artists Year Book*). However, any agent will want to see that you have potential and an interesting idea to market. In the early days, establishing yourself as a writer can be very hard work, but an ever-growing market does mean there is room for those with talent and persistence.

How much will I make?
It is important not to give up your day job before you have established that there is a demand for your writing, or you may find yourself with financial problems. The amounts earned by freelance writers vary hugely. At one end of the scale there are the handful of millionaire novelists and the top columnists paid £80,000 a year. At the other end, there are the people scraping to survive by writing for publications which pay very little. Most earn somewhere in between, though it has to be said that the first year is likely to be the hardest since this is when you will be establishing your reputation.

Pros:

> Fulfilling, varied and flexible work – you can choose how much you do.
> ___
> Some potential for fame or fortune and possibly both.
> ___
> Can be lonely.
> ___

Cons:

> Overcrowded market means that it is difficult to get into, and that even the most talented writer is vulnerable to a change of editor.
> ___

Jenny Hulme has been a freelance journalist for three years.
Jenny's career as a freelance writer started almost by accident. She'd previously been a successful editor, but felt, 'that I needed a change. I thought working freelance from home would be a temporary measure but have found it suits me down to the ground. I like my own

company, but my husband is also a freelance writer and so there are other advantages – like seeing more of each other.'

Jenny thinks it helps to have previous experience in the publishing world, 'because you have a better idea of what an editor is looking for and how to approach him. If you are a newcomer, then it's a good idea to study the publications you want to write for carefully and be prepared to be persistent. Write all your ideas down before you forget them and don't think of time spent in libraries researching as "wasted," but as an investment.'

Jenny feels that a lot of writers think of themselves as 'creative' and tend to ignore the business side of their profession, or turn down less interesting – but well-paid – jobs. 'But I put my heart into all the jobs I get and if some are not as interesting as others, well there are boring bits in every office job. The people who are not doing well are those who are too fussy about what they are prepared to do.'

Although, Jenny enjoys her job, she is well aware of the disadvantages. 'It is absolutely vital to have outside interests if you are writing at home or you could start to feel very boring. My husband also writes from home, and we both make sure we spend time outside – not just interviewing and seeing contacts, but going to the gym and generally being sociable. You do need to be self-disciplined, you need to like your own company, but for me it's an excellent way to make my career.'

Useful addresses

National Union of Journalists, Acorn House, 314 Grays Inn Road, London WC1X 8DP. Tel: 0171 278 7916

The Society of Authors, 84 Drayton Gardens, London SW10 9EB. Tel: 0171 373 6642

The Writers Guild of Great Britain, 430 Edgware Road, London W2 1EH. Tel: 0171 723 8074

TEN

Traditional homeworking

One of the reasons why many people are dubious about working from home is that some traditional kinds of homeworking have had a very bad press. The vast majority of Britain's one million homeworkers are women, who sit at home doing piecework sewing (the most common of all forms of homework), knitting, assembling or packing. Most do it because they need to earn – but do not have access to childcare facilities. As most homeworking is unskilled it can (theoretically anyway) be done at times when the children are in bed or otherwise occupied (see chapter 4 for more about childcare and employment).

A survey for the National Group on Homeworking showed that homeworkers assembled things which ranged from dog collars to first aid kits to Father Christmas Hats. Not surprisingly much of the work is seasonal and it is generally low-paid. There is also confusion as to whether homeworkers are self-employed or employed. Many companies claim that their homeworkers are self-employed since this reduces the companies' liabilities towards them. Only a few actually have homeworkers on their books as employees.

The National Group on Homeworking found that that the average national rate for homeworkers is £1.28 an hour although they have come across a few being paid as much as £5 an hour – mainly skilled machinists – and a few being paid as little as 20p an hour. Such a rate may seem risible but Peg Alexander of the NGH points out that for a single mother (who does not lose benefit if her earnings are below a certain amount), it can mean buying an extra pair of shoes for her children or more food. That people are willing to work for such a pittance (and that employers are happy to offer it) says something extremely sad about the current employment situation.

However, few people would knowingly set out to work for such rates. They are often disguised by the fact that homeworkers are paid per piece made up (or kit assembled) rather than by the hour. It is vital that if you intend to do this kind of homework, you work out just how much sewing or assembling you are expected to do in an hour and then work out whether the job is worth doing.

Most homeworking opportunities are spread by word of mouth. If you know someone who is already a homeworker and has reasonable conditions, ask if she can get you on the waiting list. You may also find other opportunities through local newspaper advertisements. Or you could create your own opportunities by going through the Yellow Pages and approaching local firms – particularly if you are a machinist. If you are disabled, the National Register of Disabled Homeworkers gives an outlet to self-employed disabled people making crafts at home and also has its own homeworking scheme (see next chapter).

Before you decide to take a job, here are some do's and don't's to consider:

Do ensure you work out the rate of pay per hour.

Do get the name and address of your employer or agent in writing.

Do find out on what basis you are employed. Are you to be self-employed or employed? (Employed workers have their tax and national insurance deducted from their wages, have the right to a contract of employment and certain other rights such as maternity leave and redundancy payments after a qualifying period.) If you are to be self-employed you will have to be responsible for your own tax and national insurance and will need to tell the Department of Social Security.

Do get a statement from your employer as to how and when you will be paid and how much. Keep a detailed note of any payments made. If an employer says they cannot pay you for a particular piece of work, notify the Citizens Advice Bureau.

Do find out exactly what is expected of you. What will happen if you fail to sew the required number of teddy bears, for instance? What will happen if your work is not up to scratch?

Do ask for any training or supervision you may need to help you do the work.

Do quiz telesales companies carefully. Will they pay for all your business calls whether or not leads turn into sales? How much of your pay will be made up of commission and how much basic?

Don't pay out any money for the chance to be introduced to homeworking opportunities unless you have some idea of what you will get for the money. It is quite common for adverts to ask for people to send a certain amount of money in order to find out more about a scheme. These may be genuine – or you may get nothing at all.

Don't spend large sums of money on equipment supplied by the firm you are working for. If the firm wants you to do work, they should either be prepared to give the equipment to you free, OR rent it to you on a weekly basis OR ask you for a deposit to ensure its security. It is unfair to ask you to pay outright for the equipment unless you are allowed to act as a freelance operator.

Another major factor to consider is the *health and safety* aspect of becoming a homeworker. If, for instance, you are sewing garments, you will need a guard for your machine to keep it away from prying little fingers, and somewhere to store materials. It is vital to make sure they are stored away from appliances which could ignite them.

However, the issues become more vexed if you are expected to work with chemicals, such as *glues, solvents, or paints*. If you are supplied with these, you should be given relevant information such as:

- whether they catch fire easily or are toxic

- whether they give off fumes

- how they should be stored (and do you have the room to store them safely?)

- whether you need protective clothing, gloves etc.

If you are working with chemicals and feel sick, giddy or develop an allergy, you can take the substance along to your local Health and Safety Officer (who can be found through your local phone book), who will inspect it for free and in confidence. If you are working with any substances that you have been told are dangerous, it is important that your working space is well ventilated and that all necessary precautions are taken. Your supplier must supply you with any protective clothing required.

If you are working with chemicals etc., it is vitally important that they are stored out of reach of children in clearly marked containers. Every year children die as a result of drinking poisons that have been decanted into squash bottles.

If you are working with tools, you should establish:

- Will the equipment be regularly maintained and by whom?

- Does it use electricity? Do you need a power breaker?

- Do you need protective equipment or clothing?

This list may seem rather daunting, particularly if you are desperate to get work. However, it is well worth ensuring that you are working for a reputable employer and protecting your own – and your family's health – at the same time.

At best, homeworking can provide an excellent way for a mother who cannot – or does not want – to find childcare, to earn money. Unfortunately, at worst, it is merely exploitation.

Useful addresses

The National Group on Homeworking (a campaigning group which does not keep addresses of people employing homeworkers; however, it can give information about homeworking and refer you to your local homeworking office) 102 Batley St, W. Yorks, WF17 5DP

ELEVEN

Homeworking and the disabled

Working at home has been held out as an excellent way for disabled people to enter the employment market. In fact, there is a great deal of investment currently being put into training schemes to this end. However, there are drawbacks – not least that you may lose entitlement to benefits. Currently, disabled people are allowed to do 'therapeutic work' provided they earn less than £44 a week, work less than 16 hours and the work is done on doctor's advice, without losing their entitlement to incapacity benefit or severe disability allowance. The definition of therapeutic work is that it 'improves or prevents a deterioration in the disease or bodily or mental disablement which causes incapacity for work.' However, therapeutic earnings are taken into account in assessing income support, housing benefit or council tax benefit, with the result that you may not end up, much better off although you may be very glad of the chance to work. Schemes such as that run by the Guild of Disabled Homeworkers (address below) provide therapeutic employment. On the plus side, you may also be entitled to money from the Access to Work Scheme, run by the government, to provide equipment which can help you work successfully – such as adapted computer screens.

Setting up your own business can be immensely rewarding, but Sue Maynard-Campbell, herself a self-employed disability consultant, points out that there may be pitfalls. She warns that any business which takes a loan generally has to provide some form of security, 'and that could well be your house. It's bad enough for anyone to lose their house, but mine has been specially adapted for me so I can make maximum use of it. To lose that and have to start trying to get the same facilities elsewhere would be very difficult.'

Sue also points out the potential problems of isolation. She works with her sister, but feels she meets less people through her work than she would do if she were employed in an office. 'Disabled people are often isolated enough without being pushed into doing something which makes them feel more isolated. There are plenty of people like myself running a business successfully, but people shouldn't be pushed into it.'

Mick Kirk works as a teleworker for Humberside County Council. Mick has been disabled since childhood. His muscle weakness means he requires help with feeding and other functions. Until his mid twenties, he was unable to get a job, concentrating instead on educating himself. Then he was given a computer and began to train on it. Some time later, he heard that Humberside County Council had a vacancy computerizing their occupational health records. 'It wasn't like a proper interview,' he recalls, 'because there were all these agencies who came to see me as well, to see if they felt I could hold the job down. I was also in the middle of getting married and moving house!'

Mick was given a six-month trial. Eight years later, his job has expanded enormously and he now also devises and develops software applications. 'It would be hard to work in an office full-time,' he says. 'But I go into the office twice a month or so to help out and keep in touch.'

Mick feels he is much more effective than an office worker. 'I'm less tired by travelling and I don't get interrupted all the time.' But he also points out that he suffers exactly the same disadvantages as any able-bodied teleworker. 'When you are not in the office it can be easy for people to forget you. There's a newsletter that goes round with everyone's birthday on it and one time mine wasn't there – simply because I wasn't in the office, I'd been forgotten. There is also a danger of doing valuable work that isn't recognized, so I make follow-up calls to find out how my work has been received. Teleworkers need to be assertive.'

Mick enjoys his job, 'there are down sides in that you lose benefits, but the boost to your self-esteem and the freedom, far outweigh the benefits trap. When you are disabled and not working you are treated almost as a perpetual child by the law and you can start to feel that way yourself. Working gives you adult status and for me working at home was the very best option.'

Useful addresses

Association of Disabled Professionals, 170 Benton Hill, Horbury, Wakefield, West Yorkshire WF4 5HW. Tel: 01924 270335

Disability Alliance (helpline for queries on benefit) Tel: 0171 247 8763

Instant Muscle (a training group which has done a project on job opportunities for the housebound) 84 North End Road, London W14 9ES. Tel: 0171 603 2604

National Guild of Disabled Homeworkers, Market St, Nailsworth, Gloucestershire, GL5 OBX. Tel: 01453 835623

RADAR (information on services for disabled people)12 City Forum, 250 City Road, London EC1V 8AF. Tel: 0171 250 0212

Note: your local Job Centre should have a Disability Employment advisor and a Placement, Assessment and Counselling Team who can keep you up to date on opportunities.

The Telecommuters, Francis Kinsman (John Wiley)

Teleworking Explained, ed. Noel Hodson (John Wiley)

Teleworking in Britain, Ursula Huws (Department of Employment)

Changing Times – A Guide to Flexible Work Patterns (New Ways to Work)

Working Mother Marianne Velmans and Sarah Litvinoff (Simon and Schuster)

The Working Parent's Handbook, (Parents At Work)

The Daily Telegraph Guide to Working for Yourself, Godfrey Golzen (Kogan Page)

Taking up a Franchise, Godfrey Golzen and Colin Barrow (Kogan Page).

The Lloyds Guide to Running a Small Business

The New Guide to Working From Home, Sue Read (Headline)

101 Ways to Start Your Own Business, Christine Ingham (Kogan Page)

Running Your Own Mail Order Business, Malcolm Breckman (Kogan Page)

Career Couples, Suzan Lewis and Cary L. Cooper (Unwin)

Working From Home, Paul and Sarah Edwards (Tarcher Putnam)

The Which? Guide to Earning Money At Home, Lynn Underwood (Which? Books)

All Pan Books are available at your local bookshop or newsagent, or can be ordered direct from the publisher. Indicate the number of copies required and fill in the form below.

Send to: Macmillan General Books C.S.
                Book Service By Post
                PO Box 29, Douglas I-O-M
                IM99 1BQ

or phone: 01624 675137, quoting title, author and credit card number.

or fax: 01624 670923, quoting title, author, and credit card number.

or Internet: http://www.bookpost.co.uk

Please enclose a remittance* to the value of the cover price plus 75 pence per book for post and packing. Overseas customers please allow £1.00 per copy for post and packing.

*Payment may be made in sterling by UK personal cheque, Eurocheque, postal order, sterling draft or international money order, made payable to Book Service By Post.

Alternatively by Access/Visa/MasterCard

Card No.

Expiry Date

Signature _____

Applicable only in the UK and BFPO addresses.

While every effort is made to keep prices low, it is sometimes necessary to increase prices at short notice. Pan Books reserve the right to show on covers and charge new retail prices which may differ from those advertised in the text or elsewhere.

NAME AND ADDRESS IN BLOCK CAPITAL LETTERS PLEASE

Name _____

Address _____

_____

_____

_____

8/95

Please allow 28 days for delivery.
Please tick box if you do not wish to receive any additional information. ☐